U.S. NAVY
Pirate
COMBAT
SKILLS

Further Reading in Military Irregular and
Supernatural Combat Training

U.S. Army Zombie Combat Skills

U.S. Army Werewolf Sniper Manual

U.S. NAVY
Pirate
COMBAT
SKILLS

Department of the Navy

Edited by Adam Reger
Illustrations by David Cole Wheeler

Pirate Combat Consultants to the U.S. Navy

LYONS PRESS
Guilford, Connecticut
An imprint of Globe Pequot Press

Lyons Press is an imprint of Globe Pequot Press

Text design: Libby Kingsbury
Layout artist: Kevin Mak

Library of Congress Cataloging-in-Publication Data
Reger, Adam.
   U.S. Navy pirate combat skills / Department of the Navy ; edited by Adam Reger ; illustrations by David Cole Wheeler, Pirate Combat Consultants to the U.S. Navy.
     p. cm.
   ISBN 978-0-7627-7037-3
   1. Pirates—Humor. 2. United States. Navy—Humor. I. Wheeler, David Cole. II. Title.
   PN6231.P53R44 2011
   818'.602—dc22
                                        2011000578

Printed in the United States of America

10 9 8 7 6 5 4 3 2 1

Contents

LIST OF ILLUSTRATIONS

GUEST FOREWORD
by
(Retired) Admiral I. I. Scuttle,
Commander of the Fighting 44th Anti-Pirate Assault Force,
the Most Decorated Anti-Piracy Unit in U.S. Navy History

Call them privateers. Buccaneers. Sea rovers. Call them criminals, cockroaches of the seven seas, swashbucklers, corsairs. Call them scurvy mariners under the black flag.

Call them what you will, these treacherous curs have only one proper name, and it is *pirate*. Scourges of the open water, nuisance to navies, merchants, and pleasure boaters alike, pirates have always been with us. For centuries the crisp billow of the skull-and-crossbones, the knocking of a peg leg upon the decks, the nearby murmur of pirates' salty anachronistic language, have troubled the sleep of many an honest sea captain.

But no longer must these vivid dreams become nightmarish realities. Sailor, you hold in your hands the most complete guide yet assembled to confronting the pirate enemy and driving him to the far corners of this watery globe.

It may be true, as some say, that pirates will always be with us, that the Jolly Roger will sail forevermore. But if it is, then it is also true that we possess the capabilities and the knowledge to beat back the murderous sea dogs, to keep them forever in fear of capture.

For you will find, sailor, working your way through these pages, that the anti-pirate game has become primarily one of offense rather than defense. Gone are the days of pitched cannon battles on the open sea, both sides filling the air with acrid gunpowder and the sickly sweet stench of rent flesh, while bloodthirsty marauders swing from deck to deck, knives clenched in their teeth. Simply put, this ain't a manual for your grandpappy's pirate-fighting force. The Navy's superior technological capabilities allow it to sail circles around the antiquated sloops and galleons of the corsair foe. More to the point, these capabilities allow today's anti-pirate assault force to quite literally "hit the pirates where they live," trailing them to far-flung coves and island protectorates. Antipiracy is now a global mission, and one that no longer entails waiting for the pirate to make the first move. Reconnaissance, stealth infiltration, and asymmetrical warfare are now the name of the game.

Or, as the Pirate Fighter's Creed puts it:

> *The pirate may catch the tradewinds*
> *The pirate may ride the gulf stream*
> *The pirate may dock safe in harbor*
> *But he won't escape me or my team.*

Still, despite the Navy's overwhelming advantages in the technical arena, the sailor underestimates the buccaneer enemy at his peril. Wily, worldly, and wise with centuries spent traversing this watery world, the pirate has his stratagems. Sneak attacks, counter-ambushes, and cunning booby traps are all in the game. The buccaneer is expert at hand-to-hand combat, and does not give up control of his ship easily.

There are dangers, to be sure, and chief among them is to be taken captive by the swashbucklers. Then, there's pirate impressment. A disturbing trend in the world of anti-piracy operations is the appearance of former Navy men aboard the decks of the Jolly Roger, hoisting the main sail and calling "yo ho ho for a bottle of rum." Leaner, with missing teeth, appendages, and eyes, these men caked in dirt and sporting the unsightly growth of vermin-occupied beards are nonetheless identifiable as former naval officers. No one knows what makes these men turn—perhaps it is the unfettered freedom of the pirate lifestyle, the wild romance of life upon the high seas, the perceived promise of a deeper brotherhood aboard the pirate vessel than is attainable belowdecks on the Navy ships. Perhaps . . .

But I digress. The "Why" is not important, so much as the "Why not." The manual set before you contains all the seeds of "Why not" you should require: turn rogue at pain of death, sailor, by means of tireless hunting unto extinction.

At great expense, in blood and treasure, has this manual been assembled. Value its wisdom, sailor, and honor those fallen pirate-fighting sailors who have preceded you in this sacred mission by keeping the waterways safe, and chasing all pirate enemies to the very edges of this world.

Now then, join me, if you will, in a spirited rendition of that age-old pirate-fighter's anthem, "Pirate Slayers We."

PIRATE SLAYERS WE

Nowhere on earth can the pirate hide,
Be it cove or cave or sea.
Nowhere but we shall have his hide,
For pirate slayers we,
For pirate slayers we.

No weapon has he, strong enough
To vanquish Sam's Navy.
Though he bethink himself rough and tough,
Pirate slayers we,
O pirate slayers we.

Though his sloop was never so fast
With sails enough for three,
He can't outrun our undersea blast,
For pirate slayers we,
For pirate slayers we.

In folly he hides in jungle coves,
Not a single luxury.
Navy men find him, our force in droves,
Pirate slayers we,
O pirate slayers we.

Come wind and hail and the monsoon's attack,
Through which no man can see,
We'll follow the pirate, who's easy to track,
For pirate slayers we,
For pirate slayers we.

Resourceful the corsair, trapped on his sloop,
No fiber, no vitamin C.
Faced with our force, he'll easily poop,
Pirate slayers we,
O pirate slayers we.

Through his skull-and-crossbones no message of love,
Nor hope nor charity.
We'll gladly donate death from above,
For pirate slayers we,
For pirate slayers we.

No pirate shall ever lie snug in his bed,
Nor slip into safe reverie.
Visions of Us shall dance in their heads,
For pirate slayers we,
O pirate slayers we!

PREFACE

This field manual provides information needed to prepare and equip members of the anti-pirate assault force and to aid them in their missions against pirates, herein referred to as buccaneers, swashbucklers, corsairs, privateers, sea dogs, sea rovers, freebooters, filibusters, and scurvy seamen. It is intended for use by admirals, vice-admirals, rear-admirals, lieutenants, commanders, sub-commanders, field commanders, captains, pilots (of ships, planes, and helicopters), divers, weapons-locker operators, demolitions experts, jumpmasters, parachutists, snipers, and sailors.

This manual is organized as a reference for anti-pirate assault force members and leads the trainer through the material needed to drill and prepare the anti-pirate force for operational readiness. Subjects include boarding a pirate ship, searching a pirate ship and detaining prisoners, hand-to-hand and hand-to-hook combat skills, ship-to-shore assault procedures, inland waterway interdiction measures, special operations, diving, parachute maneuvers, the undersea planting of explosives and other sabotage operations, weapons, demolitions, general defensive strategies, medical evacuations, survival at sea, and escape from captivity. The appendices cover nautical abbreviations, a list of the sailor's standard wardrobe and equipment, and specific loadout lists for anti-pirate operations. General Navy personnel guidelines are covered at length in NAVPERS 15560D, and instruction specific to marksmanship can be obtained in the *U.S. Army Werewolf Sniper Manual.*

Note that the pirate enemy referred to in the text is the ever-present, persistently dangerous pirate of yore—e.g., Blackbeard, Captain Kidd, the dread Bartholomew Roberts, etc.—and not the imitative johnnies-come-lately operating out of Somalia, Malta, or the Seychelles.

Unless this publication states otherwise, masculine nouns and pro-ouns do not refer exclusively to male sailors or pirates.

Part One

OFFENSIVE STRATEGIES

The manual you hold in your hands exists because the problem it addresses is a grave and ever-present one. If you harbor doubts about the scurrilousness of the pirate foe, sailor, put down this book and consult a newspaper. There, you will read about the misdeeds of the marauding mariners you will soon be facing, about frigates left to burn and sink slowly into the briny deep, about the orphaned children of honest merchant marines, and of loyal Navy men like yourself and your companions.

Do not read further in this manual until you are suitably outraged at the behavior of these scurvy privateers. The following chapters will tell you in exhaustive detail the myriad ways of terminating the pirate foe. Whether you meet him at sea or on land, approaching his dreaded ship from the skies or beneath the waves, brandishing high-powered explosives or just your own two hands, this Part One will provide instruction. As a general principle, however, you need only know that the bloodthirsty savages are never to be pitied, and have never been innocent. Consider yourself the bearer of their justice, sailor. If you wish to pay them some kindness, make it that their judgment be swift.

Chapter 1

PIRATE SHIP BOARDING ASSAULTS

1.1. Background

The following are fundamental tactics for anti-pirate assault. Standard operating procedures (SOPs) for in-ship insertion, deck infiltration, actions at objective, integration of anti-pirate forces, and consolidation are included. Because the variety of tactics used in ship/hostage recapture are target-specific, the individual pirate scenario will dictate the applicability of the general guidelines listed below. These SOPs provide a general overview of anti-pirate operations, including (but not limited to) buccaneer termination, hostage extraction, and treasure reclamation; they are not intended to restrict the options of the tactical commander.

1.2. Pre-assault

Insertion of anti-pirate snipers and/or observers, when practical, should be executed at the earliest opportunity to provide intelligence updates on the pirates' activity, potential sailing plans, and environmental data. See Figures 1-1 and 1-2. From a position proximate to the pirates' ship (or cove, as in land-based operations; see Chapter 4 for land-based assaults), intelligence is communicated via satellite to higher headquarters and anti-pirate assault forces staging at a Floating Sea Base (FSB). Real-time data may be passed on to planners regarding pirates' defensive capacity, movement (both with respect to ship's position on sea and the position of various high-value pirate targets within the ship, when such intelligence is available), and habits, and provide "eyes on" information vital to operational planning and mission success.

Figure 1-1. The anti-pirate sniper can also conduct reconnaissance missions.

1.3. Insertion/Infiltration

a. Insertion into the area of operations—i.e., the immediate vicinity of the pirates' ship or cove—may be accomplished by air, surface, or sub-surface platforms. Following insertion, infiltration of the target area is usually undertaken. This permits anti-pirate water assault forces to maintain communications prior to main body launch and facilitates swimmer scout/lead climber insertion. The low freeboard and small radar signature of inflatable craft make them especially well suited to infiltrate swimmers into the target area.

Figure 1-2. The sailor must make use of his environment when conducting sniper missions.

b. Swimmer scout/lead climber launch should be coordinated with anti-pirate sniper/observer personnel to preclude compromise. See Figure 1-3. Prior to insertion, a tide and current check should be conducted in the vicinity of the objective. In areas of high pirate activity known for short currents (i.e., the Caribbean, West Indies, and the area surrounding Madagascar), this procedure is of particular importance. Swimmer scouts/lead climbers may communicate with the main body to adjust the location of main anti-pirate force swimmer release. When major items of pirate assault force equipment are to be carried, and/or tactical considerations require long swims, a broad communication window should be established. Current, illumination, and environmental factors will determine the distance at which swimmer scouts and the main anti-pirate body will be launched. In conditions of low illumination, 1,000 to 500 meters distance is usually sufficient.

c. When doing so will not compromise the mission, it is advisable to order the assault force's sniper to terminate a ship's night watch personnel in advance of approach on the pirate ship. This is particularly the case when a night watchman is stationed in the ship's crow's nest, as this vantage gives the pirate watchman a particularly clear view of the sea surrounding the ship. Termination of the night watchman should be expected to open only a small window of time, however, as the discovery of a fallen comrade will elicit alarm among the pirate crew. See Figure 1-4.

Figure 1-3. The sniper must exercise creativity in blending in with his surroundings.

NOTE: Pirates depend heavily on the element of surprise. Ironically, this can often lead to smugness and complacency, as the pirate crew believe themselves unseen and alone upon the high seas. This arrogant attitude often makes pirate vessels nicely susceptible to surprise attack. While this is a point in favor of the anti-pirate assault team member, it must be reiterated how vitally important are the three S's of pirate assault: Stealth, Speed, and Silence

d. Once on target, anti-pirate swimmer scouts/lead climbers mount the pirate ship (typically a sloop or schooner, with wood sides and railings well suited to grappling hooks and other climbing devices) by any available means, reconnoiter the immediate vicinity, and rig ladders and climbing aids for the main body approach. See Figure 1-5. Lead climbers

Figure 1-4. Instances of good and bad opportunities for taking out pirate watchmen.

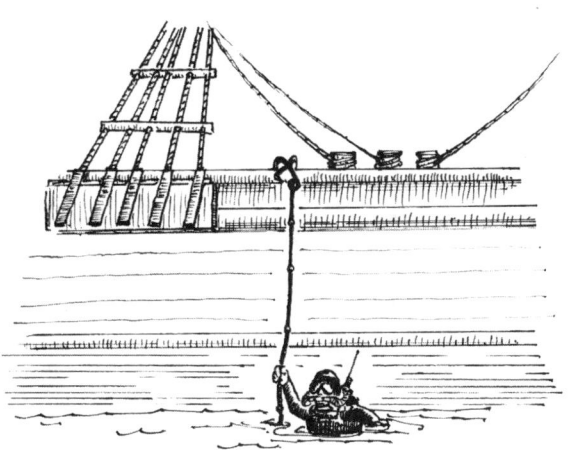

Figure 1-5. The lead swimmer attaches a ladder for the assault force to use.

are responsible for security during the main body climb, and for the selection of a secure location on the ship in which swimmers can consolidate and rig for the main anti-pirate assault.

e. Main body swim should be conducted with each shooting pair designated a swim partner. Following swimmer insertion, force members loiter downwind of the objective, coming no closer than 1,500 meters to the pirate ship. At the time of the actual assault, force members proceed to the target and are directed there by the on-scene commander.

f. Upon arrival at the objective, assaulters remove fins, secure them to the ladder or rig put in place by the lead swimmer, and climb aboard. It may be necessary to secure the bottom of the ladder to the ship's sidewall to prevent any attached equipment from pulling the ladder into view—be aware that pirate ships typically station at least one crew member on deck for night watch.

g. Following the climb, assaulters consolidate in the area designated by lead climbers and rig for assault, bridge-taking, and room clearance. As soon as team members are safely over the rail, preparations should be made for immediate shipboard assault. Weapons, lights, and communications equipment should be readied while lead climbers maintain security.

1.4. Actions at Objective

a. At earliest opportunity, communication should be made with follow-on assault forces. When the first team begins infiltration of the pirate ship, follow-on forces should be notified and move into position to react in the event of compromise. See Figure 1-6.

b. While executing a soft approach to the hostage site, assaulters should be prepared to conduct an immediate assault.

c. At the time the waterborne element approaches, air assault forces should be in a downwind orbit 4 to 5 nautical miles from the platform, prepared to assault (if necessary). This distance places follow-on forces far enough from target to avoid detection of rotor noise, and sufficiently close to arrive on scene within 90 to 120 seconds from call.

d. Waterborne element continues soft approach and calls in follow-on team to hostage site. In the event of compromise—most likely in the form of a disorganized pirate force emerging from below

Figure 1-6. Snipers provide support throughout the mission.

deck—assault teams engage the opposing force, neutralize it, and proceed immediately to the hostage site. Soft approach may be continued if, in the opinion of the tactical commander, the initial infiltration of the pirate ship has not compromised the assault force's mission. In a deliberate assault, assault teams stage at entrances to the hostage site. The air assault team is called in by prearranged signal. Room entry is executed immediately upon hearing rotor noise of the approaching aircraft.

e. Air assault teams fastrope or perform helo land insertion at designated points. Snipers cover crow's nests, towers, and decks. Command and control elements position themselves to control the recapture operation and communicate with higher authority.

f. The specific mission of the assault forces will be stated in the operation order. In general terms, it may be expected to be prioritized as follows:

(1) Rescue and secure the hostages.
(2) Neutralize the buccaneer threat.
(3) Confiscate any illegally obtained pirate treasure.

(4) Safeguard pirate ship and onboard equipment. (Remember that in the vast majority of cases, the pirate ship has been hijacked from honest merchants.)

g. As soon as operations are completed, a full report should be communicated to the on-scene commander.

h. Hostages should be secured and consolidated in an area separate from neutralized privateers. The expeditious removal of hostages from the pirate ship is the responsibility of the tactical commander. Explosive devices, booby traps, and booby-trapped hostages are common occurrences and should be reported immediately and referred to command personnel. See Figure 1-7. Hostages should be removed from any spaces where such threats exist.

i. The possibility of "sleepers," unaccounted-for pirates and fire/explosive/mechanical hazards, should be considered and anticipated. See Figure 1-8. Once the hostages are secure, unaccounted-for or escaped pirates may continue to pose a significant threat to hostages, assault forces, and the ship itself. If, following SOP, these conditions exist:

(1) Additional measures should be taken to safeguard hostages at consolidation points.

(2) Teams should be dispatched to locate any remaining, or hidden, swashbucklers. Cargo holds, galley cabinets, and other tightly enclosed spaces are likely hiding places.

Figure 1-7. Beware of "booby traps" planted on pirates' hostages.

Figure 1-8. Be on the lookout for "sleeper" pirates.

(3) Measures should be taken to safeguard helicopters, the host Navy ship, and landing sites from pirate assault or intervention. All cannons should be seized and disabled as swiftly as possible.

(4) Steps should be taken to ensure the security of the route along which hostages will be traveling from consolidation point to extraction.

j. Wounded hostages and assault personnel receive priority over wounded sea dogs for exfiltration and should be stabilized on scene. Following the removal of the hostages, the assault team will be exfiltrated as directed on scene at the discretion of the commander.

1.5. Communications

a. A plan to overcome lost communications is mandatory. So, too, are contingency signals. Covert/overt lights, pyrotechnics, and relay networks may be necessary to ensure communications reliability.

b. Communications equipment should be waterproofed, secured, and made buoyant for swimmer operations. Where possible, waterproofing material should not interfere with the operation or function of equipment. Command and control communication personnel should be positioned to establish satellite or line of sight (LOS) communications without delay.

Aircraft Preparation and Pilot Brief

1. Insertion Aircraft Preparation

a. The insertion aircraft used in pirate shipboarding operations are normally limited to fleet assets. These assets consist of SH-3, CH-46, SH-60, and the CH-53 aircraft. The CH-46 is the preferred insertion platform because of its ability to carry a fully loaded-out sixteen-man anti-pirate assault force, and because of its superior navigation abilities at the very low heights needed for on-deck insertion operations.

b. The disadvantages: The SH-3 without its electronic package is limited to eight passengers. The SH-60 is normally limited to three passengers because of its electronic package for antisubmarine warfare. The CH-53 should not be used because its rotorwash could blow personnel off the ship's deck when fastroping. However, the SH-60 and the SH-3 are suitable for a sniper platform, making them ideal for air support of the anti-pirate assault team. In most cases, the assault force commander will not be given the option of what aircraft he wants to use.

c. When using the CH-46 for insertion, a number of things have to be done prior to the mission:

(1) Remove the right and left front side doors.
(2) Install fastrope on SAR boom. The fastrope should be rigged for quick release.
(3) Special Patrol Insertion/Extraction (SPIE) rig should be rigged to fit the hell hole.
(4) Caving ladder should be rigged for deployment from right front side door.
(5) ICS should be made available to the fastrope master and assault force commander.
(6) All communications should be tested with all assault forces prior to liftoff.

(7) Mission, SPIE rig, and fastrope briefs should be conducted with aircrew and pilots prior to liftoff.

d. Most pirate ships don't have the surface area required for landing a helicopter on deck. Even in cases where the required landing diameter is present, it should be assumed that the deck will be susceptible to volleys from pirate muskets and rifles, as well as close-in assaults by means of swords, daggers, cudgels, etc. The extraction of the assault force and hostages from the deck of a pirate ship may require the use of a SPIE rig. See Figure 1-9. Also, the SPIE rig's primary function is for emergency extraction of the assault force if, for whatever reason, it has to abandon ship and go into the water.

e. The caving ladder is used for the same reasons: It allows the assault force the ability to escape from the deck of the pirate ship and get back into the insertion aircraft without it having to land.

Figure 1-9. The SPIE rig can be used to extract assault force members from perilous situations.

2. Sniper Aircraft Preparation

a. The sniper aircraft should have both sides of the aircraft rigged so the sniper can move freely while sniping at sea dogs. The removal of the aircraft door and windows will most likely be required, depending on the aircraft type.

b. Communication should be installed and checked between pilot and sniper prior to takeoff.

c. Fastrope should be installed on aircraft in case the sniper has to be inserted on deck of the pirate ship.

d. The sniper aircraft's secondary mission is Search and Rescue (SAR). It should have a fully functional hoist and horse collar for the recovery of personnel from both on-deck and in-water situations.

e. Mission, SPIE rig, fastrope and sniper briefs should be given to the aircrew and pilot prior to aircraft liftoff.

3. Sniper Employment

a. The employment of anti-pirate snipers during a shipboarding operation is a valued asset, which should be made available to the assault force commander. Normally, an anti-pirate assault force platoon should have two qualified military snipers. The snipers tasked to support a shipboarding operation should be experienced assault team operators who can be trusted to work independently without directions, and make quick and competent decisions in regards to the use of deadly force as they apply to the current rules of engagement.

b. During a shipboarding operation, two snipers will be employed. Each sniper will be assigned his own aircraft. The primary responsibility of the sniper element is to provide close-in and highly accurate supporting small arms fire for the duration of that specified mission.

c. The sniper aircraft will link up with the assault force insertion aircraft 5 miles astern of the pirate ship. The two sniper aircraft will take station ahead of the assault force's insertion aircraft. All aircraft will proceed to the pirate ship at an altitude of 50 feet above ground level.

d. Upon reaching the stern of the pirate ship, the sniper aircraft will flare and maneuver port and starboard of the assault force's fastrope insertion point. The insertion aircraft should immediately follow the sniper aircraft and take station for inserting the assault force. The sniper aircraft will maintain a 45- to 60-degree attack angle while providing security. This attack angle prevents the skipping of rounds into friendly forces. In addition to providing cover fire, the sniper elements are required to pass timely information to the members of the assault force, including pirates' location; the number of pirates, booby traps, and weapons; the most direct and accessible routes to the pirate ship's bridge; and all movement of unknown personnel and their description—including movement of swashbucklers from the ship, or the movement of the pirate ship itself (something that may be difficult for assault force members to detect).

e. Once the assault force has inserted and has started its movement to the bridge, the sniper element will engage any and all perceived pirate enemies, clearing the way for the assault force as it conducts its movement to the bridge.

f. Once the assault force has taken and secured the bridge, the sniper element will remain in place, providing security for any additional insertion of follow-on forces or for the clearance of outside and internal spaces. The sniper element will not leave its station unless so directed by the assault force commander.

1.6. Prisoner Handling

a. The handling of captured pirates is a primary concern in the mission concept. Normally, the enemy crew aboard a pirate ship will consist of forty or more personnel. Pirate crews are, without exception, hostile. The assault force must be fully skilled in the tactics and procedures of prisoner handling and crowd control.

b. When handling captured pirates, the amount of force used to subdue an individual is in direct relation to the amount of force the prisoner uses to resist. In other words, use only the amount of force that is necessary to secure the individual. Unfortunately, in the case of the typical captured pirate, for whom captivity and the threat of prosecution are justifiably dreaded, quite a bit of force will be needed. You are not, however, authorized to use deadly force on any individual who does not present a threat of bodily harm to yourself or others around him.

c. The six rules of prisoner handling are:

(1) Speed
(2) Secure
(3) Search
(4) Silence
(5) Separate
(6) Safeguard

These are basic rules to live by when handling pirate prisoners. The two-man rule should always be utilized: one man to set security while the other man handles the prisoner.

d. To better understand the six rules of prisoner handling as they apply to the shipboarding mission, further explanation is as follows:

(1) **Speed.** This goes without saying. The faster you handle a pirate prisoner, the less time he has to escape his manacles, reach for your service pistol, jump overboard, etc.

(2) **Secure.** The securing of pirate prisoners during a shipboarding operation can be performed by any member of the assault force during any phase of the mission. Each member of the assault force should have in his possession prior to the mission enough prisoner handling gear to fully secure six prisoners, either by handcuffs or ties. The force member should also be equipped to secure pirates with hook prostheses using the hookcuff. See Figure 1-10.

(a) During the initial assault, if a detainee is encountered while the assault force (hereafter referred to as the

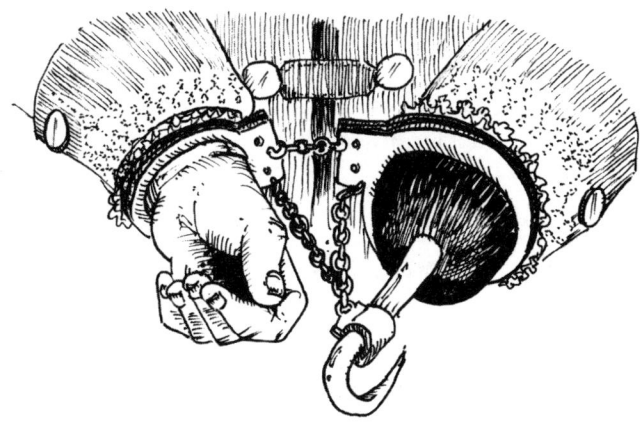

Figure 1-10. Hookcuffs are essential when detaining pirates with hook prostheses.

"train") is moving to the bridge, the first two men in the train will move to the appropriate flank (this is done so the Number Three man in the train can pick up the point and the train does not have to stop) and secure the prisoner, while the remainder of the train continues to the bridge. The two men who have remained behind secure the prisoner, handcuff him to a secure surface on the ship's deck, and fall back into the train as quickly as possible.

(b) The same holds true if a detainee is encountered in a confined space during the initial assault and the first two men cannot step to the flank to secure the prisoner. The Point Man will knock the pirate to the ground and the train will go over him. The last two men in the train will stop and secure the prisoner, handcuff him to the ship, and quickly fall back into the train.

(c) If there are a large number of captive pirates who can effectively hinder the assault force by leaving them short-handed during the final assault onto the bridge, the train will blow past them and continue toward its objective.

(d) Once the bridge has been assaulted, all prisoners on the bridge must be secured by handcuffs or ties before any movement of the prisoners or questioning. After the bridge has been secured, the requirement of securing swashbuckler prisoners to a ship's surface no longer exists.

(e) When moving prisoners, always maintain bodily control.

(f) Always handcuff pirates' hands and hooks behind the back.

(g) If it can be avoided, do not place a blindfold on a captive corsair. Doing so may make him harder to move around, and causes many pirates to lose control where they might otherwise not.

(h) Be aware of the deck of the ship—it can become so hot at times that if the pirate's bare skin comes in contact with it, he may lose control (again, where he might otherwise not have).

(3) **Search**

(a) Place the captive pirate on his stomach with his legs spread. Always approach from the rear, placing your foot inches from his crotch. At this point, if he moves you can disable him with a swift kick to the groin. With your foot between his legs, kneel down, placing your knee into the small of his back and placing one hand on his head, forcing it into the deck. With the free hand, start a detailed search of his body. See Figure 1-11.

NOTE: *It is strongly advised to wear gloves while conducting a search of the buccaneer enemy. Pirates are notorious for their poor hygiene, and stories abound of military personnel afflicted with fleas, crabs, scabies, and a whole host of exotic rashes, simply from coming into fleeting contact with captured pirates.*

(b) When searching a captive swashbuckler, search him completely, starting either from the head or the feet

Figure 1-11. Items discovered during search of pirate detainees.

and working toward the opposite end of the body. After searching the first half, search under the pirate for possible booby traps. When done, roll the prisoner over. Always roll him in a direction such that, if there is a booby trap, his body will serve as a shield against the blast.

(c) Once the prisoner is on his back, complete the detailed search, again starting from one end of the body and working toward the other. The main rule is to have a logical order when searching a pirate prisoner, so you don't forget a portion of the body or overlook an interior pocket or fold on the pirate's person. Do not omit any of several common hiding places on the pirate's person (see Figure 1-12).

(4) **Silence**

(a) Never allow prisoners to talk, especially with each other. By allowing pirates to talk with one another, they can become organized. By allowing them to talk to you, your fellow assault force members, or hostages, you permit them comfort; pirates thrive on nastiness and "head games." You want the pirate prisoner to remain off-guard and disoriented as much as possible. Improvised gags, made of any rags or other materials near at hand, are generally acceptable.

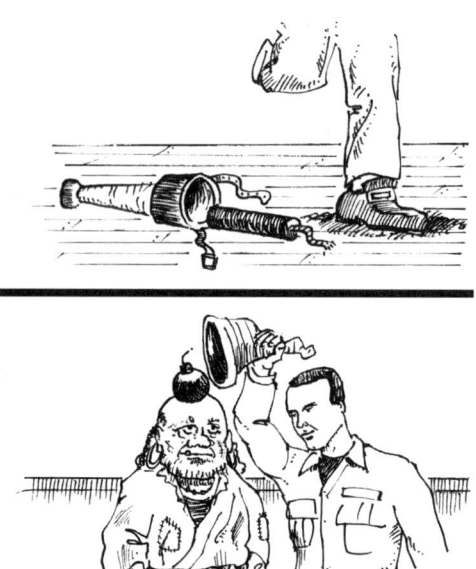

Figure 1-12. Remember to search the prisoner thoroughly.

(5) **Separate**

(a) During a shipboarding mission, this is hard to maintain. You are dealing, typically, with large numbers of pirates and limited space. Normally, buccaneer detainees will be consolidated at one or more staging points.

(6) **Safeguard**

(a) It is the assault force's responsibility to provide security to all pirate prisoners—no matter how noxious and objectionable. Prior to the movement of any prisoner, security must be set along the route the prisoner is to follow. If a shortage of personnel doesn't allow adequate security along the entire route to the next staging point, the pirate detainee will be moved in a "leap-frog" movement. Security will be placed as far as tactically feasible along the route toward the next staging point. Prisoners will then be restaged. Security will then be set again along the prisoner's route toward the next staging point. Again prisoners will be moved. This process will be repeated as many times as necessary to complete the movement to the final detainee processing and staging area (generally on board the assault force's main vessel).

(b) While the above mandate to safeguard all pirate prisoners should be absolutely clear, it is unfortunately true that pirate prisoners have a remarkable tendency to throw themselves overboard rather than be taken ashore as captives. Because the assault force will often be undermanned to begin with, the wisest course of action is to refrain from "saving" these detainees, lest an assault force team member be carried overboard along with him. There is a small chance that a Search and Rescue (SAR) support team will be able to search the waters surrounding the ship, scooping up any wet swashbucklers. As with all other areas of the mission, the individual member must exercise his best judgment, doing all within his power to safeguard the prisoner, yet stopping short of compromising the overall mission.

e. **Follow-on Security Force**

(1) The security follow-on forces should be brought on board after the anti-pirate assault force has established initial control of the topside spaces—deck, bridge, crow's nest, etc.— and before undertaking internal clearance operations of the Contact of Interest (COI)—i.e., the pirate captain, in almost all cases.

(2) Additional follow-on forces should be detailed to secure communication facilities, aft steering, and assist with the control of pirate detainees. As described above, pirates are often adept

at evading capture, and it is not unknown for one to creep out of an unexamined crate or niche and assault security forces or even begin steering the ship.

(3) Supporting surface ships should close the intervening distance as quickly as possible and prepare to serve in a Search and Rescue capacity, or otherwise support the mission as directed. It is these ships' responsibility to rescue any sea dog captives who may have jumped overboard during detainee transfer. See Figure 1-13.

(4) Follow-on personnel should join with the initial assault force and exfiltrate with same, if practical. If follow-on personnel cannot fastrope in with the assault force, they should have first priority to board after the initial infiltration.

(5) The decision to send the ship's boarding party aboard the pirate vessel will be made by the acting commander based upon recommendation of the assault force commander (AFC) and other relevant factors.

(6) Detailed clearance of the pirate ship by the anti-pirate assault force then begins and will require significantly more time. During the detailed clearance, medical assistance may fast-rope on board or come aboard with the ship's boarding party and establish a triage facility, if required. The wounded will be evacuated as necessary. Assembly areas shall be established and all pirate crew and hostages accounted for, searched, and marshaled to safe areas in the event that they require evacuation.

(7) When appropriate, the assault force commander will call for responsibility for the pirate ship and crew to be transferred to the appropriate authority, and the assault force will depart the pirate ship—unless security is required.

f. **Establishment of the Detainee Staging/Processing Area**

(1) Prior to the establishment of a staging and processing area for pirate detainees, communications between the assault force commander and follow-on force commander must be established. It is the AFC's responsibility to establish a secured

Figure 1-13. If possible, support crew should rescue any pirates who have jumped overboard.

detainee staging area for consolidating all privateer detainees encountered while the remainder of the team conducts detailed clearances of the internal spaces and compartments of the pirate ship.

(2) The assault force and follow-on force should have a detainee turnover point somewhere along the route to the detainee staging/processing area. (Normally the detainee staging/processing area will be located externally, usually on the ship's deck or, preferably, on board a supporting ship, if one has arrived on the scene.) Prior to any prisoner movement, a security corridor will be established to safeguard and assist in controlling the movement of pirate prisoners.

g. The assault force should possess the capability to conduct the entire shipboarding mission without the assistance of a follow-on force.

1.7. Clearance of Internal and External Spaces

Two-Man Room Clearance

a. On most maritime pirate ship assaults, the basic two-man clearance is the most widely used room clearance procedure. This is due to the limited size of most compartments and spaces found on most shipping vessels. (Remember that in nearly every case, a pirate ship will have been seized from an honest merchant.) Obviously there are exceptions to every rule (i.e., bridge, mess deck, dungeon space, opium den and/or grog chamber).

b. The standard operating procedure for conducting a basic two-man room clearance is as follows:

(1) Assault team (aka the "train") stacks outside the entrance of the room that is to be cleared. Security is maintained to the rear by the last man in the stack, who must be vigilant against assault by "sleeper" pirates. Front security is maintained by the Point Man, door security is the Number One man's job, and breaching of the door is the Breacher's responsibility. No clearance should be attempted unless there is at least a two-man backup team in the stack prepared and ready to assist the primary two-man clearance team.

(2) Each member in the stack quickly preps himself prior to entering the room. See Figure 1-14.

(3) Once each member of the room clearance team is ready, starting from the rear of the train the last man gives a "squeeze signal" firmly to the man in front of him. This signals that he is fully ready to conduct the room clearance. This squeeze signal is passed in order to the front of the stack until it reaches the Number One man. The squeeze signal will not be passed unless that particular man is fully ready.

(4) Once the squeeze signal reaches the Number One man, he knows everyone behind him is fully ready and standing by to enter and clear the room of privateers. The Number One man then makes eye contact with the Breacher. The Number One man nods his head three times and the door is breached. The two-man team enters the room, shouting "Avast, me

Figure 1-14. The two-man team prepares to clear a room.

hearties!" or "Shiver me timbers!" in an effort to confuse any swashbucklers who may be inside. (This strategy is part of so-called "Pirate Psychological Operations" or "PiPsyOps.") The team then conducts clearance.

(5) Standard operating procedure for any room clearance is as follows: the Number One man always moves left, staying between 12 to 18 inches off the wall. The Number Two man always moves to the right, staying 12 to 18 inches off the wall.

(6) The "fields of fire" for the first two men entering a room will never change, no matter how many men are conducting a room clearance. The Number One man's initial field of fire will always be straight down the wall. The Number One man will then sweep right across the room all the way over to the other side of the room, just short of his partner. The Number Two man will then carry out the exact opposite procedure, sweeping to his left.

(7) As soon as each man's field of fire is cleared, each will respond with a verbal signal of "Clear."

(8) As soon as the door is breached, the Breacher and Point Man will move down the hall to the door of the next room to be breached, and restage themselves as before. The Point Man will maintain security and the Breacher will stand just to the

left or right, depending on the orientation of the door, and wait for the train to catch up. As before, members of the train must be vigilant against rearguard assault by any remaining swashbucklers. The Number Three and Four men will assume the Number One and Two responsibilities for the next room. After the first room is cleared, the former Number One and Number Two men will fall into the rear of the train and assume the former Number Five and Number Four men's responsibilities.

Four-Man Room Clearance

a. The four-man room clearance is conducted in the same manner, except that there are two additional men. A four-man room clearance is the standard operating procedure employed for larger compartments found onboard a pirate vessel (i.e., mess hall, rum lair, infirmary, shipboard aviary).

b. The procedure for conducting a four-man room clearance is as follows:

(1) Stack the train.

(2) The stack will then prep as described above for a two-man room clearance.

(3) "Squeeze signal" is passed. When ready, Breacher breaches door. Point Man and Breacher then move to the next door.

(4) Four-man team enters the room (again employing "PiPsyOps" by shouting out common pirate phrases) and conduct clearance.

(5) The Number One and Number Two men conduct standard room clearance, as described above. Number One moves left, then sweeps right, clearing his field of fire. Number Two moves right, then sweeps left, clearing his field of fire.

(6) The Number Three man enters the room directly behind the Number Two man, moving to the left along the wall. Number Three should be between 12 to 18 inches off the wall. Number Three's field of fire is directly to the center of the room, then sweeping to the left and stopping just short of Number One.

(7) Number Four enters the room directly behind Number Three, moving to the right along the wall. Number Four

should also be between 12 to 18 inches off the wall. Number Four's field of fire is directly to the center of the room, then sweeping to the right and stopping just short of Number Two.

(8) After the room is cleared, the room clearance team withdraws from the room. First man in is the last man out. The order of withdrawal should be 4, 3, 2, 1. The last man out should use a piece of chalk or other writing implement to mark the room as cleared. Acceptable signs include a large "X," or any short phrase that can be written swiftly, such as "No pirates inside" or "This room has been confirmed to be a buccaneer-free zone," followed by the force member's signature, including rank and unit number.

(9) The four-man room clearance team should fall back into the stack.

The Train

a. The train will continue this procedure until all spaces and compartments are cleared, and all remaining sea rovers rousted and detained.

b. During the initial internal room clearance, the first room or passageway on each level is designated as the "detainee staging area." This area will be used as a consolidation point for any pirates taken captive during the level-by-level, room-to-room clearance. Two men will then be designated as security for the temporary detainee staging area. Normally, these are the first two men who initially cleared the compartment.

c. If during a room clearance a pirate is discovered (and if he does not present a threat), he should be secured and searched in the compartment where he was found. A surprisingly large proportion of pirates are cowards who prostrate themselves when caught, and thus this procedure may be possible more often than expected. Meanwhile, the train will continue to clear spaces, moving past the room where the captured corsair was encountered.

d. If it is a four-man room clearance, the last two men who entered the compartment (the Number Three and Number Four men) will be responsible for securing the prisoner and for his transfer to the detainee staging area. The last man to initially enter the compartment (the Number Four man) during the clearance will be responsible for the movement of the pirate detainee to the staging area. If the room has been cleared and no longer poses a threat, the remainder of the clearance team will leave the room and fall back into the rear of the train. On a two-man room clearance, the Number Two man assumes the responsibilities of handling the captured pirate. The Number One man maintains room security. In general, the rule is that the last man in assumes responsibility for the pirate detainee.

Passageway Clearance

a. The L-shaped passageway should be cleared by conducting a one-man clearance. See Figure 1-15. Rear security is always the responsibility of the last man in the train.

b. The T-shaped passageway is found only occasionally on pirate vessels, most often around the area of the galley and the pirates' sleeping quarters. It should be cleared by conducting a two-man clearance. See Figure 1-16. On this type of passageway, the Breacher should take one step to the outside of the train during the forming of the stack prior to clearing the passageway. This enables the Breacher easier access to the front of the train. The Breacher's normal position in the train, by contrast, is behind the Point Man.

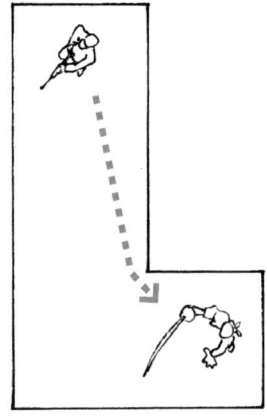

Figure 1-15. Clearance of an L-shaped room.

c. The four-directional passageway is rarely found on a pirate ship, but presents unique dangers to the assault force team. It should be cleared by conducting a four-man clearance. See Figure 1-17. Again, the Breacher steps to the side.

d. Gamesmanship can be a factor in room and passageway clearance.

By the mission stage at which the train is clearing interior rooms of the pirate ship, the element of surprise, in nine out of ten cases, has been compromised. Therefore it makes sense to attempt simple vocal ruses to draw the pirate enemy out, and into a disadvantageous position. In a gravelly bass voice, call out likely pirate phrases. Ideas include "Arr, who goes there?" "Ahoy, matey," and "Yo ho ho." Often, nonsensical or garbled phrases will suffice, if spoken in a reasonably "pirate-y" voice. You may be able, by employing this simple gambit, to draw a concealed pirate out of his hiding place. Or, if he is lying in wait around a corner, you may be able to trick the crusty mariner into lowering his guard momentarily or calling back to you, thinking you are one of his mates.

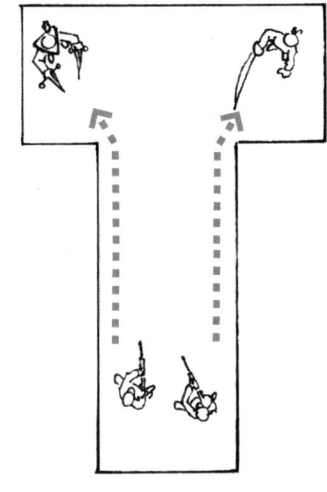

Figure 1-16. Clearance of a T-shaped room.

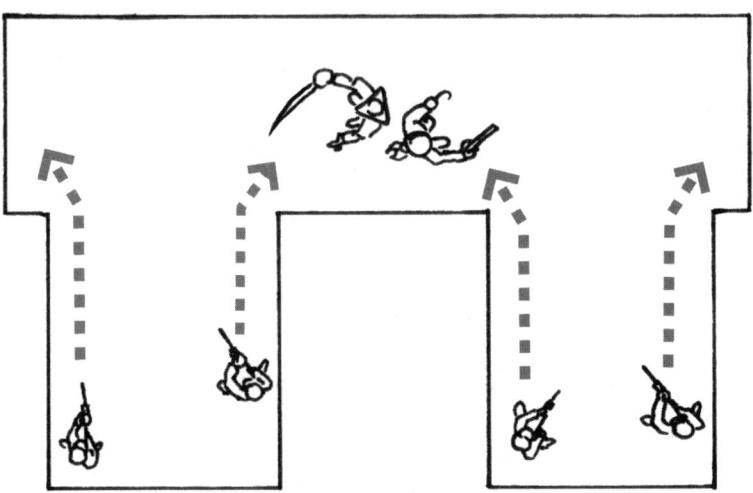

Figure 1-17. Clearance of a pi-shaped room.

Internal Stairs

a. Stairs are normally cleared using a one-man clearance. The Point Man will clear ahead of the train. See Figure 1-18. However, if the train is to enter through a door onto a particular level of the pirate vessel utilizing the stairs, a two-man clearance will be conducted. First the train will stop, prep for the clearance, and pass squeeze signals. Once ready, the Point Man and Breacher conduct the clearance. The Point Man moves past the door, taking a position so he can cover the remainder of the stairs below him. The Breacher moves forward where he can cover the door and, if needed, breach the door without interfering with the clearance team's ability to go through the door to clear the passageway at that level. Special care should be taken to clear the areas beneath internal staircases, as these tight, dark spaces make appealing hiding places for sneaky seafaring rogues and—more perilously—provide them with the perfect opportunity to slash and stab at the ankles and Achilles tendons of assault force members.

Figure 1-18. Proceed with caution along internal stairways.

External Stairs

a. External stairs are primarily located on the main superstructure. The best method for clearing a flight of stairs is with a four-man clearance team.

b. The standard operating procedure is as follows: left, right, forward, and back. The Number One man always clears left, the Number Two man always clears right. The Number Three man in the stack clears forward. The Number Four man clears back. This way, 360 degrees of security are maintained. Note that the Number Four man is also responsible for visually clearing the crow's nest and fo'csle (if any). While these parts of the ship should have been cleared earlier by sniper fire, they make attractive vantage points for pirates and must be periodically rechecked throughout the mission.

c. The remainder of the train sets up below the four-man clearance team.

d. The Number Five man becomes the Point Man for the remaining members of the train. The Number Five man and the remainder of the train will move halfway up onto the stairway, but not before the four-man clearance team makes their move onto the next level of stairs to be cleared. Again, the shouting of pirate phrases may help expedite stairway clearance—but only insofar as such noise does not interfere with team communications.

e. Once the Number Five man hears an "All clear," he will lead the remainder of the train past the stationary clearance team to the next level of stairs and stop. The clearance team will maintain their position until the last man in the train has passed. The clearance team will then collapse and fall back into the rear of the train.

f. The Number Five man now becomes the Number One man. As soon as the new Point Man has four men, he can repeat the four-man clearance procedure.

g. This tactic enables the train to establish a "bounding overwatch" as they move to their objective. Remember, the remaining members in the train pick up their normal fields of fire.

h. Take care not to strand the entire assault force team at the top of a flight of stairs. The concentration of so much weight upon a flight of stairs is unwise and is considered an unnecessary risk. Collecting the entire team in one place also opens the possibility of some hidden sea dog peppering the force with musket fire or setting the stairs ablaze.

Weatherdeck

a. Normally the movement onto the weatherdeck is in association with the assault force's insertion and its movement to the pirate ship's superstructure. When planning an insertion point onto the weatherdeck, plan (if possible) for the shortest and most direct route to the bridge. The movement to the bridge should be as far as possible to the port or starboard side of the ship's weatherdeck. This allows the assault force to cut down on their fields of fire and concentrate their security to the front, back, and to one flank.

b. During the assault, the movement from the insertion point to the bridge should be accomplished in a "bounding overwatch"-type movement. The clearance of the weatherdeck as the assault force makes its way to the bridge should be viewed as a multiple-room clearance. That is, all dead spaces and structures encountered along the route should be cleared utilizing basic assault force skills.

Bridge

a. The primary objective when raiding any pirate vessel is the bridge and, ultimately, the wheel of the ship. On most merchant shipping vessels, if you control the bridge, you control the ship. Normally the pirate ship's captain will be located in close proximity to the bridge, provided he has not gotten wind of the assault force's approach and high-tailed it (a not-uncommon occurrence among the privateer class, infamous opportunists). The bridge area should be secured by the assault force in the least amount of time possible. This will cut down the pirate ship's crew reaction time. Don't sacrifice your assault force's security for blinding speed, however: Be forewarned that many pirate captains will put up a ferocious, often nasty fight prior to ceding control of the bridge.

b. The bridge is normally a four-man room clearance with at least a two-man backup team.

c. The possibility of needing to mechanically or explosively breach the bridge's hatch or door is always there. Plan for it. A good rule of thumb for breaching is that every door or hatch is a breaching problem. Train for it. Flex liner, data sheet, explosive foam, and 12-gauge 00 buck are just some of the explosives that can be used. Hooligan tools, sledgehammers, buc busters, crowbars, and fire axes are a few items that should also accompany any assault force on a shipboarding operation. These items are backpacked by the Breachers. In addition, two men should be designated as "Torch Operators."

d. Once the bridge is secured, the following sequence of events should take place in the following order:

- Bridge is secured by four-man room clearance team.
- Communications are established to higher authority.
- All detainees on the bridge are secured.
- The pirate ship's captain is identified and brought to the bridge, instructed to stop the ship, and present a complete sailing list of the crew and all documentation of cargo his ship is carrying. This is, in virtually every case, merely a formality: The pirate captain seems to take as a point of pride his ability to curse, threaten, and spit at members of the assault force team. These acts of defiance must be properly understood as the desperate acts of a deposed leader to hearten his men; the last thing an assault force member should do in this situation is rise to the crusty swashbuckler's bait.
- If the pirate ship's captain will not immediately stop the ship, the assault force will stop the ship.
- C-2 element is fully established within close proximity to the bridge. Normally the C-2 element consists of the assault force commander and his radio communicator.
- Security force is left on the bridge along with the C-2 element. This is to guard against any escaped detainees, who will sometimes make a run on the ship's bridge in a misguided effort to "take back" control of the ship. Again, it cannot be overstated that pirates are singularly adept at hiding in the unlikeliest of spaces. Thus, security must remain vigilant against the appearance of these stealthy buccaneers.
- Follow-on force is inserted and employed.
- Assault force commander directs his force to start internal clearance.
- Internal clearance is completed. All pirate detainees are accounted for and cargo inventoried. Special notations are employed on the outside of any treasure chests or troves, for greater ease of location and transfer later on.

- Detainees are turned over to the follow-on force for search and processing.
- Assault force extracts. Force members often feel the strong temptation to insult or provoke captive pirates upon exiting, but should be reminded of the higher standards of the U.S. Navy. This goes double for the impulse to vandalize or damage the pirate ship upon leaving; sailors must be reminded that this ship is now the property of the U.S. Navy.

The assault force should be able to accomplish any portion of the shipboarding mission, or the entire pirate detention and room-clearance mission, without the aid of a follow-on force in case the follow-on force cannot be inserted onto the deck of the pirate ship for whatever reason.

1.8. Shipboarding (Subsurface Assault)

This section provides future guidance for anti-pirate assault force personnel in advanced maritime instruction involving the boarding of pirate ships from subsurface platforms—i.e., from the water.

The two-week period of shipboarding instruction given to all anti-pirate assault force team members was the first subsurface shipboarding instruction. The following discussion is directed toward the problems involving these procedures, not the obvious tactical deficiencies or the potential dangers presented by the likely presence of the pirate enemy during shipboarding.

a. The obvious hazard to the diver is the potential of entanglement with the ascent lines used to connect the diver's Underwater Breathing Apparatus (UBA) to the derigging line. In subsurface derigging under controlled conditions involving a swimming pool or combat training tank, where the divers do not have to deal with any environmental or visibility problems (or hostile fire from cannons or muskets), the above procedures do not present any problems.

Under normal environmental conditions at night and in open water, the derigging procedures have a potential for entangling divers. Naturally, this is exacerbated by the need for speed and stealth, and the imagined presence of murderous privateers peering down at one from the pirate ship's deck. The main problem is the ascent lines. If a group of divers encounter any type of current or surge, there is an extreme possibility of diver entanglement when ascending to the surface.

Once on the surface, the procedure is to drop the UBA while still attached to the ascent line. (In most cases, the divers do not surface exactly together.) Again, if there is any surge or current, poor diver positioning due to restricted visibility, or loss of body contact with other divers while ascending, there exists more than a reasonable chance of a UBA being blown into a nearby diver. For example, if a diver becomes entangled after he drops his own UBA and the rest of the eight-man element has done the same, the weight of all the dive rigs would pull the entangled diver down as surely as if he had an anchor around his neck.

If this procedure is attempted around a pirate ship, the chances of this happening on a scale of 1 to 10, due to the heavy surge encountered around most pirate ships, would be a 7. Divers must also be aware of the buccaneer's affinity for dumping great quantities of chum overboard, thereby attracting large schools of sharks (whom the pirates like to shoot at and urinate on, for "fun"). This can complicate the shipboarding mission. See Figure 1-19.

b. The second problem is swimming an element on a derigging line (aka "lizard line"). Under most simple derigging situations, the current derigging procedures present no apparent problems. However, training for the worst-case scenario is how an assault force should approach their training. Train under conditions where limited visibility is a factor and obstacles such as ship screws, struts, barnacles, floating corpses, amputated limbs, the aforementioned man-eating sharks, and enormous squid are a major problem. This training will help a swimming element eliminate any confusion while it locates and rigs its securing point for its derigging line.

Under conditions where there are many obstacles (such as pirate ships in relatively shallow water or in the presence of reefs), swimming an eight-man element on a derigging line should be eliminated. All members should be attached by buddy line. An echelon formation is recommended with the attack board diver leading the formation. The secondary job of the attack board diver is to maintain the derigging

Figure 1-19. Attacking by way of subsurface approach presents significant dangers.

line. Once on the target, the derigging line man finds his first securing point for the derigging line. After snapping one end of the derigging line to the securing point with a snap link, the derigging line man then places the Number Two man's hand on the securing point. Next, the derigging man detaches his buddy line and hands it to the Number Two man. The derigging man swims the derigging line's end out to the second securing point, secures the line, then swims back to the first point by following the derigging line back to the element waiting on the first securing point. This method gives the derigging line man the freedom to search for the second derigging point without dragging seven other swimmers down to Davy Jones's locker with him. This method keeps the confusion factor to a minimum, maintaining focus where it belongs: on preparing to fight pirates.

After returning to the securing point, the derigging line man places the Number Two man on the line. This procedure is repeated for each man as the swimmer line moves down the derigging line toward the second securing point. After the element moves down the derigging line and the first man reaches the second securing point, the derigging line man places his hand on the second securing point where the derigging line is attached. The Number One man places his hands on the derigging line and slides his hand back down the line until he feels the first derigging line securing point. Next, the Number One man snaps himself into that securing point with a snap link, then slides his hands down the derigging line toward the man next to him until he locates the next securing point. The Number One man then grabs the Number Two man's hand and places it on that securing point and squeezes his hand, signaling to him that this is his securing point. The Number Two man snaps himself into the derigging line securing point. This procedure is repeated for each man.

It is imperative that this process be conducted as noiselessly as possible. Remember that derigging often must be carried out fewer than 15 feet from the deck of the pirate ship, where one or more crew members should be assumed to be standing watch. See Figure 1-20. Assault force members should not assume that snipers have removed watchmen, any more than they should assume watchmen to be dead drunk on gut-rot whiskey and home-brewed grog (though both are, as a rule, strong possibilities).

Figure 1-20. The element of surprise is crucial to the mission's success.

Chapter 2

ON-DECK HAND-TO-HAND
AND HAND-TO-HOOK COMBAT

A sailor cannot count on starting in a superior position in every encounter with the pirate enemy—especially on board the enemy's ship, where the buccaneer naturally maintains the element of surprise. There are any number of reasons why the sailor may be separated from his weaponry or unable to wield it during a lightning-fast attack by a pirate. To survive, the sailor must have simple hand-to-hand and hand-to-hook combat techniques that will bring him back into his fight plan and turn the tables on his swashbuckling foe.

SECTION I. UNARMED PIRATE

Most grasping type attacks will leave your pirate enemy in striking range. Therefore, elaborate defenses are not necessary. You should simply attack the pirate with strikes and force him to either close with you, or, when he attempts to respond with strikes of his own, take the opportunity to close or escape yourself. The techniques in this section are directed at escaping from several positions, favored by the pirate class, that are more difficult.

A Note of Caution about Facing an "Unarmed" Pirate: Though he may be without a traditional weapon, the average pirate will as likely as not have some manner of prosthesis—a hook hand, for example, or a heavy wooden peg leg—that may give him a deadly advantage. The following techniques should be followed when battle is joined with the pirate enemy, but caution must always be exercised, as the pirate is not shy about using his so-called handicap to his advantage.

2.1. Defense Against Chokes

a. **Standing Rear Naked.** At the moment you feel the arm of the pirate enemy around your neck, your hands should immediately grasp it to keep him from tightening the choke, and you should hang your weight on his arm to feel where his weight is. If he is close to your back, simply lean forward at the waist and, using your hips to lift, throw him straight over your back. See Figure 2-1.

Figure 2-1. Defense against the standing rear naked choke.

b. **Standing Rear Naked Pulling Back.** If, when you hang your weight on the pirate enemy's arm, you feel that he is pulling you back over one of his legs, you should reach back with your leg and wrap it around the outside of his leg on the same side as the choking arm. You can weaken the pirate by forcing him to hold this position indefinitely. Underfed, and often suffering the beginnings of scurvy or some tropical malady, most pirates are ill equipped for prolonged close-in combat. As your opponent tires from holding you up, use your leg as a guide and work your way around to the position shown. Your leg must be behind his, and you must be leaning forward, controlling his arm. Twisting your body, throw him to the ground. See Figure 2-2.

Figure 2-2. Defense against the standing rear naked pulling-back choke.

c. **One-Hand Neck Press Against the Wall.** Should a pirate pin you against the wall or a mast with one hand, strike his arm with the palm of your hand on the side where his thumb is pushing toward his fingers. This will make his arm slide off of your neck. Follow through with your strike, and when your arm is in position, strike with a backward elbow strike to the head. Again, special caution must be taken in the case of the pirate with a hook or metal prong in place of a hand. See Figure 2-3.

Figure 2-3. Defense against the one-hand neck press against the wall.

d. **Two-Hand Neck Press While Pinned Against the Wall.** If a pirate uses both hands against your neck to press you into the wall, grasp under his elbows with both hands. You may utilize the pirate's elaborate dress—often including long coat, breeches, ruffled shirt, etc.—to gain a solid grip. Step out to either side and throw him against the wall. Finish with a knee strike. See Figure 2-4.

2.2. Defense Against Bear Hugs

a. **Front Bear Hug Over Your Arms.** The bear hug, ideal for the close conditions of shipboard combat, is a special favorite among the ruffled-shirt crowd. When a pirate attempts to grasp you in a bear hug from the front over your

Figure 2-4. Defense against the two-hand neck press while pinned against the wall.

arms, move your hips back and use your arms as a brace between his hips and yours. Short, sharp blows to the swashbuckler's groin should prove as effective against him as against any other male foe. Your hands should be on his hip bones, and your elbows should be braced against your hips. Keeping one arm as a brace, step to the opposite side to achieve the clinch. Finish with a takedown. See Figure 2-5.

b. **Front Bear Hug Under Your Arms.** If the pirate enemy attempts to grasp you under your arms, step back into a strong base and use both hands to push his chin upwards to break his grasp. Finish with a knee strike. If he is exceptionally strong, push upwards against the nose. You may also gain an advantage by grasping any facial hair or jewelry the pirate might be wearing around the head and neck. See Figure 2-6.

Figure 2-5. Defense against the frontal bear hug (over the arms).

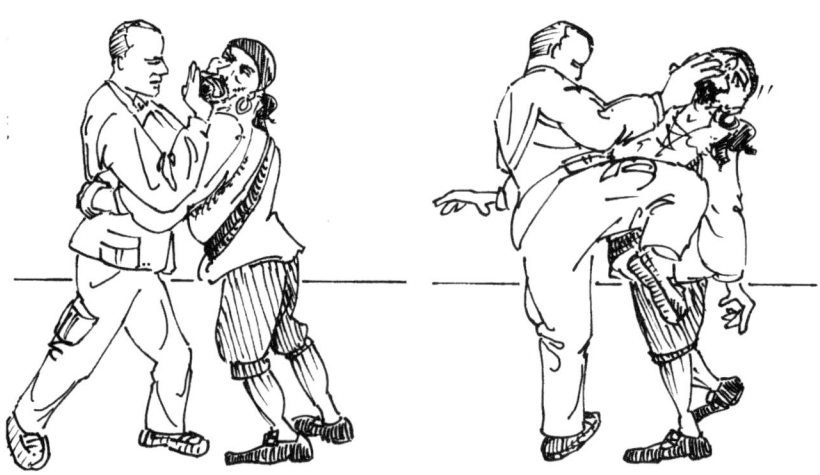

Figure 2-6. Defense against the frontal bear hug (under the arms).

c. **Bear Hug from the Rear, Over Your Arms.** When a pirate attempts to grab you from behind over your arms, drop down into a strong stance and bring your arms up to prevent him from controlling them. Step to the outside and then around his hip so that your legs are behind him. At this point you may attack his groin, or you may lift him with your hips and throw him. Be advised, too, that the average pirate holds woefully outdated social views and will be susceptible to "PiPsyOps" in this situation: Suggesting that he is attempting to initiate sexual congress with you will fluster and anger him immeasurably. Utilize his irritation to throw him or otherwise gain the advantage. See Figure 2-7.

Figure 2-7. Defense against the rear bear hug (over the arms). Beware the hook.

d. **Bear Hug from the Rear, Under Your Arms.** When a pirate grasps you from the rear under your arms, he will probably try to lift you for a throw. If he does so, wrap your leg around his so that you are harder to maneuver for the throw. The above note regarding the pirate's inferior physical conditioning applies here: His general lack of nutrition should translate to a lack of stamina. Take advantage by forcing him into a lengthy grappling session, steadily tiring him out. When the pirate sets you down, or if he proves unable to lift you at all, lean your weight forward and place your hands on the ground. Move to one side until one of his legs is between yours. Push backward slightly and reach one hand back to grasp his heel. When you have a good grip, reach back with the other hand. Pull forward with your hands, and when the corsair falls, break his knee by sitting on it as you pull on his leg. See Figure 2-8.

Figure 2-8. Defense against the rear bear hug (under the arms).

SECTION II. ARMED PIRATE

A sword or dagger, properly employed, is a deadly weapon; in the hands of a veteran pirate, any stick or blunt object can be used as a cudgel. However, using proven defensive techniques, such as maintaining separation, will greatly enhance the sailor's ability to fight and win.

2.3. Defense Against an Armed Pirate

An unarmed defender is always at a distinct disadvantage when facing an armed pirate. This is doubly true in the close quarters of shipboard combat. It is imperative, therefore, that the unarmed defender understands and uses the following principles to survive:

a. **Separation.** Maintain a separation of at least 10 feet plus the length of the weapon from the piratical attacker. This distance gives the defender time to react to any attempt by his privateering foe to close the gap. The defender should also try to place stationary objects—chairs, lanterns, rum jugs—between himself and the attacker. Here again, the defender may take advantage of the pirate's handicap by moving to terrain a peg-legged combatant may find difficult to navigate.

b. **Unarmed Defense.** Unarmed defense against an armed pirate should be a last resort. If it is necessary, the defender's course of action includes:

(1) **Move the body out of the line of attack of the weapon**. Step off the line of attack or redirect the buccaneer's attack of the weapon so that it clears the body.

(2) **Control the weapon**. Maintain control of the pirate's leading arm by securing the weapon, hand, wrist, elbow, or arm by using joint locks, if possible.

(3) **Stun the attacker with an effective counterattack**. Counterattack should be swift and devastating. Take the vigor out of the sea dog with a low, unexpected kick, or break a locked joint of the cur's attacking arm. Rip a prized gold earring from the pirate's ear. Jam a thumb into the already-damaged eye socket lying behind his patch. Strikes to motor nerve centers are effective stuns, as are skin tearing, eye gouging, and attacking of the throat. The defender can also take away the pirate's balance (though this is trickier, since pirates are famously nimble).

(4) **Ground the attacker**. Take the privateer to the ground where you can continue to disarm or further disable him.

(5) **Disarm the attacker**. Break the attacking pirate's locked joints. Use leverage or induce pain to disarm the oceanic marauder and finish him, or simply to maintain physical control.

(6) **Mock the attacker**. Do not hesitate to verbally assault the pirate with the foulest of language. Pirates have notoriously thin skin, and remarks, especially about their mothers and wives, tend to enrage them. This loss of composure could be all the edge you need to take the pirate down.

c. **Precaution.** Do not focus full attention on the weapon because the attacker may have other weapons affixed to his body (possibly including dangerous hook- and prong-hands, or heavy oak peg legs, which serve as ideal cudgels). There may even be other attackers that you have not seen. Also do not overlook sudden airborne attacks from the pirate's disease-ridden parrot.

d. **Expedient Aids.** Anything available can become an expedient aid to defend against an armed attack. The Kevlar helmet can be used as a shield; similarly, the load-carrying equipment (LCE) and shirt jacket can be used to protect the defender against a weapon. An empty grog jug, a concertina found lying around, a pair of breeches awaiting darning—all can be picked up and thrown at the pirate's eyes.

2.4. Defense Against a Dagger

When an unarmed sailor is faced with an enemy armed with a dagger, he must be mentally prepared to be cut. The likelihood of being cut severely is less if the fighter is well trained in knife defense and if the principles of weapon defense are followed. A slash wound is not usually lethal or shock inducing; however, a stab wound risks injury to vital organs, arteries, and veins and may also cause instant shock or unconsciousness.

a. **Types of Dagger Attacks.** The first line of defense against a pirate armed with a dagger is to avoid close contact. The different types of knife attacks are:

(1) **Thrust.** The thrust is the most common and most dangerous type of knife attack used by pirates, as dictated by the close quarters of shipboard fighting. It is a strike directed straight into the target by jabbing or lunging.

(2) **Slash.** The slash is a sweeping surface cut or circular slash. The wound is usually a long cut, varying from a slight surface cut to a deep gash.

(3) **Tear.** The tear is a cut made by dragging the tip of the blade across the body to create a ripping-type cut.

(4) **Hack.** The hack is delivered by using the dagger to block or chop with.

(5) **Butt.** The butt is a strike with the dagger handle. This attack may also be frequently encountered during close-in fighting with pirates.

b. **Dagger Defense Drills.** Dagger defense drills are used to familiarize sailors with defense movement techniques for various angles of attack. For training, sailors should be paired off; one partner is designated the "pirate" and one is the defender. It is important that the "pirate" make his attack realistic in terms of distance and angling during training. Mimicking the crudeness of the buccaneer, in his guttural speech and offensive personal odor, can help to prepare a sailor. The "pirate's" strikes must be accurate and hit the defender at the intended target if the defender does not defend himself or move off the line of attack. For safety, the attacks are delivered first at one-quarter and one-half speed, and then at three-quarter speed as the defender becomes more skilled. Variations can be added by changing grips, stances, and attacks.

(1) **Defense #1 Against Armed Opponent—Check and Lift.** The pirate delivers a slash along the No. 1 angle of attack. The defender checks the pirate's thrust with his elbow and forearm, striking the pirate's outside forearm and wrist area (Step 1). The defender's right hand immediately follows behind the strike to lift, redirect, and take control of the pirate's dagger arm (Step 2). The defender brings the attacking arm around to his right side where he can use an arm bar, wrist lock, and so forth, to disarm the pirate (Step 3). He will have better control by keeping the dagger hand as close to his body as possible. See Figure 2-9.

(2) **Defense #2 Against Armed Opponent—Check and Ride.** The pirate slashes with a No. 2 angle of attack. The defender meets the attacking arm with a strike from both forearms against the outside forearm, his bone against the pirate's muscle tissue (Step 1). The strike checks the forward momentum of the attacking arm. The defender's right hand is then used to ride the attacking arm clear of his body (Step 2). He

redirects the attacker's energy with strength starting from the right elbow (Step 3).

Figure 2-9. Defense #1 against armed opponent: Check and Lift.
Note: **Beware parrot attack.**

(3) **Defense #3 Against Armed Opponent—Curb and Lift.**
The attacking corsair delivers a horizontal slash to the defender's ribs, kidneys, or hip on the left side (Step 1). The defender meets and checks the attacking arm on the left side of his body with a downward circular motion across the front of his own body. At the same time, he moves his body off the line of attack. He should meet the attacker's forearm with a strike forceful enough to check its momentum (Step 2). The defender then rides the energy of the attacking arm by wiping downward along the outside of his own left forearm with his right hand. He then redirects the pirate's dagger hand around to his right side where he can control or disarm the weapon (Step 3). See Figure 2-10.

STEP 1

STEP 2

STEP 3

Figure 2-10. Defense #3 against armed opponent: Curb and Lift.

(4) **Defense #4 Against Armed Opponent—Check.** The buccaneer slashes the defender with a backhand slashing motion

to the right side at the ribs, kidneys, or hips. The defender moves his right arm in a downward circular motion and strikes the attacking arm on the outside of the body (Step 1). At the same time, he moves off the line of attack. The strike must be forceful enough to check the attack. The left arm is held in a higher guard position to protect from a redirected attack or to assist in checking (Step 2). Again, the sailor may wish to use his greater conditioning and the pirate's malnourishment to tire the pirate out before proceeding. The defender then moves his body to a position where he can choose a proper disarming maneuver (Step 3). See Figure 2-11.

Figure 2-11. Defense #4 against armed opponent: Check.

(5) **Defense #5 Against Armed Opponent—Parry.** A lunging thrust to the stomach is made by the pirate along the No. 5 angle of attack (Step 1). The defender moves his body off the line of attack and deflects the attacking arm by parrying with his left hand (Step 2). He deflects the attacking hand toward his right side by redirecting it with his right hand. As he does this, the defender can strike downward with the left forearm or the wrist onto the forearm or wrist of the pirate—his goal should be to fracture the bone (Step 3). The defender ends up in a position to lock the elbow of the attacking arm across his body if he steps off the line of attack properly (Step 4).

(6) **Defense #6 Against Armed Opponent.** The pirate lunges with a thrust to the face, throat, or solar plexus (Step 1). The defender moves his body off the line of attack while parrying with either hand. He redirects the attacking arm so that the knife clears his body (Step 2). He maintains control of the cur's weapon hand or arm and gouges the eyes of his seafaring attacker, driving him backward and off balance (Step 3). Biting the pirate about the nose and cheeks is also advantageous, though by doing so the sailor risks contracting any number of exotic maladies or skin infections. If the pirate is much taller than the defender, it may be a more natural movement for the defender to raise his left hand to strike and deflect the attacking arm. He can then gouge his thumb or fingers into the pirate's jugular notch and force him to the ground. Still another possibility for this angle of attack is for the defender to move his body off the line of attack while parrying. He can then turn his body, rotate his shoulder under the elbow joint of the pirate, and lock it out (Step 4).

(7) **Defense #7 Against Armed Opponent.** The attacking pirate strikes straight downward onto the defender with a stab (Step 1). The defender reacts by moving his body out of the weapon's path and by parrying or checking and redirecting the attacking arm (Step 2). The reactions may vary as to what is natural for the defender. The defender then takes control of the weapon and disarms the attacker (Step 3).

c. **Follow-up Techniques.**

(1) **Defend and Clear.** When the defender has performed a defensive maneuver and avoided a pirate attack, he can push the attacker away and move out of the sea dog's reach.

(2) **Defend and Stun.** After the defender performs his first defensive maneuver to a safer position, he can deliver a stunning blow as an immediate counterattack. Strikes to motor nerve points or to the pirate's limbs, low kicks, and elbow strikes are especially effective stunning techniques.

(3) **Defend and Disarm.** The defender also can follow up his first defensive maneuver by maintaining control of the pirate's weapon arm, executing a stunning technique, and disarming the salty dog. The stun distracts the pirate and gives the defender some time to gain possession of the weapon and to execute his disarming technique.

2.5. Unarmed Defense Against a Sword

Defense against a pirate's sword involves the same principles as knife defense. The sailor considers the same angles of attack and the proper response for any attack along each angle.

a. Regardless of the type of weapon used by the piratical enemy, his attack will always be along one of the nine angles of attack at any one time. The sailor must get his entire body off the line of attack by moving to a safe position. A sword provides the buccaneer with two weapons: a blade at one end and a butt stock at the other end. The sailor will be safe as long as he is not in a position where he can be struck by either end during the attack.

b. Usually, he is in a more advantageous position if he moves inside the length of the weapon. He can then counterattack to gain control of the situation as soon as possible. The following counterattacks can be used as defenses against a sword; they also provide a good basis for training.

(1) **Unarmed Defense Against No. 1 Angle of Attack.** The pirate enemy prepares to slash along the No. 1 angle of attack

(Step 1). The defender waits until the last possible moment before moving so he is certain of the angle along which the attack is directed (Step 2). This way, the swashbuckler cannot change his attack in response to movement by the defender. It is also smart to approach one-eyed pirates on their "blind side." See Figure 2-12. When the defender is certain that the attack is committed along a specific angle (No. 1, in this case), he moves to the inside of the attacker and gouges his eyes (Step 2) with one hand while the other hand redirects and controls the weapon. He maintains control of the weapon and lunges his entire body weight into the eye gouge to drive the buccaneer backward and off balance. The defender now ends up with the weapon, and the attacker is in a poor recovery position (Step 3).

Figure 2-12. Approach the patch-wearing buccaneer on his blind side.

(2) **Unarmed Defense Against No. 2 Angle of Attack.** The pirate makes a diagonal slash along the No. 2 angle of attack

(Step 1). Again, the defender waits until he is sure of the attack before moving. The defender then moves to the outside of the pirate attacker and counterattacks with a thumb jab into the right armpit (Step 2). He receives the momentum of the attacking weapon and controls it with his free hand. The defender uses the attacker's momentum against him by pulling the weapon in the direction it is going with one hand and pushing with his thumb of the other hand (Step 3). The corsair is now completely off balance, and the defender can gain control of the weapon. If possible, the sailor can now grip the pirate's wrist and thrust the weapon into his face, using the sword butt to deliver a blunt blow to the pirate's face, which will often break his nose.

(3) **Unarmed Defense Against No. 3 Angle of Attack.** The pirate directs a horizontal slash along the No. 3 angle of attack (Step 1). The defender turns and moves to the inside of the pirate attacker; he then strikes with his thumb into the jugular notch (Step 2). His entire body mass is behind the thumb strike and, coupled with the incoming momentum of the attacker, the strike drives the privateer's head backward and takes his balance away (Step 3). The defender turns his body with the momentum of the weapon's attack to strip the weapon from the attacker's grip (Step 4).

(4) **Unarmed Defense Against No. 4 Angle of Attack.** The attack is a horizontal slash along the No. 4 angle of attack (Step 1). The defender moves in to the outside of the pirate's attack (Step 2). He then turns with the attack, delivering an elbow strike to the greasy throat of the buccaneer (Step 3). At the same time, the defender's free hand controls the hilt of the sword and pulls it from the attacker as he is knocked off balance from the elbow strike. See Figure 2-13.

(5) **Unarmed Defense Against Low No. 5 Angle of Attack.** The pirate thrusts his sword at the stomach of the defender (Step 1). The defender shifts his body to the side to avoid the attack and seizes the opportunity to gouge the eyes of the salty sea dog (Step 2). The defender's free hand maintains

control of and strips the weapon from the attacker as he is driven backward with the eye gouge (Step 3). This counterattack is doubly effective when the pirate enemy has already lost an eye (and is wearing an eye patch). While there are numerous one-eyed pirates, privateers who have lost the use of both eyes and survived for any length of time thereafter are virtually unheard of. See Figure 2-14.

Figure 2-13. Unarmed defense against a sword-wielding opponent, No. 4 Angle of Attack.

Figure 2-14. Defense against a sword-wielding opponent, Low No. 5 Angle of Attack.

(6) **Unarmed Defense Against High No. 5 Angle of Attack.**
The pirate delivers a thrust to the throat of the defender (Step 1). The defender shifts to the side to avoid the attack, parries the thrust, and controls the pirate's sword with his trailing hand (Step 2). He then shifts his entire body mass forward over the lead foot, slamming a forearm strike into the ocean thug's throat (Step 3).

(7) **Block the Opposite Knee.** If the pirate turns away from you, maintain control of his leg and reach between his legs to block his opposite leg. See Figure 2-15. Use pressure with your shoulder on the back of his leg to bring him face down on the ground. In the case of peg-legged foes, do not hesitate to focus your kicks and punches on the point of weakness. Alternately, you may wish to attack the pirate's good leg, forcing him to concentrate his weight on his wooden prosthesis—setting up a quick, toppling blow.

Figure 2-15. When grasping a pirate's peg leg, be sure to block his other leg to protect against blows.

(8) **Leg Sweep.** Reach your outside arm under the pirate's leg and with your outside hand reach down and gain control of his ankle. Pull his leg up with both of your arms and use your foot to sweep his post leg. The leg sweep should be your first option when facing a peg-legged foe.

2.6. Takedowns from Against a Wall

If you are having difficulty gaining control of the buccaneer enemy, a good technique is to push him hard against a wall, mast, railing, or any other vertical surface near at hand.

a. **Position and Strikes.** Push the pirate against the wall with one shoulder. One arm should be around the pirate's waist, and the other should be on the inside of his knee to deflect knee strikes to your groin. One of your legs should be back to push, and the other one should be inside of the pirate's knee to deflect knee strikes. From this position, you can deliver strikes to the pirate's ribs by turning your hand over and attacking with the knuckles. When he attempts to cover his ribs, with a sharp movement, push your shoulder into him to gain enough space to strike his head.

b. **Leg Drag.** Should a pirate attempt a knee strike on the side you are facing, capture his leg. Step back with the foot on the same side, pulling him from the wall. If you are executing the leg drag in proximity to the ship's railing, be on guard against the pirate's attempting to escape overboard. As mentioned earlier, all reasonable effort should be made to capture pirates alive and prevent them from finding sweet release in a watery grave.

2.7. Double Leg Attacks

Going under a pirate's arms and straight to his legs is a very useful type of attack. There are several ways to finish, depending on the pirate enemy's actions, but the initial attack is the same. When you find yourself relatively close to the enemy, change your level by bending both of your knees and drive into his midsection with your shoulder. One of your feet should penetrate as deep as the pirate's feet. Continue to drive and control the legs to end in side control.

a. **Finish from the Double Leg Attack.**

(1) **Lift.** Drive your hips under the pirate and arch your back to lift him up. Push up with your head and, by controlling his legs with your arms, gain side control.

2.8. Attack from the Rear

In a perfect world, you should be boarding the pirate ship only after all pirate watch personnel have been removed, ideally by sniper fire. However, as missions must often be conducted in an imperfect world, sailors must be prepared to incapacitate pirate sentries. In the rear attack, the unsuspecting pirate watchman is knocked to the ground and kicked in the groin, or rear mounted. The sailor can then kill the sentry by any proper means, or may prefer to muzzle him so as to prevent the watchman from alerting his confederates. Using the pirate's bandana as a muzzle is quick and efficient. Since surprise is the essential element of this technique, the sailor must use effective stalking techniques (Step 1). To initiate his attack, he grabs both of the pirate sentry's ankles (Step 2). Then he heaves his body weight into the hips of the sentry while pulling up on the ankles. This technique slams the sentry to the ground on his face. The sailor may follow with a kick to the groin (Step 3) or by achieving the rear mount.

SECTION III. STRIKES

Striking is an integral part of anti-pirate combat. Practicing ground-fighting techniques exclusively without strikes is a common mistake.

2.9. Pass the Guard with Strikes

Step 1. Keeping your head close to the pirate's chest, drive both hands up the center of his body and then out to control his arms at the biceps.

Step 2. Give the privateer enemy a couple of head butts.

NOTE: Ensure that head butts are not given with the center of the forehead, which could result in injuring your own nose.

Step 3. Stand up one leg at a time, and change your grip to one hand on the sea dog's jacket. Your hips should be pushed slightly forward.

Step 4. With your free hand, strike the pirate a couple of times in the head. (At this point he may release the grip with his legs. If he does, continue with Step 5.)

NOTE: With both hand strikes and head butts, avoid prolonged contact with the pirate's beard. Pirates are notorious for their poor hygiene and their beards and hair are breeding grounds for vermin of all types.

Step 5. Press inward with your knees. This will cause his legs to stick out so that you can reach behind one of them. Gain control of the leg and pass normally. (If he does not release his legs, go to Step 5 (Alternate).

Step 5 (Alternate). While the pirate enemy is distracted by your strikes, step back with one leg and push your hand through the opening. Place your hand on your own knee and squat down to break the grip of his legs. Gain control of his leg and pass normally. If needed, do not hesitate to apply manual pressure to the pirate's testicles and/or twist the scrotum. Again, you may wish to play on the pirate's innate homophobia by suggesting that he is familiar with this kind of treatment, enjoys it, or is "responding" to your touch, etc. You may use his aggravation to gain further advantage of the situation.

2.10. Basic Takedown

This is the basic tackle.

Step 1. From the clinch, step slightly to the front of the pirate enemy and change your grip. Both palms are pointed down and your hands are at the enemy's kidneys.

Step 2. Pulling with your hands and pushing with your head and shoulder, break the pirate's balance to the rear.

Step 3. Step over the puffy-shirted thug and release your grip, ending in the mounted position.

NOTE: It is very important to release your hands to avoid landing on them.

a. **Hook the Leg.** If the pirate attempts to pull away, use your leg closest to his back to hook his leg. When he begins to fall, release the leg and finish as before.

b. **Hip Throw.** The piratical enemy may attempt to avoid the tackle by leaning forward.

Step 1. With the leg that is behind the pirate, step through until you are standing in front of him with your legs inside of his. Your hip should be pushed well through.

c. **Rear Takedown.** Frequently, you will end up after the clinch with your head behind the pirate's arm. When this happens, grasp your hands together around his waist by interlocking your fingers, and place your forehead in the middle of the small of his back to avoid strikes. From this secure position, you can attempt to take the pirate enemy down.

Step 1. Step to one side so that you are behind the pirate at an angle.

Step 2. With the leg that is behind the pirate, reach out and place the instep of your foot behind the pirate's far side foot so that he cannot step backward. Sit down as close to your other foot as possible and hang your weight from the buccaneer enemy's waist.

Step 3. The pirate will fall backwards over your extended leg. As he does so, tuck your elbow in to avoid falling on it, and rotate up into the mounted position. Again using "PiPsyOps," a pithy quip, delivered from this dominant position, will drive the typical pirate mad with frustration. (Examples: "Fancy meeting you here" or "Hello, beautiful.")

2.11. Finishing Moves

When dominant body position has been achieved, the sailor can attempt to finish the fight secure in the knowledge that if an attempt fails, as long as he maintains dominant position, he may simply try again.

a. **Rear Naked Choke.** Chokes are the most effective method of disabling a pirate enemy. This technique should only be executed from the back mount after both leg hooks are in place.

Step 1. Leaving the weak hand in place, the fighter reaches around the pirate's neck and under his chin with the strong hand. In hand-to-hand and hand-to-hook combat, there's no time to worry about contact with the pirate's disease- or vermin-infested beard. Just get your choke hold in place!

Step 2. The fighter now places the biceps of the weak hand under the strong hand, moves the weak hand to the back of the pirate's head, and completes the choke by expanding his chest. See Figure 2-16.

b. **Cross Collar Choke from the Mount and Guard.** This technique can only be executed from the guard or the mount.

Figure 2-16. The rear naked choke.

Step 1. With the weak hand, the fighter grasps the pirate's collar and pulls it open. Most pirates own only one or two shirts—if yanking the collar open should cause a rip in the shirt, or pop off a number of buttons, so much the better for the purposes of demoralizing the pirate enemy.

Step 2. While keeping a hold with the weak hand, the fighter now inserts his strong hand, fingers first, onto the collar. The hand should be relaxed and reach around to the back of the pirate's neck grasping the collar.

Step 3. After grasping the back of the pirate's collar, the fighter inserts the weak hand under the strong hand and into the pirate's collar, fingers first, touching or very close to the first hand. As with conducting a search of the pirate's beard and clothing, the sailor should exercise caution to avoid infection or vermin infestation from close contact with the buccaneer.

Step 4. The fighter turns his wrists so that the palms face toward him, and brings his elbows to his side. He will complete the choke by expanding his chest and pulling with the muscles of his back. From this position, he can also begin pestering the pirate into surrender by attacking the pirate's pressure points. See Figure 2-17.

NOTE: *If the fighter is applying this choke from the mount, he should put his head on the ground on the side of the top hand and relax into the choke.*

Figure 2-17. Pirate pressure points.

c. **Front Guillotine Choke.** Many times this technique may be used as a counter to the double leg takedown.

    Step 1. As the pirate shoots in toward the fighter's legs, the fighter should ensure that the seafaring enemy's head goes underneath one of his arms. The fighter wraps his arm around the pirate's head and under his neck. The fighter's palm should be facing his own chest.

    Step 2. With the other hand, the fighter grasps the first hand, ensuring that he has not reached around the buccaneer's arm, and pulls upward with both hands.

2.12. Defense Against Headlocks

The headlock is a very poor technique for anything more than immobilizing a pirate. It is, however, a very common technique used by pirates in combat; therefore, knowing how to escape from it is very important for a sailor. See Figure 2-18.

a. **Form the Frame**

    Step 1. The fighter's first step in escaping from a pirate headlock is to ensure that his arm is not captured. With a short jerky motion, the sailor pulls his elbow in and turns on his side.

    Step 2. If able, the fighter forms a frame under the buccaneer's chin. The sailor's top arm should be under the pirate's jawbone, and his top hand should rest comfortably in the grasp of the other hand. At this point, the sailor's bone structure should be supporting the pirate's weight.

    Step 3. By pushing with the top leg, the fighter moves his hips back away from the pirate.

    Step 4. The fighter reaches with both legs to grasp the pirate's head. If the sea dog lets go of his headlock, the fighter squeezes the pirate's neck with his legs.

    Step 5. If the pirate does not release the headlock, the sailor rotates around until he is on both of his knees behind the privateer's back.

    Step 6. The fighter uses his top hand to clear the pirate's legs out of the way and steps over, bringing his foot in tight against the pirate's hip. The fighter establishes his base by putting both hands on the ground.

Figure 2-18. The headlock is a favorite move of pirates.

Step 7. The fighter forces the pirate to release his grip on the fighter's neck by forming the frame and leaning toward the pirate's head, driving the bone of his upper arm under the pirate's jawbone.

b. **Follow the Leg.** Although the fighter should always try to form the frame, sometimes the pirate will tuck his head in, making it impossible.

Step 1. After ensuring that his arm is not captured as in the first technique, the fighter moves as close to the pirate as possible and places his leg over him. The fighter's heel should find the crease at the pirate's hip formed by his leg. Pirates' bones, plagued by a chronic lack of calcium, are famously brittle and can sometimes be broken by the mere application of pressure from the fighter's foot to this crease.

Step 2. The fighter pulls his bottom arm free and places his weight on it. Holding the pirate tightly at the other shoulder, the fighter crawls over him using his own leg as a guide.

Step 3. At this point the pirate has the option to either roll with the fighter or not. If he does not, the fighter uses all of his body to apply pressure to the pirate's shoulder. This will break the seafaring wretch's grip and leave the fighter behind the pirate. If the pirate rolls with the fighter, the fighter brings his foot into the buccaneer's hip as before and breaks his grip by forming the frame and applying pressure toward his head.

c. **Roll Toward the Head.** If the pirate should succeed in capturing the fighter's arm, the fighter can use the pirate's reaction to his attempts to free it to his advantage. With short jerky motions, the fighter attempts to pull his arm free. The pirate will have to adjust his position by leaning toward the fighter. Immediately after the fighter attempts to pull his arm free and feels the pirate pushing, the fighter arches toward his head and then over his opposite shoulder, tossing the corsair over.

NOTE: The roll must be timed correctly and must be toward the fighter's head and not straight over his body.

Chapter 3

HANDHELD WEAPONS

Handheld weapons provide the anti-pirate assault force team member with a significant advantage when fighting a pirate opponent. As sailors progress in their training, basic techniques that are taught in initial entry training will merge with the other elements of hand-to-hand fighting to produce a sailor who is capable of combating pirates across the full range of force.

SECTION I. OFFENSIVE TECHNIQUES

In most combat situations, small arms and grenades are the weapons of choice. However, in some scenarios, sailors must engage the pirate enemy in confined areas, such as on-deck combat or room clearing, or situations where hostages are present. In these instances, or when your primary weapon fails, the bayonet or knife may be the ideal weapon to dispatch the crusty corsair. Sailors must transition immediately and instinctively into the appropriate techniques based on the situation and the weapons at hand.

3.1. Rifle with Fixed Bayonet

The principles used in fighting with the rifle and fixed bayonet are the same as when knife fighting. The principles of timing and distance remain paramount; the main difference is the extended distance provided by the length of the weapon. It is imperative that the sailor fighting with rifle and fixed bayonet use the movement of his entire body behind all of his fighting techniques—not just upper-body strength. Whether the pirate is armed or unarmed, a sailor fighting with rifle and fixed bayonet must develop the mental attitude that he will survive the fight. He must continuously evaluate each moment in a fight to determine his advantages or options, as well as the pirate's. He should base

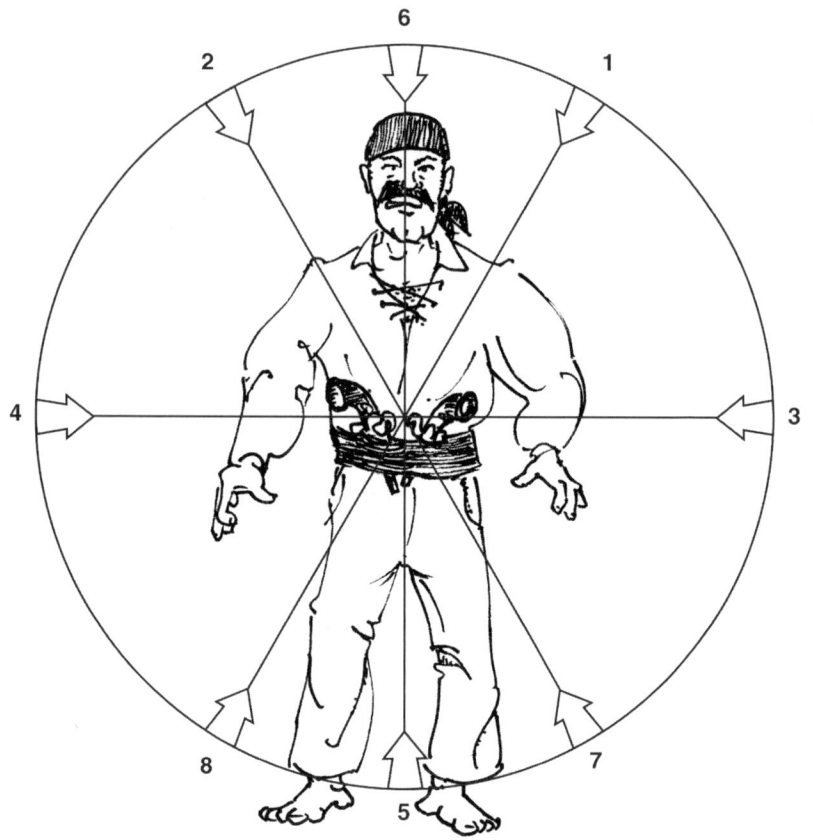

Figure 3-1. Angles of attack on the pirate enemy.

his defenses on keeping his body moving and off the line of any attacks from the pirate. The sailor seeks openings in the buccaneer's defenses and starts his own attacks, using all available body weapons and angles of attack. See Figure 3-1.

a. **Fighting Techniques.** New weapons, improved equipment, and new tactics are always being introduced; however, firepower alone will not always drive a determined pirate from his position. Remember that in most cases, the anti-pirate assault team will be confronting the privateer on his "home court"; i.e., on the pirate's own ship. He will have a superior grasp of the ship's layout, as well as already having his "sea legs" about him. The swashbuckler will often remain in defensive emplacements until driven out by close combat. The role of the sailor, particularly in the final phase of the assault, remains relatively unchanged: His mission is to close with and kill, disable, or capture the pirate. This mission remains the ultimate goal of all individual training. The rifle with fixed bayonet is one of the final means of defeating a pirate in an assault.

(1) During infiltration missions at night, when secrecy must be maintained, the bayonet is an excellent silent weapon.

(2) When close-in fighting determines the use of small-arms fire or grenades to be impractical, or when the situation does not permit the loading or reloading of the rifle, the bayonet is still the best weapon available to the sailor.

(3) The bayonet serves as a secondary weapon should the rifle develop a stoppage.

(4) In hand-to-hand encounters with the piratical enemy, the detached bayonet may be used as a handheld weapon.

(5) The bayonet has many nonfighting uses, such as to probe for onboard booby traps, poke at piles of potatoes or scraps that may conceal hiding pirates, or to cut vegetation in the case of shipwreck.

b. **Development.** To become a successful rifle-bayonet fighter, a sailor must be physically fit and mentally alert. Mental alertness entails being able to quickly detect and meet a swashbuckler's attack from any direction. Aggressiveness, accuracy, balance, and speed are essential in combat situations. These traits lead to confidence, coordination, strength, and endurance, which characterize the rifle-bayonet fighter.

c. **Principles.** The bayonet is an effective weapon to be used aggressively; hesitation may mean sudden death. The sailor must attack in a relentless assault until his buccaneer foe is disabled or captured. He should be alert to take advantage of any opening. If the pirate fails to present an opening, the bayonet fighter must make one by parrying the pirate's weapon and driving his blade or rifle butt into the sea scourge with force.

(1) The attack should be made to a vulnerable part of the pirate's body: face, throat, chest, abdomen, groin, or any area displaying a handicap—eye patch, peg leg, or the shoulder where an amputation was performed.

(2) In both training and combat, the rifle-bayonet fighter displays spirit by sounding off with a low and aggressive growl. This instills a feeling of confidence in his ability to close with and disable or capture the pirate.

(3) The fighter may also call out insults to his pirate enemy. Though famously tough-skinned, the pirate is nonetheless susceptible to mockery of his style of dress: e.g., "Nice bandana, Axl Rose." The pirate's sense of being mocked, and in particular of *not understanding* the insult, is often enough to discourage him and throw him off his game.

(4) The instinctive rifle-bayonet fighting system is designed to capitalize on the natural agility and combative movements of the sailor. The alert sailor must adapt his movements to the natural rocking of the pirate ship, keeping his equilibrium at all times.

d. **Positions.** The sailor holds the rifle firmly but not rigidly. He relaxes all muscles not used in a specific position; tense muscles cause fatigue and may slow him down. All positions and movements described in this manual are for right-handed men. A left-handed man, or a man who desires to learn left-handed techniques, must use the opposite hand and foot for each phase of the movement described. All positions and movements can be executed with or without the magazine and with or without the sling attached.

(1) **Attack Position.** This is the basic starting position from which all attack movements originate. It generally parallels a boxer's stance. The sailor assumes this position when running or hurdling obstacles.

(a) Take a step forward and to the side with your left foot so that your feet are a comfortable distance apart.

(b) Hold your body erect or bend slightly forward at the waist. Flex your knees and balance your body weight on the balls of your feet. Your right forearm is roughly parallel to the ground. Hold the left arm high, generally in front of the left shoulder. Maintain eye-to-eye contact with the pirate, watching his weapon and body through peripheral vision.

(c) Hold your rifle diagonally across your body at a sufficient distance from the body to add balance and protect you from pirate blows. Grasp the weapon in your left hand just below the upper sling swivel, and place the right hand at the small of the stock. Keep the sling facing outward and the cutting edge of the bayonet toward the swashbuckler foe.

e. **Movements.** The sailor will instinctively strike at openings and become aggressive in his attack once he has developed instinctive reflexes. His movements do not have to be executed in any prescribed order. He will achieve balance in his movements, be ready to strike in any direction he finds swashbuckling enemies, and keep striking until he has disabled his pirate opponent. One of the most used is the whirl movement.

(1) **Whirl Movement.** The whirl, properly executed, allows the rifle-bayonet fighter to meet a challenge from a pirate attacking him from the rear. At the completion of a whirl, the rifle remains in the attack position. The fighter spins his body around by pivoting on the ball of the leading foot in the direction of the leading foot, thus facing completely about.

(2) **Attack Movements.** There are four attack movements designed to disable or capture the pirate: thrust, butt stroke, slash, and smash. Each of these movements may be used for the initial attack or as a follow-up should the initial movement fail to find its mark.

(a) **Thrust.** The objective is to disable or capture the swashbuckler by thrusting the bayonet blade into a vulnerable part of his body. The thrust is especially effective in areas where movement is restricted—for example, trenches, a ship's galley, or the floor of the crow's nest. It is also effective when a buccaneer opponent is lying on the ground or in a fighting position.

Lunge forward on your leading foot without losing your balance and, at the same time, drive the bayonet with great force into any unguarded part of your pirate opponent's body. To accomplish this, grasp the rifle firmly with both hands and pull the stock in close to the right hip; partially extend the left arm, guiding the point of the bayonet in the general direction of the pirate's body. Quickly complete the extension of the arms and body as the leading foot strikes the ground so that the bayonet penetrates the target.

To withdraw the bayonet, keep your feet in place, shift your body weight to the rear, and pull rearward along the same line of penetration. Next, assume the attack position in preparation to continue the assault. This movement is taught by the numbers in three phases:

1. **Thrust and Hold, Move.**
2. **Withdraw and Hold, Move.**
3. **Attack Position, Move.**

(b) **Butt Stroke.** The objective is to disable or capture the pirate by delivering a forceful blow to his body with the rifle butt. The aim of the butt stroke may be the pirate's weapon or a vulnerable portion of his body. The butt stroke may be vertical, horizontal, or somewhere between the two planes.

1. **Butt Stroke to the (head, groin, kidney) and Hold, Move.**
2. **Attack Position, Move.**

At combat speed, the command is, **Butt Stroke to the (head, groin, kidney) Series, Move.**

(c) **Slash.** The objective is to disable or capture the pirate by cutting him with the blade of the bayonet.

Step forward with your lead foot, extend your left arm, and swing the knife edge of your bayonet forward and down in a slashing arc. To recover, bring your trailing foot forward and assume the attack position.

(d) **Smash.** The objective is to disable or capture the swashbuckler by smashing the rifle butt into a vulnerable part of his body. The smash is often used as a follow-up to a butt stroke.

Step forward with the trailing foot, as in the butt stroke, and forcefully extend both arms, slamming the rifle butt into the pirate. To recover, bring your trailing foot forward and assume the attack position.

(3) **Defensive Movements.** At times, the sailor may lose the initiative and be forced to defend himself. He may also meet a pirate who does not present a vulnerable area to attack. Therefore, he must make an opening by initiating a parry or block movement, then follow up with a vicious attack. The follow-up attack should be immediate and violent.

(a) **Parry Movement.** The objective is to counter a thrust, throw the corsair off balance, and hit a vulnerable area of his body. Timing, speed, and judgment are essential factors in these movements.
- **Parry right.** If your pirate foe carries his weapon on his left hip (left-handed), you will parry it to your right. In execution, step forward with your leading foot, strike the pirate's musket or sword, deflecting it to your right, and follow up with a thrust, slash, or butt stroke.
- **Parry left.** If the pirate carries his weapon on his right hip (right-handed), you will parry it to your left. In execution, step forward with your leading foot, strike the sea rover's musket, deflecting it to

your left, and follow up with a thrust, slash, or butt stroke. A supplementary parry left is the follow-up attack.

- **Recovery.** Immediately return to the attack position after completing each parry and follow-up attack.

The movement is taught by the numbers in three phases:

1. **Parry Right or Left, Move.**
2. **Thrust, Move.**
3. **Attack Position, Move.**

(b) **Block.** When surprised by a pirate, the block is used to cut off the path of his attack by making weapon-to-weapon contact. A block must always be followed immediately with a vicious attack. Extend your arms using the center part of your rifle as the strike area, and cut off the pirate's attack by making weapon-to-weapon contact. Strike the rogue's weapon with enough power to throw him off balance. Blocks are taught by the numbers in two phases:

1. **High, Low, or Side Block**
2. **Attack Position, Move.**

- **High block.** Extend your arms upward and forward at a 45-degree angle. This action deflects a pirate's slash movement by causing his bayonet or upper part of his musket to strike against the center part of your rifle.
- **Low block.** Extend your arms downward and forward about 15 degrees from your body. This action deflects a pirate's butt stroke aimed at the groin by causing the lower part of his musket stock to strike against the center part of your rifle.
- **Side block.** Extend your arms with the left hand high and right hand low, thus holding the rifle vertical. This block is designed to stop a butt stroke

aimed at your upper body or head. Push the rifle to your left to cause the butt of the pirate's musket to strike the center portion of your rifle.

- **Recovery.** Counterattack each block with a thrust, butt stroke, smash, or slash.

(4) **Modified Movements.** Two attack movements have been modified to allow the rifle-bayonet fighter to slash or thrust at a pirate without removing his hand from the pistol grip of the M16 rifle should the situation dictate.

(a) The modified thrust is identical to the thrust with the exception of the right hand grasping the pistol grip.

(b) The modified slash is identical to the slash with the exception of the right hand grasping the pistol grip.

(5) **Follow-up Movements.** Follow-up movements are attack movements that naturally follow from the completed position of the previous movement. If the initial thrust, butt stroke, smash, or slash fails to make contact with the buccaneer's body, the sailor should instinctively follow up with additional movements until he has disabled, subdued, or killed the pirate. It is important to follow up the initial attack with another aggressive action so the initiative is not lost.

(6) Instinctive, aggressive action and balance are the keys to offense with the rifle and bayonet.

3.2. Bayonet/Knife

As the bayonet is an integral part of the anti-pirate combat sailor's equipment, it is readily available for use as a multipurpose weapon. The bayonet produces a terrifying mental effect on the pirate when in the hands of a well-trained and confident sailor. The sailor skilled in the use of the knife also increases his ability to defend against larger pirates and multiple attackers, who will most likely try to ambush and/or gang up on the sailor. Both these skills increase his chances of surviving and accomplishing the mission. (Although the following paragraphs say "knife," the information also applies to bayonets.)

a. **Grips.** The best way to hold the knife is either with the straight grip or the reverse grip.

    (1) **Straight Grip.** Grip the knife in the strong hand by forming a V and by allowing the knife to fit naturally, as in gripping for a handshake. The handle should lay diagonally across the palm. Point the blade toward the scurvy sea dog, usually with the cutting edge down. The cutting edge can also be held vertically or horizontally to the ground. Use the straight grip when thrusting and slashing.

    (2) **Reverse Grip.** Grip the knife with the blade held parallel with the forearm, cutting edge facing outward. This grip conceals the knife from the pirate's view. (If the pirate should be wearing an eye patch, you can utilize his considerable "blind spot" to more easily conceal the knife from his vision.) The reverse grip also affords the most power for lethal insertion into the swashbuckler's person. Use the grip for slashing, stabbing, and tearing.

b. **Stances.** The primary stances are the knife fighter's stance and the modified stance.

    (1) **Knife Fighter's Stance.** In this stance, the fighter stands with his feet about shoulder-width apart, dominant foot toward the rear. About 70 percent of his weight is on the front foot and 30 percent on the rear foot. He stands on the balls of both feet and holds the knife with the straight grip. The other hand is held close to his body where it is ready to use, but protected from being knocked away by the pirate.

    (2) **Modified Stance.** The difference in the modified stance is that the knife is held close to the body with the other hand held close over the knife hand to help conceal it from the buccaneer's view.

c. **Range.** The two primary ranges in knife fighting are long range and medium range. In long-range knife fighting, attacks consist of figure-eight slashes, horizontal slashes, and lunging thrusts to vital areas on the pirate's torso. Usually, the straight grip is used. In medium-range knife fighting, the reverse grip provides greater power. It is used to thrust, slash, and tear along all angles of attack.

3.3. Knife-Against-Knife Sequence

The knife fighter must learn to use all available weapons of his body and not limit himself to the knife. The free hand can be used to trap the pirate's hands, gouge his eyes, or otherwise distract the swashbuckler in order to create openings in his defense. The pirate's attention will be focused on the weapon; therefore, low kicks and knee strikes will seemingly come from nowhere. The knife fighter's priority targets are the eyes, throat, abdominal region, and extended limbs. Focused yanks on the pirate's beard and earrings, if any, may also prove effective.

3.4. Advanced Weapons Techniques and Training

Anti-pirate assault team members can execute attacks along multiple angles of attack in combinations. The attacker must attack with a speed that overwhelms his buccaneer opponent.

SECTION II. FIELD-EXPEDIENT WEAPONS

To survive, the anti-pirate sailor in combat must be able to deal with any situation that develops. His ability to adapt any nearby object for use as a weapon in a win-or-die situation is limited only by his ingenuity and resourcefulness. Possible weapons, although not discussed herein, include candles or ink pens; grog or rum jars tied to string to be swung; metal clamps and casings at the end of sections of rope; wooden detritus from the ship's masts; stray lengths of rope from the pirate ship's rigging; parrots' cages; dirt, rocks, bird feed, liquor, chum, parrot excrement, or other liquids and semi-liquids that can be thrown into the pirate's eyes; and any food, cutlery, or dishware that may be lying around. The following techniques demonstrate a few expedient weapons that are readily available to most anti-pirate sailors.

3.5. Three-Foot Stick

Since a stick can be found almost anywhere, the anti-pirate assault force team member should know its uses as a field-expedient weapon. The stick is a versatile weapon; its capability ranges from simple pirate captive control to lethal combat. The 3-foot stick can be found among the detritus on the pirate ship's deck, in the galley, or in extraordinary cases, may be obtained by forcibly removing a pirate's wooden prosthesis. (Although tales of anti-pirate assault team members "beating a pirate to death with his own leg" are unconfirmed, the actual feat is well within the bounds of the possible.) See Figure 3-2.

a. Use a stick about 3 feet long and grip it by placing it in the V formed between the thumb and index finger, as in a handshake. It may also be grasped by two hands (aka "baseball style") and used in an unlimited number of techniques. The stick is not held at the end, but at a comfortable distance from the butt end.

b. When striking with the stick, achieve maximum power by using the entire body weight behind each blow. The desired point of contact of the weapon is the last 2 inches at the tip of the stick. The primary targets for striking with the stick are the vital body points. Effective striking points are usually the buccaneer's wrist, hand, knees, and other bony protuberances. It goes without saying that the swashbuckler's peg leg is an especially vulnerable target. Soft targets include the side of the neck, jugular notch, solar plexus, and various nerve motor points. Attack soft targets by striking or thrusting the tip of the stick into the area. Three basic methods of striking are:

(1) **Thrusting.** Grip the stick with both hands and thrust straight into the privateer's body with the full body mass behind it.

(2) **Whipping.** Hold the stick in one hand and whip it in a circular motion; use the whole body mass in motion to generate power.

(3) **Snapping.** Snap the stick in short, shocking blows, again with the body mass behind each strike. Snapping is ideal for knocking a dagger or old-timey musket from the pirate's hand.

Figure 3-2. Combat with the 3-foot stick. This weapon can be found virtually anywhere.

c. When using a 3-foot stick against a musket, the defender grasps the stick with two hands, one at each end, as the attacker thrusts forward to the chest.

(1) The defender steps off the line of attack to the outside and redirects the weapon with the stick.

(2) He then strikes forward with the forearm into the attacking pirate's throat. The force of the two body weights coming together is devastating. The pirate's neck is trapped in the notch formed by the stick and the defender's forearm.

(3) Using the free end of the stick as a lever, the defender steps back and uses his body weight to drive the stunned pirate to the ground. The leverage provided by the stick against the crusty buccaneer's neck creates a tremendous choke with the forearm, and the pirate should lose consciousness completely in a matter of seconds.

3.6. Six-Foot Pole

Another field-expedient weapon that can mean the difference between life and death for a sailor in an unarmed conflict is a pole about 6 feet long. Examples of poles suitable for use are mop handles, pry bars, tent poles, and the oars from pirate lifeboats hanging over the ship's side. A sailor skilled in the use of a pole as a weapon is a force to be reckoned with. The size and weight of the pole requires him to move his whole body to use it effectively. Its length gives the sailor an advantage of distance in most unarmed situations, and has the potential to take out multiple swashbucklers in one go. There are two methods usually used in striking with a pole:

a. **Swinging.** Becoming effective in swinging the pole requires skilled body movement and practice. The greatest power is developed by striking with the last 2 inches of the pole. Swinging may, however, be impossible given the frequently tight quarters aboard the pirate ship.

b. **Thrusting.** The pole is thrust straight along its axis with the sailor's body mass firmly behind it.

    (1) A pirate tries to thrust forward with a sword or dagger. The defender moves his body off the line of attack; he holds the tip of the pole so that the swashbuckler runs into it from his own momentum. He then aims for the jugular notch and anchors his body firmly in place so that the full force of the attack is felt at the sea rover's throat.

    (2) The defender then shifts his entire body weight forward over his lead foot and drives the pirate off his feet, ideally against a mast, wall, or other hard surface.

NOTE: *During high stress, small targets, such as the throat, may be difficult to hit. Good, large targets include the solar plexus and hip/thigh joint.*

Chapter 4

RIVERINE ASSAULT OPERATIONS

"Riverine assault operations" refers to inland or inlet strikes on the pirate enemy. Most often this will mean trailing the targeted pirate ship to its "cove" or hideaway some distance inland along a narrow riverway. However, it can also mean chasing the pirate vessel along a similar waterway, or even storming a "pirate bay"—a safe harbor for pirates—with the intention of rounding up privateers.

Though much has changed since the days of Blackbeard, Captain Kidd, etc., the same dangers remain. The anti-pirate assault force sailor will do well to remember his history and recall the heavy casualties inflicted upon Lieutenant Robert Maynard and his ships during their defeat of Blackbeard at Ocracoke Island. The pirate's cove, often tucked away in dense jungles teeming with native life, always presents the pirate with "home field advantage," and thus stealth and caution are as important in this theater—perhaps more so—than in attacks waged on the open sea.

4.1. Scope

A riverine assault operation commences when the anti-pirate assault force begins tactical assault loading to depart the riverine base for an operation and terminates when all forces involved have returned to the base (generally meaning the Navy ship from which anti-pirate operations are based). See Figure 4-1.

In any assault landing against a hostile pirate contingent, several options rest with the assaulting force. In all options and phases, the assault must support and contribute to the attainment of the mission. The phases of the mobile riverine force assault operations are movement, landing attack, subsequent operations, and planned withdrawal.

a. Safety Precautions

Loading and unloading of troops is a hazardous operation, especially at night. There is always a danger of personnel falling into the water

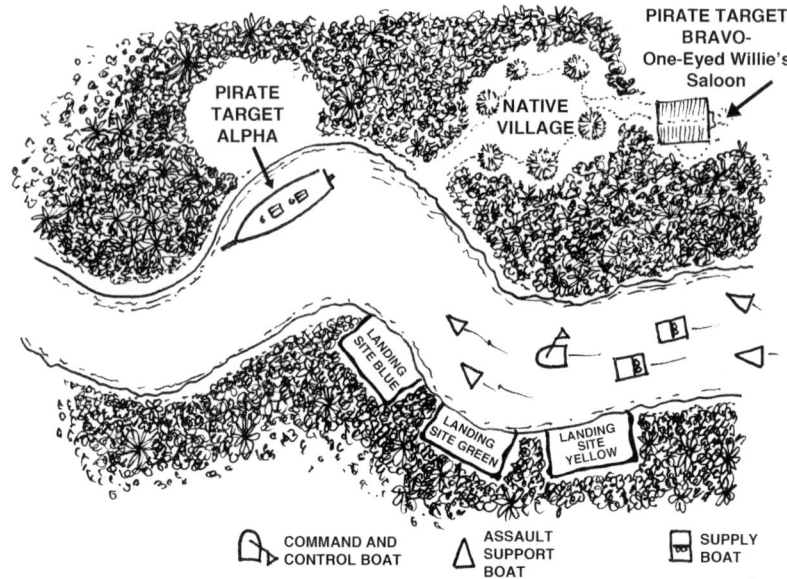

Figure 4-1. Diagram of landing site in a pirate cove.

and being carried away by the current. Where possible, a safety boat equipped with a swimmer in harness, portable floodlights, and life rings attached to lines, shall be positioned close downstream during loading or unloading operations. Troops and boat crews must don life preservers prior to loading and unloading. All harness gear will be unbuckled while loading and unloading, and all troops and boat crews will wear life preservers during loading and unloading. To the maximum extent, all troops should have both hands free; they should pass heavy equipment between river assault craft and pontoon piers prior to loading and unloading. Personnel required at each loading or unloading area are:

- One hospitalman or medical aid man
- The ship/craft loading officer
- One safety officer
- Two swimmers with harnesses rigged
- Two men for each loading/unloading station to handle troop equipment.

4.2. Movement of the Assault Force

When transiting waterways to an area of operations, riverine assault forces must be prepared for unforeseen situations. As rivers and canals narrow or shoreline vegetation increases, so increases the danger from cannon fire, pirate ambush, and mining. During movement to an area of operations, unit commanders will maintain a readiness posture consistent with the pirate force's capabilities and threat.

a. Tactical Organization for Movement

The Navy elements of the riverine assault force are task organized to provide an advance guard, a main body, and rear guard. Essential tasks such as reconnaissance, minesweeping, fire support, troop lift, and escort are assigned to movement groups and units as appropriate.

b. Preparation for Movement

Prior to departing the riverine base, the Navy commanders will thoroughly familiarize themselves with the waterways to be transited and the size and capabilities of the buccaneer contingent being targeted. All available navigational information including water depths, river and canal widths, bridges and obstructions en route, tides, and currents will be studied. Latest intelligence including the pirate threat en route, possible mining and ambush locations, population concentrations, and shoreline characteristics should be obtained. In view of the fact that independent action is frequently required by individual boat crews, task group/unit commanders will ensure that boat crews are adequately briefed on the topics enumerated in this paragraph.

c. Techniques

The following techniques may be applicable during movement to and from the area of operations:

(1) **Escort.** Whenever possible during both daylight and night transport movement, an escort should be provided. Escorts may be riverine assault craft, river patrol boats, or attack helicopters, depending upon the tactical situation and the location of the pirate target(s).

(2) **Avoiding Patterns.** When operations are being conducted over an extended period, times of transits and routes for

troop rotation or resupply should be varied, consistent with operational requirements.

d. **Reaction to Unforeseen Situations**
  (1) **Target of Opportunity.** Targets of opportunity may occur during movements to and from the objective area. These may be waterborne or on land. Rules of engagement may require that authorization be obtained before engaging such targets. Consideration must be given to the assigned mission before taking action that may delay movement of the force or potentially alert other pirates of the assault force's presence.
  (2) **Attack on the Force.** If the force is attacked during movement, immediate action will be taken to neutralize the hostile buccaneer fire. Command and control boats and armored troop carriers (with troops embarked) should clear the area of attack at best possible speed, unless the decision is made to assault the pirate enemy. If required, naval gunfire, artillery, and air support will be requested. When the tactical situation permits, a quick-reaction force may be landed to conduct follow-up operations. If the decision is made to counterattack the filthy curs, river assault craft will land previously designated counter-ambush forces.

    It is always desirable, and often necessary, to control both banks of streams on which riverine forces operate. However, it is especially important to control the shore opposite the area in which landings take place. At a minimum the opposite shore must be controlled by fire and, in many instances, it will be necessary to have troops physically occupy the opposite shore to provide the necessary rear security for the landing force making the main attack.

4.3. Landing Attack and Subsequent Operations

The landing attack phase begins with the arrival of the main body of the riverine assault force in the landing area and ends with the seizure of initial objectives. It encompasses preparation of the landing area, landing, initial ground and waterborne maneuver, and special operations in support of the landing attack.

The organization for landing is designed to maintain the tactical integrity of assault units, to provide flexibility in reacting to the situation encountered, to maintain the assault force's security against ambush by pirates, and to facilitate control of subsequent maneuvers. The basic unit is the boat team.

a. **Landing Plan**
   (1) **Purpose.** The landing plan supports the main assault force. It includes the sequence, time and place of arrival of combat unit(s), combat support and combat service support units in the landing area(s), plans for reorganization, and securing initial objectives.
   (2) **Landing Areas.** Landing areas that encompass one or more river sites are selected to avoid hostile defensive positions prepared in advance by the buccaneer enemy. Plans for landing in unsecured areas must assume that the units will have to conduct an assault landing. The force commander recommends landing areas to the mobile riverine force commander on the basis of initial objectives, plans for subsequent tactical ground operations, and the capability of assault craft to support the landing attack. Alternate landing areas are selected whenever practicable. The selection and location of landing areas are influenced by:
   • Mission and size of waterborne units
   • Pirate situation and capabilities
   • Characteristics of the waterways, adjacent land areas, and airspace
   • Available river landing sites and assault river landing points within these sites
   • Capabilities and limitations of naval craft
   • Nature of subsequent ground tactical operation
   • Possible presence of civilians.

   (3) **Riverine Landing Sites.** When the riverine landing sites within the selected river landing area are insufficient or inadequate, several elements may have to use the same site in turn. When a single site is used, combat elements are generally delivered first, combat support elements next, and combat service support elements last.

b. Landing

The landing is an exacting operation, requiring combat and combat support elements to be landed as rapidly as possible. Every element must be prepared to contribute its combat power in a coordinated effort to seize and defend the landing area.

(1) **Time.** The force commander recommends the time for the waterborne landing to the mobile riverine force commander. In selecting the time for landing, consideration must be given to pirate capabilities, weather, tides, visibility, characteristics of watercraft being used, availability of fire support and the plan for supporting fires, and the security of the force in transit. Units may land at first light to take advantage of darkness during the water movement while conducting the ground tactical operations in daylight. Or they may land at last light to facilitate landing and consolidation of forces, then conduct ground tactical operations during darkness. Waterborne landings during daylight present fewer command and control problems and can be better supported by available supporting arms. Waterborne landings may be made at night, or under other conditions of reduced visibility to gain tactical surprise and reduce the effectiveness of hostile fire. In general, nighttime landings are slightly preferable because there is a higher likelihood that some or all of the pirate force may be in "recreation mode" and imbibing great quantities of alcohol, thus impairing the pirates' collective ability to defend their ship or land-based safe haven.

(2) **Initial Objectives.** Rapid assembly and reorganization ashore are essential following the landing attack. Assignment of initial objectives to subordinate units will facilitate assembly of the units and provide for initial defense of the landing area. Characteristics of initial objectives should include:
- Protection from pirate observation and attack
- Sufficient size for dispersion
- Proximity to assault landing areas.

(3) **Landing Techniques.** In the final approach to the pirate ship or land-based pirate safe haven, preparatory fires may

be delivered by artillery, river assault craft gunfire, and air and naval gunfire. If light conditions allow, pinpoint sniper assaults may also be used against strategic sea dog targets. While the pirate ship's weapons are outmatched by Navy capabilities, from close proximity cannon, musket, and small-arms fire can be devastating, and thus covering fire is of crucial importance. A command and control boat should be stationed in the vicinity of the landing of the transport craft. Escort craft are stationed to protect the transport craft. Escort duties may include establishing patrol barriers up- and downstream from the riverbank site to seal river approaches and along the opposite bank to protect the rear of the force from hidden or sympathetic pirate forces.

When the transport craft of the first wave reach positions opposite the river landing points, they turn (independently or upon signal) and beach on the shore where troops are landed. After debarkation, the transport craft retract, clear the river landing site, and move to act as a blocking force or transit to an assembly area by prescribed routes, avoiding interference with succeeding waves. During landing operations, riverine assault craft may also provide afloat command facilities, close fire support, evacuation, and selective resupply.

If available, assault amphibian vehicles (AAV) may be used to land troops. Depending on the situation, troops may be debarked or stay aboard AAVs to achieve the objective ashore.

When the landing is completed and the mission is to operate ashore for a specified period, river assault craft will assemble at a designated staging area; take up patrol, blocking, or fire support stations; conduct minesweeping and booby-trap sweeping operations; and perform other assigned tasks. If the assault force is to remain ashore, all or part of the supporting riverine assault craft may be returned to the riverine base, depending upon the mission and the tactical situation.

(4) **Scheme of Maneuver.** Riverine assault operations are strike operations. Riverine schemes of maneuver are normally designed to fix, entrap, and destroy or detain a hostile pirate force in a given area of operations. The lack of definite

intelligence may make it necessary to base the selection of objectives on terrain rather than on the pirates' location. However, the primary objective is the swashbuckler force, not the terrain itself.

Pressure must be maintained once contact is made, and forces must deploy rapidly to fix the hostile force in a killing zone where maximum fire support can be used.

Riverine assault operations capitalize on supporting watercraft capabilities and the tactical flexibility inherent in the continuous availability of assault support craft to support tactical maneuver. Naval craft may:

- Withdraw or redeploy troops
- Act as, or in support of, a blocking force against buccaneer assault
- Conduct waterborne reconnaissance, security, and combat patrols
- Transport a raiding force
- Transport detained pirates
- Serve as mobile aid stations
- Provide direct and indirect fire support
- Perform damage control, salvage, and explosive ordnance disposal (EOD) operations (on a limited basis).

To take maximum advantage of available watercraft and exploit terrain characteristics, planners must consider all possible uses of watercraft and water routes when selecting objectives. They must also determine short-term requirements for watercraft by other units participating in the operation, and provide for pre-positioning, security, and control of such craft.

c. **Reserve/Reaction Force**

(1) **Planning.** As in all military operations, the retention of a reserve force is highly desirable in all riverine operations. Riverine operations normally have destruction of the pirate forces as their primary mission and do not orient on terrain objectives to the extent that most other operations do. While

the reserve force may be committed to assist other elements of the force, its primary employment should be to capitalize on opportunities to detain or destroy pirate forces. In this regard, the reserve force can be more appropriately thought of as a reaction force. Reaction operations require flexibility, careful planning, coordination, and reliable communications between all elements.

(2) **Evaluating Requirements.** The commander must ensure that a valid requirement for commitment of the reaction forces exists before he requests or commits it. Helicopter-borne reaction forces can deploy directly against located pirate positions and are usually the preferred type. Elements on airborne alert are expensive in terms of resource expenditure; therefore, their use is infrequent even though they are the most responsive type of reaction force. Waterborne reaction forces can be available for rapid and effective commitment in the riverine environment and will often be the only type available. Reaction forces, in the desired condition of readiness, are maintained in assembly areas either at land bases or at afloat bases. To facilitate immediate employment of the reaction forces, the commander ensures completion of all possible preparations in advance.

4.4. Supporting Arms

Supporting arms are used during the landing attack primarily for close support of the riverine assault force, and require the coordinated employment of artillery, assault craft fire, naval gunfire, and close air support.

a. **Artillery**

Standard artillery procedures should be followed, and each battery should be capable of conducting independent fire direction from craft, barges, or ashore.

The use of all means of mobility is a key factor when employing artillery in riverine operations, since artillery frequently must be repositioned prior to the assault landing. This usually requires that artillery displacements be supported by air and other artillery during movement.

The rough terrain and dense foliage of most pirate-cove locations (typically in Caribbean and other tropical locales) may deny use of the quantity and caliber of artillery normally dictated by hostile strength and area characteristics. Positions will usually be relatively small and established in insecure areas. The absence of firing positions in defilade, lack of cover and concealment, and positioning in insecure areas will frequently require use of direct fire techniques and heavy expenditures of anti-personnel ammunition for self-defense.

Because of lack of survey control and concurrent meteorological data, adjusted fires will be the primary method used to obtain maximum effect on the pirate enemy.

Artillery batteries may be deployed by either surface craft, helicopters, or on barges that act as firing platforms.

Buoy markers should be placed on artillery weapons and prime movers to facilitate salvage operations in the event of ship sinkage.

Normally, the lack of suitable terrain in the area of operations increases emphasis on aerial observation, particularly during waterborne movement. A combination of aerial observers with forward observers on the ground allows the best artillery coverage, coordination, and surveillance of the pirate target.

b. Assault Craft Gunfire

Assault craft gunfire is supporting direct and indirect fire provided to the assault force by naval craft. These craft deliver direct fire on the swashbuckling enemy with a wide variety of automatic weapons. Naval craft can also provide indirect fire support with naval mortars installed on selected craft. Mortar fire is usually unsuitable to the anti-pirate mission, which requires close-in fighting and stealth; however, mortar fire is effective at scaring the tar out of the swashbuckling enemy. A high degree of coordination is required to provide support of troops ashore.

The assault force commander of the riverine assault operation is responsible for coordination of all fires, including assault fires, in support of operations ashore.

Once troops begin landing, all assault craft fire on the targeted pirate ship must be either delivered at the request of the supported unit, or cleared by the assault force commander.

(1) **Direct Fire Support.** Assault craft providing direct fire in support of a specified assault force unit will normally be in direct support of that unit. The boat unit commander advises the supported commander concerning the capabilities of assault craft weapons. These weapons may be given pirate neutralization, "jungle sweep," interdiction, harassing, or destruction fire missions. They may augment infantry weapons with fires through gaps in friendly lines. Whatever the mission, their fires must be executed in coordination with the supported unit commander's fire support plan.

(2) **Indirect Fire Support.** Craft equipped with indirect fire weapons may be employed as a fire unit. With all craft in close proximity, one can direct the fires of all to provide supporting indirect fires. While less efficient than direct fire, indirect fire can provide intangible mission support by creating a "shock and awe" effect on the pirate crew. As is widely known, the typical pirate—aka "the cockroach of the sea"—is an opportunist and, above all, a survivor. An overwhelming display of force will give him pause before he rushes to engage with the anti-pirate assault force.

Chapter 5

WATERWAY INTERDICTION, SURVEILLANCE, BARRIER, AND SECURITY OPERATIONS

5.1. Purpose

Waterway interdiction, surveillance, barrier, and security operations are conducted by specially configured craft and aircraft in the waters of the riverine area. These operations are intended to support an attack on the pirate's cove. They may be used to gain control of waterways preparatory to subsequent riverine assault operations.

Waterway interdiction and surveillance and security operations serve five basic purposes:

(1) Protect friendly lines of communication
(2) Deny hostile pirate forces the use of waterways (See Figure 5-1)
(3) Collect intelligence information on pirate foe
(4) Perform security missions
(5) Enforce population and resources control.

To be effective, waterway interdiction and surveillance and security forces must include both surface craft and aircraft. The type of craft selected will depend on the environment, the pirate threat, and the assigned mission. The air and surface operations are mutually supporting and may be conducted independently or concurrently. During waterway interdiction and surveillance and security operations, close coordination is required between airborne and waterborne patrols in the employment of mutually supporting fires.

Remote sensors used in conjunction with supporting arms or remotely fired demolitions are an effective method of interdiction offering minimal risk to friendly personnel.

Figure 5-1. Take action to prevent the pirate ship from exiting the cove.

5.2. Scope of Operation

Pacification of a region requires accomplishment of three major tasks:

(1) Clearing an area by regular military forces
(2) Securing the area by indigenous paramilitary forces, thereby releasing the regular forces to focus resources and attention on the swashbuckler target
(3) Developing the secured area through political, economic, and social programs.

A vital aspect of the clearing and securing phases of pacification is the control of all resources in order to deny the corsair the means to wage war. First and foremost, this includes denying the pirates the means of selling their contraband (or "booty") and thus significantly defunding him. Isolating the pirate from his native support system levels the playing field. This greatly facilitates the clearing of an area by military forces and the identification and elimination of indigenous buccaneer supporters.

For effective control of resources, all modes of transportation must be controlled, including waterways and rivers. See Figure 5-2. Effective control of the smaller rivers and canals in the riverine area can best be maintained by controlling the banks and adjacent territory; however, connecting tributaries between major waterways may be controlled by patrol-blocking action. Waterway interdiction and surveillance and security forces will conduct patrols and inshore surveillance to enforce curfews and prevent pirate infiltration, movement, and resupply along and across the major waterways of the area.

Waterway interdiction and surveillance and security operations often will be conducted with the added hazards of operating continuously within weapon range of the pirate (i.e., within cannon range).

Figure 5-2. The "Peg-Giver" mine prevents the pirate ship from easy escape.

a. **Command Relationships**

The commander of the waterway interdiction and surveillance and security forces will be designated by the anti-pirate assault force commander, who will exercise operational control of assigned forces. The command relationship structure should be flexible, with necessary changes being implemented as required.

5.3. Tactics and Procedures

An individual waterway interdiction and surveillance and security operation may be called a "patrol" and consists of two or more craft in execution of a specific operation. This section outlines various tactical considerations and procedures; however, these are not all-inclusive, nor do they necessarily apply to all phases of waterway interdiction and surveillance and security operations.

a. **Area Familiarization**

Prior to initial patrols, commanders will arrange for area indoctrination and familiarization of crew personnel.

b. **Secondary Missions**

Patrols may be modified at times to accommodate requests for combat support of anti-pirate forces ashore, including blocking, the wrangling of buccaneers located on shore, and similar operations. See Figure 5-3.

Figure 5-3. Be aware that pirates may try to flee on land.

c. Response to Hostile Pirate Fire

The response to pirate fire must be governed by the type and volume of fire received and the rules of engagement in effect. The presence of civilian populace and/or other friendly forces in the operational area must also be considered. Rules of engagement and measures to prevent mutual interference must be observed. As a general guideline, however, fire received from the pirate ship itself may be returned indiscriminately and with maximum force.

d. Mutual Support

Multiple boat patrols are frequently useful in providing mutual support.

e. Time and Pattern of Patrols

Boats will conduct a random patrol, and not establish a pattern such as passing through the same points on subsequent passes or at regular intervals. Establishment of a pattern may invite mining or pirate ambush. In the case of operations where stealth is crucial, falling into a pattern can be fatal.

f. Readiness

Readiness condition appropriate to the area being patrolled will be maintained at all times to include alertness to ambushes or any movement of the pirate ship itself. (Remember that pirates come and go at all hours, and be prepared for the ship's attempted exit from the cove at any time.)

Locals

Note: Do not overlook the possible pro-pirate sympathies of the natives. In the case of some pirate hideaways, the entire economy of a given cove may depend on the elaborate fencing of the swashbucklers' booty. This can lead to misguided loyalties, which have been known to go as far as armed rearguard assault on the anti-pirate assault force.

Chapter 6

SPECIAL OPERATIONS

6.1. Scope of Operations

Special operations are ancillary or supporting operations conducted by the anti-pirate assault force as adjuncts to a riverine assault operation. Special operations are normally characterized by employment of procedures and techniques that require special training and equipment. The capability to conduct these operations is generally limited to specific units that have been assigned primary mission responsibility within the service organization. See Figure 6-1.

The special operations set forth in this chapter represent the minimum capability required by the assault force commander to conduct sustained operations in a riverine environment. The magnitude of a particular operation, the pirate threat, or terrain considerations may make it necessary to augment assigned units and provide specialized units in support.

Figure 6-1. The sailor's mission may include recovering stolen pirate treasure.

6.2. Reconnaissance and Waterway Clearance

a. **Determination of Waterway Characteristics**

Gathering information regarding waterway characteristics is a prerequisite to the proper use of waterways leading into and out of the pirates' hideaway. Since waterway characteristics constantly change because of seasonal effects, this requirement is continuous throughout the operation.

b. **Waterway Clearance of Barricades and Obstacles**

The mobile riverine force must have a capability for clearing navigable waterways of barricades and obstacles, including pirate mines. An orderly and continuing barricade removal program is required throughout the riverine environment. Close coordination with local officials is necessary before any barricade or obstacle is removed.

6.3. Riverine Base Security

In providing for the security of the riverine base of operations, measures must be taken to defend the mobile riverine base elements, troop installations, equipment, lines of communication, and nearby key friendly installations. Pirate characteristics, capabilities, and weaknesses must be constantly studied. Vigilance and sound security measures will reduce the rogues' threat to operations.

a. **Base Defense Planning**

The riverine base of operations must be organized for defense against attack from any direction. Plans must provide flexibility and must position reserves for rapid reaction to any pirate threat. Tasks for ground combat forces and supporting weapons are to detect, engage, and destroy or eject an attacking swashbuckler force. All elements within the base area must be appropriately tasked and/or assigned sectors of responsibility.

Combat outposts and mutually supporting strongpoints forward of the riverine base's main defense positions are employed to add depth to the defense. Defensive fires are planned throughout the area. Patrols, listening posts, and obstacles are included in the plan.

The ability to disperse is limited in most riverine base areas. This deficiency must be compensated for by increasing the depth of the security area through aggressive patrolling and the use of airborne observers. Other passive measures such as camouflage, varying normal routines, and control of entrance of local noncombatants into the base area should be employed. Remote monitored ground sensors can also increase the depth of the security area by providing an effective warning barrier against infiltration attempts.

(1) Security Area

The security area is a reconnaissance and surveillance zone that extends forward from the forward defense area to the limit of employment of security elements. These elements are far enough forward to:

- Provide timely warning of the pirate's approach
- Deny the buccaneer direct fire into the base area
- If possible, deny the pirate observed cannon fire into the base area.

Security elements also prevent unrestricted observation of the base area and the undetected assembly of pirate forces within striking distance of the base.

(2) Forward Defense Area

The forward defense area encompasses those positions and forces necessary to engage the sea dog in decisive combat to preserve integrity of the riverine base. Within this area, forces are organized to repel and destroy the pirate force and prevent his entry for destruction of the riverine base. The forward defense force is provided defense capabilities according to the swashbuckler's attack capabilities.

b. Operations Center

The mobile riverine base operations center must be able to coordinate all forms of maneuver (e.g., patrols) and defensive positions with supporting arms and integrate them into an effective defense of the anti-pirate assault force. Operations, intelligence, appropriate fire support, and other friendly force representatives should be present in the operations center.

c. Defensive Measures

The mobile riverine force (MRF) is vulnerable to virtually all direct and indirect fire weapons, with cannon fire a particularly significant threat. Fortunately, the range of cannon fire available to the buccaneer enemy is limited, and these areas can be avoided. See Figure 6-2. When formulating the plan for defense against mortar and recoilless rifles, the mobile riverine force commander considers likely firing position, intelligence reports, reports by indigenous personnel, and resources available. He plans passive defensive tactics to minimize casualties and damage and aggressive action to locate and destroy hostile buccaneer forces.

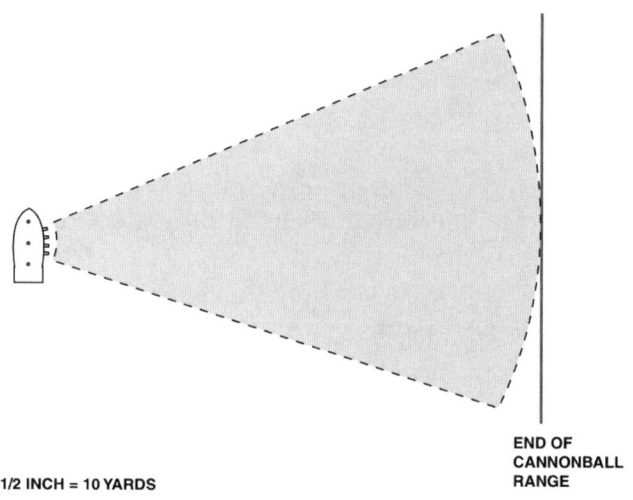

END OF
CANNONBALL
RANGE

1/2 INCH = 10 YARDS

Figure 6-2. The limited range of the pirate ship's cannons.

d. Defense of an Afloat Base

Although possibly located in hostile territory, the riverine base of operations must be relatively secure before barracks ships arrive. The base area selected should have enough room to moor the afloat force without impeding the normal flow of indigenous commercial and military traffic. Note, however, that an oversized Navy ship can be used as an effective blockade of the riverine entry point in advance of assault on the pirate stronghold.

The afloat base ships are subject to a variety of waterborne threats. The pirate can be expected to employ swimmers, limpet-type mines, drifting contact mines, suicide attack boats, sympathetic natives bearing deadly "gifts," or drifting boats loaded with explosives. The pirate may also attack with his more customary musket or pistol, firing from a discreet position among the foliage. Though ordinarily a liability, the sea dog's crude firearms can do considerable damage when fired onto the crowded deck of a Navy ship, where disparate grapeshot has the potential to wound a great many force members.

Additional considerations in preparing the defensive plan include:

(1) Congestion of personnel and vulnerability of the afloat base as they affect the choice of forces to be used for defense.

(2) Integration of all weapons into a coordinated fire support plan.

(3) Use of surveillance equipment to gauge number, movement, and location of the swashbuckling enemy force.

(4) Coordination of swimmer defense requirements employing multi-sensory systems, including radar, sonar, optics, and waterborne sensors in conjunction with explosive weapons, electrical deterrents, and physical barriers.

(5) The use of regular boat patrols to control indigenous civilian and military traffic, and detect and destroy waterborne pirate attacks via swimmers, drifting mines, or suicide boats.

(6) Contingency plans to provide for situations where tide, current, or weather has an influence on the defense of the afloat base.

(7) Use of boat patrols to protect routes of communication and resupply.

(8) Use of aircraft to conduct aerial reconnaissance.

The mission may require forces to operate on a continuing or periodic basis to achieve and/or maintain dominance of designated water routes. For example, elements of a reconnaissance unit may be used with naval riverine assault craft to conduct continuing combat patrols on the waterways.

e. Security of Anchorages

An "anchorage" is the location of ships and craft not underway, whether anchored off a riverbank, beached, secured to a pier, or otherwise made fast for a relatively long period of time. It is necessary to differentiate between temporary halts during movement and periods spent in ports and riverine bases. In the latter case, the pirate will have more time to prepare his attack. Systematic firing on all suspicious floating debris, use of patrol craft, and detonation of grenades at irregular intervals in the approaches to anchorages may be employed as defensive measures. Note, however, that pirates have been known to employ "waste warfare," sending tree branches, empty rum barrels, discarded pantaloons, etc. down the river as a means of forcing the assault force to waste ammunition and as a way to distract the attention of the force from other movements of the pirate force. Some discrimination should be used to determine whether a floating object is likely to be an explosive or is more likely a piece of pirate jetsam.

The adjacent waters should be patrolled by small craft. These craft should not operate out of sight of one another, so that individual craft are not attacked and destroyed before they can be supported or can support each other.

6.4. Mine Warfare Operations

Riverine mine warfare operations include mining and mine countermeasures. Mine countermeasures assume primary importance because of the nature of the environment, pirate tactics, and the need to keep key waterways open. In certain areas it may be tactically advantageous to restrict use of designated waterways and disrupt piratical movement by mining; however, waterway control in the riverine area of operations is normally maintained by continuous patrol, surveillance, and interdiction.

Environment will impose a variety of restrictions and limitations on mine warfare operations in inland waterways.

a. Threat

To assess the mine threat and evaluate countermeasures that might be employed, it is necessary to consider the various environmental characteristics, pirate mining capabilities and tactics, ambush threat, and waterway hydrography. Mine attacks normally are conducted against river craft in locations where the banks of waterways afford protection to the mangy corsair. Mining is frequently used in conjunction with ambushes. Conventional naval mines or land (on and around the riverbank) mines may be encountered. Pirate mines typically are constructed from gunpowder and a variety of detritus, including sharp fragments of metal, pottery, and splintered wood. Contact drift mines may be encountered as well as boats or rafts loaded with explosives, detonated almost exclusively via collision with naval craft. Although crude in technology, pirate mines are nothing to laugh at. See Figure 6-3. Because of their simple construction and low cost, pressure-activated mines may be implanted along shallow waterways. Limpet-type mines, which might be attached to the ship or anchor chain by swimmers or drift techniques, constitute a serious threat to an afloat base.

b. Mine Countermeasures

Mine countermeasures include all methods that may be used to counter the threat of a pirate mining effort. One of the most effective countermeasures is to interfere with or restrict swashbuckler mine-laying activities. Patrol and surveillance and interdiction activities must be emphasized as a preventive measure and included in mine countermeasure planning and operations.

Countermeasures employed against mines already laid require locating the mines. This can be difficult as pirate mines may not contain easily detected metals, and may sometimes be disguised as river trash. Classification of mines in the riverine environment is difficult because of waterway

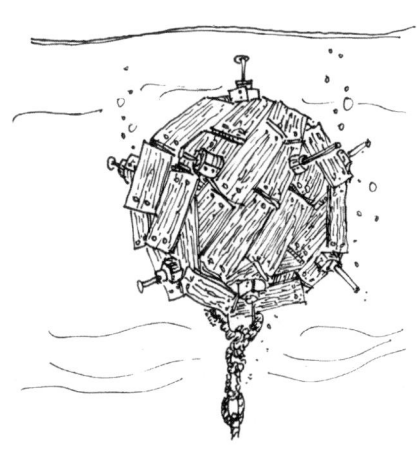

Figure 6-3. Though less technologically advanced, pirate mines are every bit as dangerous as their U.S. Navy counterparts.

characteristics. Therefore, primary emphasis is placed on minesweeping and area clearance.

c. Passive Protection

When the threat of drifting mines or explosive charges or floating pirate-delivered limpet mines is great, the use of nets and/or booms will provide some protection for anchored ships/craft. However, in swift river currents, mooring tackle must be extraordinarily heavy because the build-up of floating debris will often carry away even the heaviest equipment. The most effective countermeasure against this type of threat is an alert watch and patrol around the anchorage or base area.

6.5. Salvage Operations

Salvage operations require highly skilled personnel with specialized equipment. The salvage effort must provide for highly mobile teams that can deploy to remote areas on short notice.

A salvage capability is most important because without this capability the number of lost craft is likely to be extraordinarily high. Small craft, especially riverine assault craft (RAC), are especially vulnerable to accidental flooding. Every downed craft is a victory for the sea rogues' cause. In some instances, pirates have been known to salvage incapacitated Navy craft and use them for their own purposes, including loading them up with kegs of gunpowder, fuse lit, and floating the ill-gotten boats downriver in the direction of assault force vessels. (In some cases, these boats have been outfitted with straw-and-burlap dummies made to look like Navy officers calling out for help, luring assault force members into a cruel surprise.)

a. Mission of Salvage Units

The mission of salvage units is to provide salvage, repair, diving, and rescue services to the riverine commander. To effectively carry out its mission, the salvage unit must have a mobile lift capability to lift the heaviest craft assigned to the riverine commander.

b. Salvage Support

Salvage personnel are highly trained and skilled and require only area security and support from the AO commander. When requesting salvage support, the AO commander should provide the following information:

- Type of craft and how sunk
- Water depth, visibility, tide ranges, and sea state
- Security and support available
- Best known information on the number and attack capabilities of any pirates in the area.

Prior to commencing a salvage operation, a salvage plan is prepared by the salvage unit, taking into consideration the following factors:

- Could this vessel be utilized by the buccaneer enemy?
- Should the sunken craft be refloated, removed, or destroyed?
- Can the salvage job be accomplished using locally available assets?
- Can adequate security for the salvage forces be provided?

6.6. Cover and Deception

Riverine cover and deception operations are those special operations undertaken to deceive the pirate target in order to enhance the mobile riverine force's ability to accomplish the mission. See Figure 6-4.

a. Need for Cover and Deception Operations

The need for cover and deception operations in a riverine area is based on the following factors:

- Surprise is essential to a well-planned military operation. Cover and deception is a means of achieving the tactical advantage of surprising the privateer enemy.
- In a riverine area, the MRF may be under constant surveillance by pirate agents and/or natives either sympathetic to the pirate cause or in their employ.

b. Planning Cover and Deception Operations

Cover and deception planning should be conducted concurrently and in coordination with river assault and waterway interdiction and surveillance plans. The same analysis required for a military plan is also required for a cover and deception plan.

Figure 6-4. Blending in with the local population.

6.7. Unconventional Warfare Operations

Mobile riverine force unconventional warfare (UW) operations are normally conducted within pirate or pirate-controlled territory by specialized military and paramilitary forces. Naval UW resources assigned to the MRF normally operate clandestinely and are capable of performing the following missions:

- Interdict pirate lines of communication (including intercepting bottle-sent messages); see Figure 6-5
- Destroy or sabotage pirate craft, base areas, and caches
- Collect intelligence
- Confiscate buried treasure
- Disrupt pirate political infrastructure
- Assist with evasion and escape of friendly forces from the pirates.

Figure 6-5. Intercepting a pirate communication.

6.8. Pirate Psychological Operations

Pirate psychological operations (or "PiPsyOps") are of major importance to both the total military as well as civil affairs effort. These psychological operations include all actions and forms of propaganda designed to influence the behavior of pirate, neutral foreign, and friendly foreign target groups. Military participation in psychological operations is relative to tactical operations as well as to civil affairs and population and resources control programs.

A well-planned psychological campaign is vital in countering an insurgency, and will contribute substantially to reducing the sea dog's effectiveness and to gaining the support of friendly and neutral segments of the local population. Winning the hearts and minds of the local population can single-handedly win an encounter with the pirate enemy. The campaign can be difficult, however, as the economy of a pirate cove—or an entire island, in some cases—may be built upon the pirates' activities (e.g., fencing of stolen goods, patronage of local brothels and tattoo parlors, multiday rum benders, etc.).

Initial military operations disrupt commerce and inconvenience or even endanger large segments of the local population. The populace usually has been thoroughly propagandized by the insurgent force. Therefore, indigenous and foreign military forces will likely be greeted with hostility, suspicion, and at best, passive resistance.

a. **Fostering a Positive Impression of the Anti-Pirate Assault Force**
To obtain the support of the civilian population, the words, deeds, and actions of the military force must be carefully considered for their effect on the populace. It is not enough simply to denigrate the pirate force, broadcasting the misdeeds of the local buccaneering community. The creation of a favorable image of the national government and its military forces fosters cooperation of the civilian population, to the detriment of the insurgents' cause.

The responsibility for conduct of psychological operations rests with commanders at all echelons, from the headquarters through units in the field, and ending with the individual serviceman. Policy direction, propaganda materials, and guidance as to themes, target groups, intelligence, and specific programs can be expected from higher headquarters. Local commanders must adapt the materials available to achieve the best effect in their own areas. See Figure 6-6.

Figure 6-6. "PiPsyOps" involves both fostering a good impression of the assault force and causing stress for the pirate enemy.

b. **Wearing Down the Buccaneer Enemy**

Along with winning the sympathies of the local population, the effort should be made to "wear down" the pirate enemy by depriving them of certain comforts. Establishing a "rum ration," for example, or buying out the local saloons' liquor supplies, may put subtle pressure on the swash-buckling contingent. Ditto the local prostitution market; simply forcing the island's "escorts" to scatter to a new location each night should cause enough of a hassle to the pirate enemy to begin to fray at their collective nerves.

More commonplace PsyOps tactics, when adapted to anti-pirate campaigns, have proved successful. For example, assault force members (wearing protective earwear) may blast jarring sound effects at high volume and during all hours of the night. Music is also effective. The complex, insipid beats of much modern pop music proves highly irritating to the average pirate. But almost any song, played at high volume and on repeat, can jar the most defiant of buccaneers. Proven successful songs includes Phil Collins's "Sussudio," "My Humps" by the Black-Eyed Peas, "We Are Family" by Sister Sledge, and anything by Prince, Billy Joel, or Garth Brooks.

Chapter 7

DIVING IN SUPPORT OF ANTI-PIRATE OPERATIONS

The primary reasons all anti-pirate assault force team members are trained in diving are 1) To perform reconnaissance against the buccaneer enemy; 2) To make approaches to the pirate ship for stealth assaults; and 3) To plant explosives on or beneath the pirate ship. Diving may also be utilized to perform salvage and Search and Rescue missions. It must be remembered that the combat operation will in most cases have to be played by ear, with the general requirements kept as guidelines. Procedures should be adapted depending on the mission: riverine assaults will entail shallow dives, while recon and explosives missions on the open sea will require deeper dives conducted from a greater distance to the pirate ship.

SECTION I: THE DIVING OPERATION

7.1. Entering, Swimming, and Diving

No diver shall enter the water until he has been checked and been told to do so by the diving supervisor. Always enter the water feet first, holding onto the face mask. It is advisable to spit into the face mask and then wash it out to prevent fogging. Enter the water out of sight of any buccaneer spies and well away from cannon fire, shark schools, propeller blades, etc. Always remain on the surface for a few moments in order to accustom the body to the water. Divers should surface immediately when the reserve valve is activated or when gas pressure drops below 200 psi, whichever occurs first.

The "buddy system" is to be used during all anti-pirate missions. Each man is responsible for checking his buddy both prior to and after entering the water for possession and proper operation of equipment. It is especially important to check for indications of leaks once in the water, and to carefully watch the buddy during descent for any malfunction.

Buddies will maintain a close watch on each other at all times, and will never under any circumstances deliberately become separated.

Always watch your buddy and be prepared to assist him or to wait for him. Never rush or force; do not hold the breath on the way down.

On the bottom, do not separate from your buddy. If you become separated, stop, look, listen, bang oxygen tank (or "bottle") with your knife to alert your buddy, and immediately surface (unless doing so will attract the attention of any pirate enemy). If he is not already on the surface, bang the bottles again and inform the diving supervisor. Do not attempt to stay down and find a lost buddy.

Know when your bottom time is up; surface then. Come up immediately upon activation of reserve. Do not attempt to skip breaths to increase duration.

Surface immediately upon any sensation of medical symptoms or signs. Never try to be a hero.

a. Buddy System and Lines

Buddy lines should be fastened to the wrist in such a manner that they cannot slip off. Line signals for the buddy line should be known by all swimmers and are as follows:

1 tug: OK
2 tugs: STOP
3 tugs: SURFACE
4 tugs: PIRATES PRESENT

No line signal should ever be ignored; i.e., an OK tug should be answered with the same tug if such is the case, and the STOP, SURFACE, and PIRATES PRESENT signals must be followed immediately and without question.

b. Divers' Signals

The standard diving signals as outlined in the U.S. Navy Diving Manual shall be used as required. The most important ones are the closed fist "STOP" sign, the thumbs up "SURFACE" sign, and the pointing sign to indicate an area of difficulty (e.g., reserve, out of air, knife fouled, etc.). Anti-pirate assault force teams will also use the crook-finger (or "hook") sign to represent "PIRATES." See Figure 7-1.

STOP

SURFACE

PIRATE ON SURFACE

Figure 7-1. The divers' signals.

7.2. Diving Responsibilities

a. Diving Department

The Diving Department is responsible for ensuring that the requested equipment is ready to go at the specified time. The department will check the equipment out to the individuals going on the dive and check it back in following the dive. The Diving Department is specially trained to detect and repair any pirate-specific damage, such as tanks and tubing punctured by hook thrusts, dagger strikes, or parrot bites.

b. **OIC**

The officer in charge has overall responsibility for the operation, must be at the scene at all times, and should not enter the water with the other swimmers. He may, however, make the initial dive to determine depth and other conditions. He should conduct the briefing and oversee the check-out and return of all equipment to be used. He is responsible for all post- and pre-operational reports.

The specific planning responsibilities of the OIC are as follows:

- Make provisions for boats through appropriate external channels or through the First Lieutenant if team boats are to be used.
- Supervise extensive reconnaissance of the pirate enemy, condensing all relevant information for briefing.
- Brief all divers and medical staff on the nature of the mission, the number and location of the corsair enemy, and the desired outcome.
- Ensure that adequate medical personnel and equipment are provided.
- Notify the Diving Department of all diving equipment required.
- Assign personnel and ensure that they are informed as far in advance of the operation as possible.
- Ensure that all equipment has been signed for, tested, and properly prepared.
- Assume overall responsibility for the operation's success and safety.

7.3. Diving Problems And Emergency Procedures

a. **Exhaustion of the Air Supply**

Running out of air is not a serious situation unless the air reserve mechanism has failed to function. If the situation necessitates surfacing, do so quickly, grabbing quick breaths and submerging, so as not to draw any unwelcome attention from pirates who may be in the vicinity.

When breathing resistance becomes noticeable, open the air reserve valve and start the ascent.

If opening the air reserve valve does not restore a normal breathing supply, surface immediately. Continue to breathe normally throughout ascent, if possible. If not, exhale continuously throughout.

b. Regulator Leaks Air

This is indicated by hissing even when not in use. Surface, again using caution. (As a rule of thumb, the small amount of noise you make when surfacing can be played off by the pirate watchman as a frolicking shark or dolphin pod. Repeated splashes, however, may be harder to ignore. Thus, an effort should be made to tread water as silently as possible.)

c. Diver Rescue Procedures

The general procedure is to get behind the victim, squeeze his lungs or gut to force him to exhale, straighten him out, and start him to the surface. If this is difficult, drop his weights and actuate his life preserver if necessary. If not already done, activate his life preserver on the surface, then remove his mouthpiece and face mask, call for help, and if necessary, attempt to administer mouth to mouth resuscitation while waiting for the boat.

The primary dangers in diver rescue are embolising the victim and losing both personnel, and surfacing within range of pirate attack, thus presenting them with a "two birds with one stone (or cannonball)" opportunity. There are several procedures for rescue. The most important thing to remember in all cases, however, is for the rescuer *never* to come off diving status until he is absolutely sure that the victim is under control and will safely float by himself on the surface. The following points outline the proper rescue procedures for surface-tended divers.

(1) Ensure that the line is secured around some part of the diver's body, and is secured to itself under all of the diver's releasable equipment.

(2) When hauling in the diver, pull smoothly; do not jerk. Send a standby diver down the victim's line, if necessary, to untangle it.

(3) Be alert for the distress signal; signal for OK. Check frequently and ensure that the diver answers.

(4) Orient yourself with respect to the pirate ship, and be aware—to the extent possible—of the presence and location of any pirate crew along the ship's railing. Your pre-mission briefing should have given you some idea of the swashbuckling enemy's offensive capabilities. You should now use this

information to gauge your response. For example, if the buccaneer crew are equipped with slow-loading muskets, or cannons that cannot quickly be swabbed out, loaded, aimed, and discharged, you may be able to exercise more caution, and less blind haste, in removing yourself and your buddy from the pirate threat. In many of the tragic cases where a diver and his buddy were both lost, it was haste—and the resulting lack of caution—that was to blame. (In other cases, accurate marksmanship on the part of the dread pirates caused the fatalities.)

d. **Depth Time Limits**
The safe diving limit for the standard gear used by the anti-pirate assault force is 25 feet. The preferred depth is 15 feet. As mentioned, depth will vary based on the exact nature and setting of the anti-pirate mission being conducted. The normal depth/time limits are:

10 feet for 240 minutes
15 feet for 150 minutes
20 feet for 110 minutes
25 feet for 75 minutes

Limits for exceptional purposes, to be authorized by the officer-in-charge *only*, are:

30 feet for 45 minutes
35 feet for 25 minutes
40 feet for 10 minutes

e. **Diving Risks**
Apart from the bodily dangers the diver faces when mounting an assault on a ship inhabited by murderous and amoral privateers, the act of diving presents a number of distinct risks to the diver's health. The three basic conditions against which a diver must protect himself are:

- Hypoxia
- CO_2 buildup
- O_2 poisoning

The following rules are designed to forestall one or more of these conditions:

- Never charge the apparatus with any gas except oxygen.
- When swimming with closed-circuit gear, wear sufficient weights, and always use a buddy line and a depth gauge.
- *Do not* use controlled breathing.
- Swim at a moderate rate: approximately 1 knot per hour.
- Follow depth/time limits precisely.
- Be aware at all times of possible symptoms and signal SURFACE *immediately* if any are noted.
- Remember that fresh air is a cure for O_2 diseases. Be confident of your ability and that of your buddy; if you are not, don't dive.

f. Emergency Procedures

The following are the emergency procedures to be used during any anti-pirate diving mission. Emergencies occasionally arise in the best planned and supervised anti-pirate diving operations. Most, naturally, are due to hostile fire or other assault by the targeted swashbucklers. Many of the remaining emergencies are caused by failure to observe some safety precaution. Others are unforeseen or unavoidable. These emergencies can almost always be resolved if the diver, his buddy, his tender, or the diving supervisor stops to think. Take a second to reason the situation through to a solution. Do not act immediately on what may prove to be a blind impulse brought on by panic.

Few situations in diving are so serious as to require instantaneous action. Remember your training. Do not panic.

Above all, never abandon the breathing apparatus underwater unless you cannot ascend without doing so.

NOTE: *This section is designed to cover general emergency procedures only. See the sections on weaponry, hand-to-hand combat, sniper procedures, medical evacuation, and defensive tactics for additional emergency protocols.*

(1) Medical Emergencies

The primary treatment for the three basic O_2 divers' diseases is breathing fresh air. Surface immediately upon noticing any symptoms or signs. Close mouthpiece valve *before* taking it out of mouth or removing mask. Signal the boat; do *not* attempt to continue the swim. Again, surface with caution and, if possible, out of sight of the buccaneer enemy.

In the event of medical emergency, the important thing is to surface immediately and signal the boat. In instances where you are certain you have not yet been spotted by the pirate crew—for example, where advance sniper fire has removed any night watchmen from the situation—you should tread water, waiting to signal nearby rescue craft, and not attempt to swim. In situations where mangy shipboard rogues appear likely to take potshots at you, you should attempt to put as much distance as possible between yourself and the enemy, though this may not be advisable from a medical standpoint.

(2) **Tank Rupture Due to Pirate Assault**

Drop tank and surface immediately. Use the "PIRATES" hook-finger signal to alert fellow force members of the situation. If possible, swim clear of the pirates' cannon and/or musket range.

(3) **Flooding**

Clear mask by standard procedure. If bags flood, roll to left and blow; swim in slightly upright position and loosen straps to allow water to stay in bottom of bags. Surface if it is impossible to breathe without taking on water.

(4) **Regulator Malfunction**

This is often indicated by a bypass valve that cannot be activated and an increased flow through the metering valve; a ruptured hose will likely occur as well. Surface.

(5) **Overpressure in Bags**

Exhale through nose; allow O_2 to escape around corners of mouth.

(6) **Exhaustion of Gas Supply**

Exhaustion of the gas supply is not a serious problem. The oxygen in the breathing system is usually enough for several minutes of light swimming. Simply swim to the surface and shift to air breathing. Alternatively, if you are in possession of your snorkel, remain just below the surface but breathing through your snorkelpiece. Regardless of the course chosen, take care to make as little noise as possible, swimming below the surface when able so as to evade detection by pirates.

(7) **Emergency Ditching**

This is to be used *only* if apparatus is severely damaged or caught on an obstruction where the buddy cannot free it, and it is impossible to surface with it on. The proper ditching procedure is as follows:

- Get rid of weights.
- Pull life preserver quick releases; if it is necessary to remove it, hold it securely in your hand.
- Loosen Emerson side straps and unzip vest.
- Slip out of vest.
- Pull life preserver toggle, holding bib against chest with one hand; extend other arm over head; blow and go.
- If time allows, the tank's valve should be opened, thus allowing all oxygen to escape. This renders the tank useless to opportunistic pirates, who have been known to incorporate oxygen tanks into improvised explosive devices and mines. The empty tank can, however, still be recovered by a Navy salvage team, and after repairs re-used in a future mission.

(8) **Diver Rescue Procedure**

Should your buddy become unconscious or convulsive while submerged, the following procedure will be followed to bring him to the surface:

- Approach from the rear.
- Hold rescuee against your body with the left hand against his rib cage, right hand holding the backpack.
- Release *his weights*; this should provide sufficient buoyancy.
- Swim toward the surface, squeezing his chest.
- At the surface, or if necessary on the way up, inflate his life preserver.
- Remove his mask.
- If his buoyancy is adequate and there is *no chance* of losing him, come off diving status (ensure you close mouthpiece valve before removing it), light flare, and call boats. If you are able to (i.e., you have a free hand), make the "PIRATES" hook-finger signal.

NOTE: *Throughout the rescue, the rescuer must not do anything that would make himself unable to dive. He must never lose control of the rescuee. Remember that fresh air is the primary treatment for O₂ divers' diseases. And finally, take all necessary steps to remove yourself and your buddy from the strike range of pirate forces. Opportunistic to the core, the average buccaneer will think nothing of "shooting fish in a barrel," regardless of whether one of those fish is unconscious.*

(9) Flooding of a Separate Face Mask

Learn to dive without a face mask. Flooding of a separate face mask, or having the lens cracked by the blow or musket shot of a sea rogue, is then less of a serious problem. To clear the face mask, use the following procedure:

- Tilt the head backward.
- Hold the upper part of the face mask tight across the forehead.
- Exhale through the nose. Water will drain past the lower edge of the face mask.
- During the dive, exhale occasionally through the nose to clear the face mask of small amounts of water. This procedure will also prevent face squeeze by equalizing pressure inside the face mask.

(10) Flooding of a Full Face Mask

Flooding of a full face mask is a serious problem, but every acceptable apparatus should have a means of overcoming it. The technique depends upon the type of apparatus used. The diver, again, should be prepared to remove the face mask and let it fall to the ocean or river floor, and then carry on. If the situation allows you to operate at a shallower water level without drastically increasing the risk due to pirate assault, do so. Otherwise, it may be necessary to operate at a greater depth, despite the limitations of your vision without the face mask. In these situations, your buddy will need to take the lead in continuing the anti-pirate mission, while you assume a support role.

(11) Flooding of the Breathing Bags

The seriousness of flooding of the breathing system depends on the type of SCUBA used. In general it is less of a problem in open-circuit SCUBA.

Be alert to the possibility that the cause of flooding (e.g., a cut breathing tube, or a musket ball rattling around within the bag) may prevent successful clearing of the system.

(12) Emergency Ascent

Except in the most desperate situations, make an emergency ascent by swimming to the surface. The possibility of becoming entangled, striking an obstruction, or falling prey to cannon or musket fire from on board the pirate ship, makes it hazardous to use positive buoyancy for ascent. Swimming to the surface gives a better chance to avoid entanglement and to clear obstructions. It provides the additional security of allowing the diver to make evasive moves. Fortunately for assault force members, pirates' firearm technology is severely outdated and cannot be quickly aimed or deployed, allowing greater chances of "dodging a bullet" (or, more accurately, a load of grapeshot). In some situations the pirate ship itself, or another large object overhead, may preclude anything but swimming.

An emergency situation can become so desperate that the need to surface outweighs the need for caution. If it becomes preferable to risk entanglement or injury rather than to remain on the bottom, inflate the life preserver and ascend with the aid of its positive buoyancy. Bear in mind that the ascent will be very rapid. The danger of air embolism increases, and the possibility of serious injury upon striking an obstruction becomes very great. To the extent possible, the diver should direct his free ascent so as to emerge in a position either out of the sight of any pirates, or where the likelihood of being hit by cannon or firearm fire is low. See Figure 7-2.

Use free ascent only to resolve a life-or-death situation, and no other. Swim to the surface, and/or buddy-breathe whenever possible. If a free ascent becomes necessary, use the following procedure:

Figure 7-2. In cases of emergency ascent, try to surface in an inconspicuous location.

- Drop weight belt.
- Ditch gear if necessary.
- Look around and up. Ascertain the location of pirates, if any, and of the pirate ship or any other large objects overhead.
- Pull life preserver toggle, blow, then go. Remember that at depths below about 20 feet, the life preserver will not appear to inflate; it is necessary to kick to get started.
- Keep hands overhead and exhale continuously on the way up. If you feel comfortable, exhale sharply; you should need air all the way up.
- If possible and necessary, swim directionally so as to manipulate the trajectory of your free ascent to better your chances of evading assault—or, better yet, being sighted in the first place—by any corsair crewmen.
- Upon reaching the surface, inflate the life preserver. Decide whether to take off the breathing apparatus or to leave it on while swimming to safety. An open-circuit SCUBA becomes

very heavy when it breaks the surface. A closed-circuit SCUBA may hamper body motion. If the breathing apparatus interferes with swimming, remove the equipment and tow it to safety. A closed-circuit SCUBA can provide additional buoyancy. If it is desirable to take advantage of this characteristic, inflate the breathing bag to the fullest extent that still allows comfortable breathing. If the breathing medium is not usable, close the bag cutoff valves and use the surface breather. While carrying out this procedure, keep a low profile by hunching close to the water, bobbing your head and shoulders below the surface as often as possible to disguise your presence. In cases where a swashbuckler has discovered you, bobbing in an erratic manner is best, thus increasing your chances of escaping firearm attack.

After the above survival measures have been taken, the diver should get hold of his own offensive weapons and begin fighting back immediately. Under all rules of engagement, taking enemy fire justifies the use of all lethal force, so, "let 'er rip."

Before removing a face mask, consider the hazards of unfavorable surface conditions such as whitecaps, spray, grapeshot from pirate muskets, and the generally foul and brackish water that surrounds pirate ships and represents a danger to your eyes and mucus membranes.

Even with closed and semi-closed circuit equipment there is generally a breath or two of air left in the bags, no matter what the emergency.

7.4. Post-Dive

- Secure the cylinder valve.
- Thoroughly rinse the outside of the apparatus with fresh water. This is best done by dipping the entire *assembled* apparatus into a large can of fresh water, first making sure that the mouthpiece shut-off valve is closed and all gas delivery fittings are connected. This procedure will wash salt off the fittings.
- Thoroughly wash canister, regulator, and backpack, checking each for any unnoticed signs of attack by pirates. Even small

dents from buckshot, or from rum jugs hurled from the pirate ship's deck, can lead to major trouble when paired with the corrosive effects of salt water.

- Immediately dry and return oxygen tank to rack.
- Blow canister and regulator dry, reassemble canister leaving bottom loose, reinstall canister in backpack, and replace backpack cover.
- Allow unit to drain, and return unit to its position on rack.

General Tips

- Always charge the apparatus with a standard mixture.
- Always use fresh absorbent in the canister.
- Carefully set the injector to the proper flow for the work anticipated.
- Do not exceed the maximum depth specified for the mixture in use.
- Be constantly alert for failure of the exhaust valve to bubble.
- Watch constantly for the presence of the pirate enemy, even—*especially*—in locations you do not expect to find them.

SECTION II. DIVING ACCESSORIES

What follows is a list of equipment used in anti-pirate diving missions. Weaponry specific to individual operations will vary depending on the mission objective and specific conditions, and will be covered elsewhere. Note that precautions must be taken, when transporting firearms and explosive devices, to keep all weapons dry.

7.5. Buddy Line

The buddy line is a length of rope 6 to 10 feet in length. It is secured to each swimmer in a buddy pair in order to ensure contact between the swimmers during the anti-pirate excursion. It is to be used during conditions of poor visibility, at night, during extremely deep dives, and during all anti-pirate missions.

7.6. Compass

The MK 1 MOD 0 wrist compass is the compass utilized by Navy dive teams. It may be fastened on an attack board or worn on the wrist. Prior to using the attack board for a compass swim, ensure that the compass does not move freely on the board, the compass top does not rotate freely, and the fixed lubber's line is toward you on the board. In order to swim to a particular object, line the attack board up with the object by holding it steady and rotating the compass top, putting the north arrow over N on the compass card. Swim to the target keeping "North over North." In order to swim a given compass course, turn the compass top until the desired course (inscribed on the side in 5-degree increments) is aligned with the lubber's line. Place North over North and swim to the target, keeping the north arrow over N on the compass card.

7.7. Coral Shoes

Coral shoes are worn when it is necessary for the diver to operate in shallow water, around coral reefs, or when crawling on a beach. Coral shoes are mandatory during all riverine assault operations aimed at a pirate's cove. Depending on the pirate ship's location, coral shoes may also be necessary during open-sea missions (e.g., the Caribbean, which has many coastal reefs). The shoes are designed to protect the feet and ankles when working around sharp objects. They are constructed of a canvas upper attached to a rubber sole. Swim fins may be worn over the shoes, when necessary.

7.8. Depth Gauge

The MK 1 MOD 0 wrist gauge is presently in use by Navy dive teams. It is marked in 5-foot increments from 1 to 200 feet and has a maximum safe diving depth of 300 feet. It is accurate to within 1 foot from 1 to 50 feet and within 3 feet from 50 to 200 feet. It is non-magnetic, corrosion and shock-resistant, and is reliable from 32 to 90 degrees F.

7.9. Exposure Suit

The exposure suit is used for cold water diving. The two types of exposure suits are the wet suit and the dry suit. The wet suit is the type most often used in anti-pirate assault missions. The wet suit permits entry of water into the suit, where it is trapped and warmed by the body, thereby creating an insulating layer. The dry suit is designed to keep water out entirely, though generally a small amount seeps in. The dry suit is used while operating in extremely cold waters such as those found in the Arctic regions. Long underwear should be worn underneath to prevent suit squeeze. Both the wet and dry suits come in full length and shorty models. Although the buccaneer enemy typically will be found in warmer climes, in certain exceptional situations the exposure suit may be necessary. Even in tropical climes, during certain seasons the exposure suit may make the anti-pirate diver's life easier.

7.10. Face Mask

The standard face mask in use at the present time is the eyes-nose mask. Face mask squeeze may be caused by too rapid descent with failure to equalize by letting air out the nose. Never wear goggles; these tend to reflect light in a conspicuous manner, which risks drawing the unwanted attention of the swashbuckler.

7.11. Fins

Swim fins are a most essential item for the anti-pirate assault force swimmer, as they will provide maximum thrust through the water when used properly. The standard fin is relatively rigid with a large blade. Proper fit is essential, as a fin too large or too small may chafe and blister the feet, thereby hobbling the swimmer—strongly undesirable for missions in which the force member must climb on deck and engage the buccaneer enemy. Booties are an additional item that may prevent fin burn and are therefore highly recommended.

7.12. Flare

The flare (MK 13, MOD 0, Signal Distress, Day and Night) is carried taped to the pistol belt or knife scabbard. One end of the flare contains the day signal, which is a heavy red smoke. The opposite end, which has raised beading around the edge, contains the night signal, which is a red light. The raised beading enables the diver to locate the night signal when unable to see. Both ends are activated by means of a pull ring. This signal flare is used as a distress signal or as an indicator of the commencement or end of the phases of an operation. It should also be used to indicate that an anti-pirate operation is being aborted—for instance, if there are discovered to be significantly more swashbucklers than anticipated, or they are better armed than reconnaissance indicated, or the wretched curs have been tipped off to the mission. After either end of the signal has been pulled, the flare gun should be held at arm's length and the activated end pointed away from the diver, at an angle of about 45 degrees. The diver's body should also be upwind of the signal. At night, the diver should not look directly at the light because it destroys night vision for several seconds.

The flare will work well after submergence to any standard diving depth. The user should, however, change flares at least every six months or twenty dives, whichever comes sooner. In the event the flare does not ignite immediately, waving it will cause ignition after a few seconds. The flare will not ignite if pulled underwater.

In extraordinary situations, the flare gun may come in handy as a weapon to be used against the pirate enemy. As a spectacle, the firing of a flare tends to impress the average sea dog and may afford the diver enough time to escape or gain a combat advantage. Flares are also highly combustible, a fact that may be utilized either as a threat or—in accordance with the prevailing rules of engagement—an actual offensive maneuver. For example, the assault force team member may aim the flare gun at a stack of barrels filled with gunpowder, threatening to "blow this lousy tub sky-high."

7.13. Knife

A standard sheath knife is required on all dives. Its primary use is to prevent entanglement. It is worn on a web belt or strapped to the leg and should be securely attached to prevent loss. At no time should it be worn attached to any releasable equipment (e.g., weight belt).

Either team-issued or commercially purchased stainless steel knives are satisfactory. Note that the diving knife may come in handy in a pinch when fighting pirates, but it is *not* intended as a combat weapon, as its metal is notoriously brittle and its blade is inconveniently short (for assault on privateer targets or effective self-defense). See Figure 7-3.

Figure 7-3. The diving knife is to be used *only* during diving missions.

7.14. Life Preserver

The life preserver should be worn at all times when in the water. It should be worn under all releasable gear. The life preserver should be thoroughly rinsed, the cartridge removed, and the inflation assembly and oral tube closely inspected for corrosion after each use. The life preserver is especially prone to being slashed in close-in combat with buccaneers, and should be inspected doubly closely following any such encounter.

In order to ensure the proper working and preservation of the life preserver, periodic preventive maintenance is necessary.

7.15. Lights

The primary light associated with anti-pirate assault dives is the single-cell marker light used in the float for night compass swim training. This light is not waterproof, however, and must be well protected.

Various commercial lights, both in standard flashlight configuration and in pistol configuration (e.g., Dacor Diving Light) are available, and are used as necessary for underwater work.

A third type of light, a strobe light, is used by some commands as a distress marker. This is generally about the size of a pack of cigarettes, is watertight at depths up to 150 feet, and emits a very bright blue-white flashing light. Battery life is generally eight to thirteen hours when activated. This light is easy to pick out in areas of complete darkness, but because of the short duration of the flash, it is hard to pick out of other lights, particularly if the search must be omnidirectional.

For nighttime missions infiltrating pirate vessels, a backup light is strongly advised. Many missions will include onboard searches of unfamiliar ship chambers through pitch-black darkness (as pirate lighting technology as of yet has not advanced beyond lanterns and candles), and dependable lighting is therefore essential.

7.16. Slate

The slate is used to record information during swimming and diving operations, and is primarily used during hydrographic reconnaissances and recon missions preparatory to anti-pirate assault missions. It should be left on-ship for the mission itself.

The slate is composed of Plexiglas ¼ inch thick, 3 inches wide, and 10 inches long. Both surfaces are roughed up with fine sandpaper to give a frosted effect. This creates a surface that can be written upon with a pencil. A length of cord should be attached to the slate to permit attaching to the belt or hanging around the neck.

7.17. Snorkel

The snorkel is strongly recommended on all dives requiring surface swimming or waiting on the surface for pickup, both to preserve gas and to ease the effort of swimming. The flexible hose type is sometimes easier to hold in the mouth, but has a tendency to flatten out and restrict breathing when swimming at any speed.

It is feasible, though not advisable, that for riverine operations a diver use *only* the snorkel, staying close to the river's surface while creeping up on the pirate ship and/or the riverbank adjoining a pirate encampment or pirate-friendly village. A snorkel-only dive carries with it the advantage of a significantly lightened load for the diver (and, consequently, more rapid movement), but has the disadvantage of preventing the diver from escaping into the river depths should he be discovered by the pirate enemy. For "quick and dirty" missions, such as tossing a grenade on board the pirates' ship, this may be a suitable procedure. Otherwise, the snorkel-only dive must be strongly recommended against.

7.18. Tender Line

Required when one man is diving alone or when divers must penetrate under ice or any other substance that precludes free access to the surface. The tender line is of vital importance when a diver is attaching an underwater explosive device (UED) to the underside of a pirate ship and/or drilling a hole in the ship's hull. (This technique has largely gone out of fashion, but is worth knowing about for difficult operating conditions when the full weight of Navy weaponry cannot be utilized.) The tender line is literally a lifeline for the diver working on the underside of a pirate ship, as his buddy can tug him out should he become snagged.

7.19. Weight Belt

The weight belt provides the necessary negative buoyancy to overcome the positive buoyancy of diving equipment and wet suit. The lead weights commonly used are of varying weight; they can be attached or removed from the belt as necessary. The belt shall have a quick release buckle that can be released easily with one hand, usually a right-hand release. The weight belt is the last piece of diving equipment to go on the diver. Therefore, the first piece of equipment to be released, in case of emergency, should be the weight belt.

Stowage and Handling of Radiologically Hazardous Equipment

Due to the radioactive material used to illuminate the compass and depth gauge, certain stowage and handling requirements, as established by the Atomic Energy Commission, must be met. These instruments will be stowed in a lead-lined box constructed of CRES or stainless steel, which is located in the diving locker. They will be used only for operations and will be returned promptly upon completion thereof. The stowage box will be secured in an area away from charging stations, SCUBA tanks, and regulators, and will be appropriately marked. The gauge and compass will be tested for decontamination each six months. The test will consist of both a wipe test and monitoring with appropriate radiac equipment. Only specifically designated personnel will work on these instruments and will do so only in designated areas. Upon completion of handling, thoroughly wash the hands. The seals are not to be broken but in the event that they should accidentally be broken, notify the diving officer. Never carry these instruments in pockets or place them face down against the skin. If individual contamination is suspected, collect and submit a twenty-four-hour urine sample to the Navy Radiological Defense Laboratory for analysis. The diving officer is responsible for ensuring that all team personnel are indoctrinated in the hazards and safety precautions pertaining to radiologically contaminated underwater equipment.

7.20. Whistle

The whistle is another valuable piece of safety equipment, and when required should be worn on the life preserver's oral inflation tube.

7.21. Wristwatch

The wristwatch used by the dive team is waterproof and pressure proof. It is to be used for computing duration of water operations, for computing bottom time and decompression stops, and for controlling rates of

Diving Regulations

Fishing

If any fishing is to be conducted on a dive, be sure to check the latest edition of the Fish and Game laws and thoroughly brief all personnel on them. Ensure that proper measuring devices are carried. Remember that the game warden can come on board a Navy boat if he has reason to suspect that game is aboard. Also be sure to check the charts to determine if the dive is going to be in Mexican waters; if so, a Mexican license must be obtained.

Recreation

Team policies vary with regard to issue of equipment for recreation dives. The following is included for planning purposes:

Recreation dives should be fun, but they should be organized in the same manner as any other dive and should follow Team Safety Precautions. In no case should civilians or members of any other organization be permitted to use team-controlled equipment. This includes not only Navy-issued diving gear but swimsuits, beach balls, suntan lotion, beach umbrellas, paddle ball sets, boogie boards, swimmies, etc. If civilians are to be involved in anti-pirate assault team recreational activities, they must supply their own equipment.

It should go without saying that, in the event of sudden pirate attack during recreational activities, civilians are not to "pitch in" or "help out" in the resulting skirmish with the buccaneer enemy.

descent and ascent. The diving supervisor and a member of each swim pair must have a watch for any diving evolutions. All divers should synchronize their watches prior to the mission, agreeing to begin their return swims no later than a designated time, regardless of whether the action against the pirate enemy has been completed.

Chapter 8

PARACHUTE OPERATIONS

Training in parachuting is offered in support of anti-pirate missions that may require air-to-ground or air-to-pirate-ship entry. These missions are typically second- or third-wave insertions, conducted partway through an anti-pirate strike as a means of providing backup in the anti-buccaneer battle. However, under certain conditions parachute entry may supersede the traditional, sub-surface entry via diving. If reconnaissance indicates an unusually large swash-buckler contingent, the commanding officer may determine the need to "go big," sending paratroopers in along with divers to squash the privateer enemy. See Figure 8-1.

While there should be no confusion that the jumpmaster is in command, it is the Navy pilot of a parachute troop who makes or breaks each mission. He is tasked with the difficult and thankless assignment of flying at low altitude over a hostile cannon-equipped pirate vessel, reading wind patterns, and making a perfect overflight in order to give the parachutists their best chance to land on the deck of the sea dogs' ship. While this manual should never be understood to condone preferential treatment, in the case of the pilot, as one old buccaneer-slayer put it, "It pays to keep 'em happy."

There is only one jumpmaster in any one airplane. He has command author-ity over and responsibility for all airborne personnel in the airplane. The jump-master is normally responsible for knowledge of the pirate enemy, an inspection of the airplane and personnel, the enplaning and jumping of personnel, and the dropping of aerial delivery containers. He is responsible for seeing that all air-borne personnel aboard the airplane observe flight safety regulations and comply with instructions from the pilot. The jumpmaster may or may not jump with the planeload. The general duties of a jumpmaster include:

Designing the mission with strict attention to the observed habits—and weaknesses—of the target pirate ship and its crew of salty sea dogs.

Ensuring that the time schedule for the conduct of the operation is followed as closely as possible, primarily station time (the time at which all parachutists and other participants are in the aircraft and ready for takeoff).

Ensuring that a thorough parachutists' briefing is conducted, including a detailed description of the shipboard mission, primers on the major high-value corsair targets and/or hostages on board, and a clear restatement of the prevailing rules of engagement with regard to the pirate enemy.

Conferring with the drop zone officer on all air-ground procedures.

Conferring with the pilot on all in-flight procedures, including any anti-aircraft capabilities the pirate enemies may possess and consequent evasive maneuvers that may be taken.

Briefing the pilot on drop zone location and identification, drop altitude and speed, number and size of sticks, and number of support personnel riding the aircraft other than jumpers.

Figure 8-1. Pants are optional during anti-pirate parachute operations.

8.1. Pre-Jump Briefing

The assigned jumpmaster will conduct or supervise the pre-jump briefing. This briefing will be attended by all personnel listed in the parachute operations schedule plus any others involved in the operation. The briefing will include discussion and explanation of all material contained in the parachute operations schedule. Any special or unusual conditions will be fully explained. The briefing will include, but is not limited to, a discussion of the following:

- The method of identification of the drop zone (almost always the deck of the pirate ship), assembly area, and obstacles, using maps and photographs when available.
- Smoke and panels for day jumps, lights for night jumps, and emergency signals.
- Arrangement of snipers and/or covering fire to clear pirate sentries from the deck prior to the jump.
- Special equipment, lights, whistles, or other assembly devices.
- Method of notifying the drop zone officer that injuries have or have not occurred.

8.2. Aircraft Inspection

It may surprise some to learn that injuries are commonly sustained even before the parachutist joins the battle against his buccaneer foes. Never forget that this operation is a complex and risky one, and care must be taken even before one is in sight or firing range of the targeted sea rovers. The jumpmaster is responsible for inspection of the aircraft prior to takeoff. This inspection will include:

- The doorway, to ensure that all sharp edges and projections are well taped.
- The aircraft floor, to ensure that it is free of all obstructions.
- Inter-communication between the jumpmaster and pilot, and the jumpmaster and snipers, to ensure it is operative.
- Anchor line cable, to ensure that it is secured on both ends and that it has the proper amount of slack.
- Emergency exits, to ensure they are clear and properly marked.
- Ensuring that first-aid kits are installed in the aircraft.
- Ensuring that sick cups are available.

- Aircraft inspection for night operations will include an inspection of the lights to ensure they are of the color required and are operative.

8.3. Personnel Inspection

Immediately prior to takeoff, a designated jumpmaster will supervise two inspections of each parachutist. One of these will be conducted by a qualified parachute rigger. The other inspection will be made by a designated jumpmaster, and will ensure all personnel are well equipped with anti-pirate weapons and miscellaneous supplies. When only one rigger is available to conduct second checks, and he is assigned to jump, the second check of his equipment will be made by another jumpmaster or a jumpmaster trainee under the supervision of a jumpmaster. Following is the jumpmaster and rigger check:

a. Front

(1) **Helmet Risers.** Properly fitted and fastened. Free of turns from tray to canopy release assembly. Risers will be of equal length. See Figure 8-2.

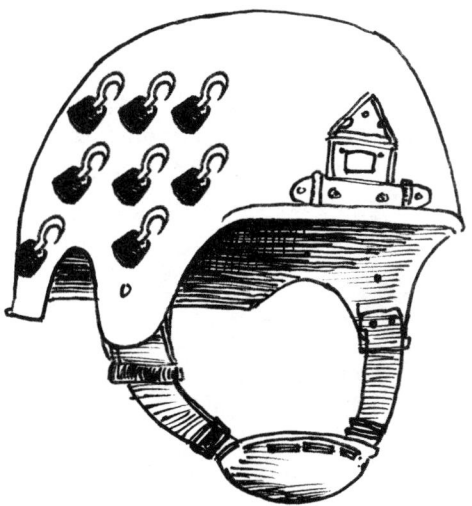

Figure 8-2. The helmet of a decorated pirate fighter.

(2) **Canopy Release Assemblies**
  (a) Remove cloth cover.
  (b) Pull down on metal cover.
  (c) Check for snug fit of the lug and ensure the release assembly is free of foreign matter.
  (d) Replace metal cover.
  (e) Pull down on cloth cover and ensure cloth cover is placed under the lower lip of the release assembly.

(3) **Chest Straps.** Free of turns and twists; lugs are properly inserted into the quick release assembly. No strap should stick out—unfortunate experience has shown that these make excellent "handles" for the pirate enemy during close-in combat.

(4) **Quick Release Assembly.** Remove safety clip and check if quick release assembly is functioning properly. Return safety clip.

(5) **Reserve.**
  (a) Snap fasteners attached to D ring with safety wire through the parachutist's right snap fastener.
  (b) Six properly attached pack opening elastics.
  (c) Ripcord locking pins through cones with riggers seal intact.

(6) **Leg Straps.** Free of turns and twists from saddle through leg strap loops; leg strap lugs are properly inserted into the quick release assembly. The same advice above regarding chest straps and their helpfulness to buccaneers applies.

(7) **Boots.** Jump type, preferably with steel-reinforced toes for "buc stomping."

b. Back

(1) **Helmet.** Properly fitted and fastened.

(2) **Back Straps.** Free of turns and twists and properly adjusted to the parachutist.

(3) **Pack Tray**
  (a) Static line breaking loop properly tied with ¼-inch cotton webbing.

(b) Static line first "stow" is going to the right side of the parachute pack tray.
(c) Static line free of turns and twists and serviceable.
(d) Static line snap fasteners will be in serviceable condition with attached safety wire.
(e) Static line placed over parachutist's shoulder (right or left) and attached to the reserve parachute carrying handle.

c. Additional Equipment Checks

- Fixed-blade knife, day/night flare, service pistol (aka "Patch Provider" [see "Weapons," Chapter 10], and life preserver as prescribed by current regulations. Other anti-pirate weapons may be substituted or added, depending on the mission.
- Static line extensions will be attached to the static line when the following aircraft is used: C-47, C-117.
- Attach the static line extension to the snap fastener of the static line. Place safety wire through hole provided and bend.
- Cover the snap fastener with cover provided on the extension and tie securely.
- Attach the snap fastener of the extension to the carrying handle of the reserve parachute, ensuring the snap fastener of the extension is of serviceable condition and the safety wire is attached. Be sure not to leave excessive slack in the safety wire, as this provides resourceful swashbucklers with a valuable strangling or garroting tool.

8.4. Duties Before Takeoff

Prior to takeoff, the jumpmaster is responsible for ensuring that all parachutists are seated in proper order, that aircraft equipment is secure, and that all personnel are seated with seat belts fastened. He may wish to lead the men in a rendition of "Pirate Slayers We" or "Bloody Knuckle Swashbuckle" before takeoff, as the engine noise during flight will become too loud to permit singing in rounds; however, this is at the jumpmaster's discretion. See Figure 8-3.

Figure 8-3. The jumpmaster fights pre-jump jitters by leading his charges in a rousing rendition of "Pirate Slayers We."

8.5. Duties During Flight

Communications between the pilot and jumpmaster are required to relay information from pilot to the jumpmaster, and from jumpmaster to snipers, who may be stationed aboard the plane or in a clandestine site nearer to the pirate ship. If the aircraft intercom system is inoperative, a system of hand signals will be used.

After the aircraft has reached an altitude of 500 feet, the jumpmaster may give the command to unfasten safety belts. He will ensure that parachutists keep safety belts fastened whenever specified by the pilot.

The jumpmaster will permit smoking only if the pilot authorizes it. (This is a part of the tactic of "keeping the pilot happy" mentioned above.) It is recommended that personnel be kept jumpy and "on edge" so as to channel these frustrations into combat with the buccaneer enemy. (One exception is the pilot, whose nerves may be steadied by the inhalation of fine Carolina tobacco.) The jumpmaster will take no emergency action unless so directed by the pilot. One of the greatest hazards during emergencies is the center of gravity shift caused by personnel moving about in the aircraft.

As the aircraft approaches the drop zone, the jumpmaster will check the aircraft alignment with the drop zone. (This may be performed via radar or electronic tracking, as a pirate ship out on the ocean in the middle of the night will be all but invisible in such heavy darkness.) Corrections in alignment will be relayed to the pilot. When the aircraft reaches the exit point, if the area is clear, the aircraft is at drop altitude, there is no visual NO JUMP signal on the drop zone, no apparent pirate activity (such as cannon fire) makes jumping inadvisable, and the surface winds are within the prescribed limits, the jumpmaster will rise to lead the jump personnel.

After determining that it is safe to jump, the jumpmaster will give all standard jump commands. He will have the assistant jumpmaster ensure each man is properly "hooked up."

If, in the opinion of the jumpmaster, an unsafe condition exists, he shall abort the jump or pass, as appropriate.

The jumpmaster, at the conclusion of each pass, will notify the pilot that the parachutists have exited and cleared the aircraft. He will then, with the help of the assistant jumpmaster, pull in the static lines, unhook, and stow them. In the event that a decisive wind change is experienced prior to the exiting of all men, wind drift indicators or wind dummy jumpers may be dropped at the discretion of the jumpmaster.

8.6. Jumping of Personnel

Four minutes from the drop zone, the red light goes on and the jump-master gives the commands: GET READY, STAND UP, HOOK UP, CHECK STATIC LINES, CHECK EQUIPMENT, SOUND OFF FOR EQUIPMENT CHECK, and STAND IN THE DOOR in sequence. The pilot notifies the jumpmaster to give the final command, GO, by turning on the green light. See Figure 8-4.

NOTE: Jumpers should remain silent as long as possible when parachuting down toward the pirate ship. However, in the event they are spotted by on-deck buccaneers, they should be prepared to produce a cacophonous battle cry, either insults and jibes directed at the swashbucklers or a more generalized yelling sound, meant to put fear in the pirates' hearts.

STAND IN THE DOOR   **GO!**

Figure 8-4. Jumping procedure. Any practice that prepares the jumper for the mission is
acceptable.

8.7. Parachute Jump

The exit from the aircraft is made by springing up and out from the door
at the command GO. This springing action is obtained by simultaneously straightening both knees and by guiding the body forward with
both hands on the outside of the door opening. The leap plus the pull
with both hands and arms should give the parachutist enough momentum to clear the door by at least 2 feet but not more than 3½ feet.

As the man clears the door, his legs are straight. He drops both hands
over the ends of the reserve parachute with the fingers spread and the
palm of the right hand over but not grasping the ripcord handle of the
reserve parachute. He holds his elbows tightly to his sides and his feet
together. His service pistol or assault rifle should be near at hand, ready
to fire upon the buccaneer enemy.

At the moment he clears the airplane, he counts aloud in normal
cadence, "One privateer, two privateer, three privateer, four privateer."
If the parachutist does not feel his main parachute open by the time he
counts "Four privateer," he activates his reserve parachute.

Number Two starts into the door as soon as Number One starts to clear the airplane. He takes a short shuffle forward, pivots into the correct door position as described above, and follows the Number One man at a 1-second interval.

Each man assumes, in succession, the Number Two and door positions previously described before making an exit. During qualification training, the command GO is given as each man assumes the door position, and at the same time he is tapped sharply on the thigh by the jumpmaster. In unit jumps, the command GO is given only once, and each man follows the Number One man without further command.

As a rule of thumb, the parachutist should have the mast of the pirate ship squarely between his feet. His feet are a "frame" he should try to keep around the ship at all times. See figure 8-5.

Figure 8-5. The parachutist should keep the pirate ship's mast between his feet as a means of staying on target.

8.8. Five Points of Performance

The five points of individual performance essential in parachute assault missions are: Check body position and count; check canopy; keep a sharp lookout during descent; prepare to land; and land.

First: Check body position and count. Upon leaving the door, assume the correct body position, check your body position, and count "one privateer, two privateer," etc.

Second: Check canopy. When you feel the parachute open, grasp the risers with your thumbs up and spread them apart. Throw back your head and inspect the canopy for malfunction, deploy your reserve parachute.

If your rate of descent is appropriate and satisfactory, reach for your service pistol or assault weapon and ready yourself. As described above, the pirate ship should remain "in frame" between your feet. This frame presents a good boundary for targeting your fire, should you catch sight of any onboard corsair activity. **Note:** *Take caution, when firing, not to nip or graze your own feet.*

Third: Keep a sharp lookout during descent. Collisions and entanglements are dangerous and must be avoided. Stay clear of other parachutists and check your landing area for obstacles. Caution is especially crucial when gunfire is involved. This uncertainty is compounded by the darkness surrounding the pirate ship. As the punchline to one old anti-pirate paratrooper's joke goes: "Drop your pants, but please—hold your fire."

Fourth: Prepare to land. At crow's-nest level or approximately 50 feet from the pirate ship's deck, prepare to land:

Extend your free (non-weapon) hand straight up, knuckles to the front, and grasp a pair of risers in each hand.

Raise your head and quickly scan the horizon. Then return your gaze to the pirate ship below you.

Hold your feet and knees together, with your knees slightly bent and toes pointed slightly toward the deck so that the balls of your feet will contact the ship's deck first. Maintain sufficient muscular tension in your legs to ensure that your feet and knees stay together throughout the fall and to prevent your legs from collapsing and allowing your buttocks to receive most of the impact.

Fifth: Land. Upon contact with the deck of the pirate ship, execute the landing fall dictated by the position of the body with respect to the line of drift. After landing, recover immediately and collapse the canopy. If you are entering a "hot" battle site, skip the landing fall and execute a landing scamper, landing skip, or landing skedaddle instead. The objective is to keep eyes open and on the lookout for buccaneer foes.

8.9. Parachute Landing Fall (PLF)

Most non-buccaneer-caused injuries in parachute jumping result from incorrect landing. The parachute landing fall (PLF) is a precise method of landing that enables the parachutist to distribute the landing shock over his entire body and reduce the chance of injury. Immediate recovery from the PLF is taught so that the parachutist will get to his feet unhesitatingly and collapse his parachute when moderate winds are blowing. This will allow the parachutist to engage in buc-battling as soon as possible.

PLF is made in the following manner: When the balls of your feet strike the ground, rotate your body to the right or left to expose the remaining points of contact to the ground and to avoid falling on your knees. When your feet strike the ground, drop your chin to your chest and bring your hands and elbows in front of your head and chest. Your feet, calf, thigh, buttock, and push-up muscles (the muscles behind your shoulder) should make contact with the ground in that sequence. The fall is executed in a fluid, coordinated, and rhythmic manner with the five points of contact following one another rapidly.

As mentioned above, in situations where pirates are waiting on deck, or a lively battle is raging aboard the buccaneers' vessel, some adjustments must be made. Rare is the scurvy sea dog who will wait patiently while you land, roll, and then rein in your parachute. The quicker landing scamper, landing skip, landing skitter, landing skedaddle, and landing moonwalk all do an adequate job of displacing the force of landing upon your joints and bone structure. In a pinch, the landing cartwheel or landing somersault may be used, though these maneuvers may cause you to take your eyes off the buccaneer enemy.

8.10. Emergencies

Following are the standard procedures to be followed when making emergency landings in crow's nests, the pirate ship's rigging, or in water:

a. Crow's Nests (and Fo'csles)

As a tradition and in the spirit of fraternal competition, the jumpmaster will typically put up some prize—a fine cigar, a weekend's leave pass, etc.—for the first parachutist able to "hit the crow's eye"; i.e., land in the crow's nest. As a result, the crow's-nest landing happens fairly regularly. The following landing position is thus valuable as a way to minimize the possibility of injury when you find yourself landing in the pirate ship's crow's nest.

To assume this position, place your feet tightly together to protect your crotch. Place your left arm over your eyes and your left hand in your right armpit, palm outward. Place your right arm across your left arm and your right hand in the left armpit, palm outward.

Fancy footwork is required to land in the crow's nest itself, rather than striking the perch a glancing blow and drifting away. When possible, try to hook the lip of the crow's nest with your feet, and/or grasp the mast at any point that is within reach. With those things accomplished, hang on for dear life and attempt to haul yourself in. At this point, realize that your parachute will become your worst enemy (unless there is a buccaneer in the crow's nest with you—in that case, he should be considered your worst enemy), as it will act as a sail, pulling you away from the crow's nest.

In the event that the crow's nest is occupied by a salty swashbuckler, job one is to terminate, disable, or otherwise forcibly remove the pirate opponent. See Figure 8-6. Job two is to land safely. It may be advisable, in this situation, to give up the dream of the jumpmaster's box of Cuban cigars and drift past the crow's nest, rather than risk your own neck falling into the arms of a waiting enemy. Often, the best option is to snipe at the crow's nest privateer well before landing. Even in the worst-case scenario, you will provide needed cover, either for yourself or for your fellow assault force members as they take the ship by air and sea.

b. Ship's Riggings

When forced to make a landing in the riggings of the pirate ship, attempt to prevent your body from becoming entangled upon contact with the ropes. This goes double for your parachute. More than once has a parachutist found himself a "fly" in the pirates' "spider web" due to his harness and chute tangling with the intricate ropes of the ship's riggings. See Figure 8-7. Place your feet together, extend your arms overhead with elbows straight, and place your hands inside and against the front risers with fingers extended and joined. Keep your head slightly down so that you may observe and at the same time avoid coming in contact with the rigging.

Figure 8-6. A "crow's eye": landing in the ship's crow's nest and disarming the watchman.

c. **Landing in Water**

Although rare, there are occasions when an air-to-water-to-ship entry will be the commander's best option, or when an aerial assault is not possible (e.g., when the pirates' stock of cannons and other firearms might endanger parachutists).

A more common occurrence is that a parachutist, aiming for the pirate ship, will be blown off course by a crosswind and find himself drifting wide of the ship, heading for a meeting with the salty sea. See Figure 8-8.

In both instances, the following procedure will be observed for preparing to land in the water and continuing with your mission:

- After the third point of performance (getting clear of other jumpers), remove waist band and loosen left side of reserve parachute.
- Put on swim fins.
- At approximately 100 feet from the water, face into the wind and put your fingers on the parachute release cord. *But do not apply pressure at this time.*

Figure 8-7. The "fly" in the "spider's web."

- When your feet touch water, release the left side of your parachute harness by applying pressure and pulling down on the
  release. If the parachute remains inflated and begins to drag
  you, release the remaining harness.

Figure 8-8. Be prepared for a water landing in the event of missing your jump target.

- Press the quick release box, free the leg straps, and remove harness. Allow the parachute to float away; it will be recovered by the salvage team.
- Swim toward the pirate ship, massing with other assault force members at the base of the climbing ladder. Report your presence to the commanding officer and await his instructions. Or, if the commanding officer has gone aboard or is not present, mount the pirate ship in support of the mission.

Chapter 9

MISCELLANEOUS ANTI-PIRATE OPERATIONS

9.1. Limpeteer Attack

The limpeteer attack is one of the oldest tactics used by underwater combat troops. Against the buccaneer enemy, it is also one of the most effective, owing to its great simplicity. The following tactics are to be learned and utilized in tandem with diving procedures (Chapter 7). The following paragraphs are designed to present a few general principles that apply to all limpeteer or "sneak" attacks.

a. **The Approach**

It is often desirable for the swimmers to swim upstream of a pirate target and drift down upon it, especially if highly phosphorescent water makes motion in the water visible. See Figure 9-1. If the wind is not extremely strong, the current can be determined by the direction in which the pirate ship tends on its anchor chain. This applies both to open-sea missions and those in which the pirate ship is anchored in a cove or pirate bay.

Proximity to a ship is indicated to an underwater swimmer by some or all of the following phenomenon:

(1) An increase in noise level.
(2) An increase in water temperature.
(3) The "darker darkness" experienced when passing under the hull of a pirate ship.
(4) The presence in the water of pirate-specific refuse, such as shark chum, excrement, amputated limbs, and discarded clothing (e.g., worn-out bandanas, faded eye patches, torn-off sleeves rendered unnecessary by amputations).

Caution must be taken to stay clear of screws, rudders, and underwater suction openings (which are usually located midships). Should a swimmer discover that his buddy has been pinned to the hull by underwater suction during an anti-pirate mission, he should not attempt to go to his aid, but should surface and notify the commanding officer immediately.

Figure 9-1. The limpeteer conserves energy by allowing the current to carry him to his destination.

Upon reaching your target, proceed to the second phase of limpeteer operations: weapon deployment. Specific information regarding weapons and explosives will be handled in chapters 10 and 11, respectively.

In the case of most explosives, phase two is straightforward: Using waterproof adhesive tape, affix explosive to the ship's hull. See Figure 9-2. It should be affixed underwater so as to ensure water entering through the hull breach upon explosion. Care should be taken to leave no daylight between the explosive and the wood of the pirate ship. The ignition mechanism should be clear of any obstructions.

Swim away quickly.

9.2. Inland Demolition Raid

This operation involves the landing of personnel on a pirate-controlled or pirate-friendly beach, movement inland to a target, loading of the

Figure 9-2. A diver affixes a bomb to the targeted pirate vessel.

target with explosives, and withdrawal to the sea. The inland demolition raid can target a docked pirate ship—i.e., attacking it from the "beach side." More often, however, the target of the attack will be a drinking establishment, meeting house, or brothel frequented by pirates, or another local establishment crucial to the buccaneers' in-cove operations. Priority should be given to operations that will cripple the piratical economy on the island; so-called "shock and awe" campaigns designed to demoralize or "shake up" the buccaneer foe are also acceptable.

When the raid is properly executed, the explosion will occur after the raiders have put out to sea.

Personnel involved in an inland demolition raid are:

Officer in Charge: He is in overall command of the raid, and remains in the delivery craft, offshore, throughout the operation.

Swimmer Scouts: The two swimmer scouts swim in to the beach, scout the area, choose an appropriate pirate-weakness point, and signal in the rest of the raiding party. They lead the powder train to the pirate target, and act as runners for Command, if necessary. Once at the objective, they attach and pull the fuses.

Powder Train: The powder train is composed of the "workhorses" of the operation. They load the powder, unload it on the beach, and carry it to the objective (usually two packs per man). See Figure 9-3.

Support Forces: The support force establishes a security perimeter to escort the powder train to its objective. Equipped with night-vision goggles and hand grenades, as well as standard-issue assault rifles, the support force engages any buccaneers who attempt to intercept the demolition squad on its mission.

a. **Conducting the Raid:** The swimmer scouts proceed to the beach, scout the area, and (if all is clear) signal in the demolition squad boat. When the boat hits the beach, Command sets up the squad and signals in the powder train boat(s).

When all hands arrive at the beach, they are informed of the location of the pirate target, and the trip to the objective begins. The swimmer scouts carry the fuses, and all hands stay at low silhouette throughout the operation.

After the powder train officers have tied the packs to the trunkline, they lead the rest of the powder train back to the point of land entry. The support force covers the powder train's withdrawal. Command conducts a muster, sends the powder train to sea, and radios the swimmer scouts (who have remained in the near vicinity of the pirate target) to pull the fuses.

The swimmer scouts radio a reply, pull the fuses, and withdraw with all due haste to the land entry point. Upon their arrival, Command calls in the support team, and all hands head to sea, admiring their handiwork as the buccaneer objective is blown to smithereens.

9.3. Sentry Stalking

As mentioned previously, the first preference of the anti-pirate assault force is to employ snipers to eliminate any buccaneer sentries observed (whether on deck, walking the dock leading up to the ship, etc.). In many instances, however, snipers will be unable to get a clean, "quiet" shot

Figure 9-3. The powder train uses extreme stealth during an inland demolition raid.

at the corsair watchman (meaning that to take the shot would rouse other pirates, mobilizing the entire swashbuckling force and defeating the purpose of eliminating the sentry).

As is true throughout this manual, all care should be taken to adhere to whatever rules of engagement are currently in force as regards the pirate enemy. Often what you may call a "pirate" will be understood by the foreign government of the pirate cove as a "privateer," an overly fine distinction that means the salty cur enjoys certain rights under that government. In certain delicate political situations, it may be necessary to muffle, detain, or "tase" the pirate sentry into unconsciousness rather than killing him.

Whenever it becomes necessary to take down a pirate sentry, two factors are extremely important:

(1) Get as close as possible to the sentry before attacking him.
(2) Dispatch him swiftly and silently. Pirates are known for raising the dead with their howls, and for their murderous pursuit of revenge.

The following paragraphs outline some points to be kept in mind while stalking a pirate sentry.

a. The Approach
Bad weather or periods of reduced visibility are best for approaching a pirate sentry undetected. All movement near man-made or natural obstacles in the presence of the pirate should be made cautiously because these areas will almost always be covered with fire. The danger of booby traps and mines on and near obstacles is a constant hazard. Utilize all available cover. Be sure to expose nothing that glitters, and attempt to blend with the background as much as possible. Move exposed parts of the body slowly; however, when changing positions move as rapidly as possible to a previously selected position, and drop quickly. Make use of all available cover and concealment when moving by creeping and crawling. Running at night should be avoided except in an emergency. Empty pockets of change and keys, which may rattle when you move. Always take advantage of natural sounds to cover up your own movements. Stop frequently (especially at night) and listen for other movement. Keep the pirate sentry within your sights at all times.

b. The Attack
If possible, get to within 6 feet of the pirate sentry before attacking him. Following are some effective weapons and techniques of using them:
- Club or sand-filled sock—often the only weapon available. With this weapon, a blow at the base of the skull will render a man unconscious.
- Cord, wire, rope, etc. can be made into a noose and used to strangle the buccaneer victim. Approach from the rear, and while placing noose over the sea dog's head, kick him behind the knee to knock him off balance. Draw the noose back tightly under his chin with one hand while keeping the other hand on

the back of his head, arm stiff. See Figure 9-4. Lower the body to the ground gently, after unconsciousness or death.

Figure 9-4. Taking down a pirate sentry.

c. Entrenching Tools
Keep the cutting edge of entrenching tools extremely sharp. They are good silent weapons and can be used in lieu of a machete. From the rear, give a powerful direct blow to the small of the pirate's back, kidney, or the base of the skull.

d. Hand-to-Hand and Hand-to-Hook Combat in Sentry Stalking
When stalking sentries and performing anti-pirate operations that involve stealth, you should always be prepared for sudden encounters with the pirate enemy. Nine times out of ten, you will not find yourself

in a position of advantage. For these occasions, you should familiarize yourself with the hand-to-hand combat techniques described earlier in this field manual for large-scale attacks (Chapter 2), plus those detailed below for stealthy sentry-stalking attacks. They are all designed to level the playing field, allowing you to escape intact or, if possible, neutralize your pirate foe and continue with the mission.

Hand-to-hand and hand-to-hook fighting is a method of combat that utilizes various techniques to disarm, disable, or kill one's pirate opponent. It involves:

- Making use of any available weapon.
- Attacking aggressively by using your maximum strength against the pirate's weakest point.
- Maintaining your balance and destroying the swashbuckler's balance.
- Using your pirate foe's momentum to your advantage.
- There are no rules of good sportsmanship in hand-to-hand combat, particularly with a pirate enemy. See Figure 9-5. Be assured, he will not hesitate to use dirty tricks or lowdown tactics to gain an advantage. It is a fight to the death.

Figure 9-5. The pirate has no sense of fair play. Be prepared for dirty tricks.

Defense Against an Attack by a Pirate Armed with a Knife (see Figure 9-6), Bayoneted Musket, or Rifle

Countering a downward knife stroke. Stop the blow by catching the corsair's wrist in the pocket formed by bending your fist forward at your right wrist. Step through with your right foot to protect your groin area. At the same time, strike the sea dog sharply in the crook of his right elbow with the thumb side of your forearm or wrist. This causes his arm to bend. Bring your left hand behind his right forearm and underneath your right wrist, and grasp your right forearm. Bring your elbow close to your body. Bend swiftly from the wrist, putting pressure on the pirate's arm. This causes him to fall backward and lose his weapon.

Countering an upward knife stroke. To block an upward knife stroke, catch the pirate's wrist or forearm in the pocket formed at your left wrist by bending your fist forward. Keep your elbow low. At the same time, twist your body to the right. As soon as you stop the blow, grasp the buccaneer's right hand with your right hand and place your thumb on the back of his hand. Reinforce this hold by grasping his wrist with your left hand and placing your left thumb on the back of his hand. Twist his wrist to your left and bend his hand toward his forearm, causing him to fall to the ground.

Countering a backhand knife slash. Bend your knees and lower your body without ducking your head. At the same time, raise your right arm and block the pirate's thrust with your forearm or wrist. As soon as you block the blow, grasp the buccaneer's knife hand with your left hand. Apply pressure with your right wrist against his right wrist or forearm. Start to twist the knife hand to your left, and then reinforce your left hand hold with a similar hold with your right hand. Both your thumbs are now in the center of the back of his hand, and your fingers are around his palm. A twist to your left, or pressure that bends the pirate's hand forward and under against his wrist causes him to lose his weapon and, in many cases, to suffer a broken or dislocated wrist.

Parry a short thrust. If the pirate attacks you with a short musket thrust, you can parry in one of two ways.

Twist your body to the left but keep your feet in place. At the same time, slap your right forearm or wrist against the barrel of his musket, deflecting the bayonet from your body. As soon as the bayonet has passed your body, grasp the pirate's left hand with your right hand. At

Figure 9-6. Disabling a pirate enemy armed with a knife.

the same time, take a long step with your left foot forward toward your pirate enemy's right, reach under the musket with your left hand and press your left shoulder against the upper handguard. With your left hand, grasp his right hand where it holds the top of the small of the stock. Pull with your left hand and push with your right hand. Keep your weight on your left foot and kick your buccaneer attacker with the calf of your right leg behind the knee joint of his right leg. Your corsair opponent will fall to the ground and loosen his grip on his weapon.

A second parry against the short thrust is: As the pirate makes his thrust, use the heel of your left hand to parry the bayonet to your right, and side-step to your left oblique. You are now in position, facing the side of the fire-arm with your groin area protected by your left leg. With your right hand, palm up, grasp the pirate's musket anywhere on the upper handguard, and with the left hand, palm down, grasp the receiver. Keep a firm hold on the musket with both hands and step through with your right foot, moving quickly past your right foot, and quickly past the swashbuckler. Jerk the weapon sharply up and backward in an arc over the pirate's shoulder, and twist it out of his hands. Whirl and smash him with the butt, ideally in the nose or eyes. You may also attack him with the bayonet.

Parrying a long thrust. Parry the pirate's bayonet to your left by slapping it with the heel of your right hand, and sidestep to the right oblique. You are now in a position facing the side of the weapon with your groin area protected by your right leg. With your left hand, palm up, grasp the pirate's left hand and the musket from underneath. Twist your body to the left in front of your pirate foe, and place your right leg in front of his body. With the right hand, palm down, grasp the sea dog's left hand and musket from above. Twist the gun and pull your pirate opponent across your right leg. At the same time, exert pressure with the right elbow against the outside of the corsair's left arm and elbow. Sufficient pressure downward with your elbow, while twisting and pulling up on the weapon, can break the brittle elbow of most calcium-deprived pirates. Continue the twisting motion, pulling your buccaneer foe completely across your leg and throwing him to the ground. Be sure to maintain control of his musket, preventing any attacks from the ground. You may also use verbal abuse to egg the pirate on, or to demoralize him (and, by extension, any other oceanic cockroaches who may be watching).

Disarming a pirate armed with a musket but no bayonet. In disarming a pirate armed with a musket to which no bayonet is attached, make each movement quickly and without hesitation. Although the swashbuckler has the weapon, you are in a good position, because you know what you are going to do (whereas he has to react to your movement). Although the pirate's reaction time is short, it is not as short as the time it takes you to act.

You can further push your advantage over the sea dog by affecting a "crazy look" and gibbering insensibly, thus conveying the idea to the buccaneer that you are a "wild man" with no boundaries. Despite his bloodthirstiness, the average corsair is an opportunist, motivated by economic necessity and self-centered greed. He will not take unnecessary risks—e.g., fighting a crazed opponent.

Countering a challenge from the front. At the pirate's order of "hands up," bring your hands to shoulder level. Then, in one motion, twist your body to your right and strike the muzzle of the musket away from your body with your left forearm or wrist. As you strike the muzzle, step forward with your left foot. Grasp the weapon's upper handguard with your right hand and the small of the stock with your left hand. Pull with your left and push with your right, and step to the swashbuckler's right with your own right foot. This knocks him off balance, and at the same time, enables you to strike him on the head and face with the muzzle of the gun, or to take the musket from him by twisting it over his right shoulder.

Countering a challenge from the rear. When the pirate has his musket in your back, start to elevate your hands as ordered. When your hands reach shoulder height, twist from the hips to your right and bring your right elbow back, striking the muzzle of the musket. See Figure 9-7. This deflects the weapon away from your body. Do not yet move your feet from their original position. Turn to the rear by pivoting on your right foot. Face the salty sea dog and bring your right arm under the musket and over the pirate's left wrist. Place your left hand on his right hand where it grasps the stock. This prevents him from executing a butt stroke. Pull with your left hand and push with your right shoulder and arm, forcing the swashbuckler to the ground and making him release his grip on the musket.

Figure 9-7. Disarming a pirate armed with a musket.

Disarming a pirate armed with a pistol

Countering a challenge from the front. The pirate orders you to raise your hands. As you do so, keep your elbows as low as possible, twist your body to the right, and strike the privateer's wrist with your left forearm. Grasp the bottom of the pistol barrel with your right hand, making certain that your hand is not near the muzzle. At the same time, strike downward on the pirate's wrist with your left fist. When applying pressure with your left fist, bend the pistol toward the pirate's body with your right hand, causing him to release his grip. The antiquated pistols used by pirates are notoriously volatile—if the pirate opponent is smart, he'll realize that and let go. If he should retain his grip, however, his index finger will be broken. From this position, you can strike the pirate on his temple with the butt of the pistol.

Countering a challenge from the rear. This counter should be used only when you are certain that the pistol is in the pirate's right hand. As you raise your hands, keep your elbows as close to the waist as possible. Twist your body to the right, and at the same time, bring your right elbow against the buccaneer's forearm. Keep your feet in place. Bring your right arm under the swashbuckler's right forearm and place it on his elbow joint, so that his forearm rests in the crook of your right elbow. Grasp your right hand with your left hand, and bend swiftly from the waist. By doing this, you force the pirate to the ground and cause him to drop his weapon.

When the pirate is holding the pistol in his right hand, against the back of your neck, raise your arms and bring your elbows shoulder high. Twist your body to the left and bring your left arm under the pirate's right elbow. Reach across with your right hand and grasp your own left hand. Twist forward and put pressure on the pirate's elbow with your left forearm. You can now either break his arm, or force him to the ground, causing him to release his weapon.

When the pirate is holding a pistol in either hand, against your back. Twist your body to the right, striking your right elbow against the swashbuckler's hand or wrist. Pivot to the right and place your left wrist against the pirate's pistol wrist, grasping the pistol barrel with your right hand, palm up. Apply pressure to his hand and trigger finger by pushing the barrel toward his upper arm. This releases his hold on the pistol and may break his index finger. You now have the pistol in your right hand, opposite your left shoulder. By twisting forcefully to the right, you can strike the dirty sea rover on the chin or neck with the butt of his pistol.

9.4. Camouflage

Camouflage is a French word meaning "disguise" and is used to describe actions taken to mislead the pirate foe by misrepresenting the true identity of an individual's position or equipment. Individual camouflage of the anti-pirate assault force team member is that personal concealment he uses in combat to surprise and deceive the buccaneer. It is important that the individual know how to use the ground for effective concealment. See Figure 9-8. He adapts his dress for the best concealment while in any position, and carefully selects his routes between positions for as much concealment as possible.

Figure 9-8. The anti-pirate assault force team member uses camouflage to gain an advantage on the buccaneer enemy.

a. **Target Indicators**

A target indicator is anything a sailor does or fails to do that will reveal his position to a swashbuckler. A knowledge of these indicators will assist the sailor in locating the pirate as well as prevent the buccaneer from locating him. These indicators are grouped into the three general areas of sound, movement, and improper camouflage.

(1) **Sound.** Although it is unlikely that a pirate will be able to pinpoint a sailor's location by sound alone, noise alerts the buccaneer sentry so that the possibility of eventual location of the sailor is increased.

(2) **Movement.** The degree of difficulty in locating moving targets depends primarily on the speed of the sailor's movement. Slow, deliberate movements are much more difficult to notice than those that are quick and jerky.

(3) **Improper Camouflage.** The improper use of, or lack of, camouflage and/or concealment provides indicators that reveal the majority of targets detected on the battlefield. Camouflage indicators are divided into the three general groups of shine, regularity of outline, and contrast with background.

- **Shine.** Items such as belt buckles and other metal objects reflect light, making them a particularly revealing signal to a pirate observer. Therefore, any object that reflects light should be camouflaged or left behind. See Figure 9-9.

- **Regularity of Outline.** The human body, rifles, helmets, and vehicles are familiar outlines and, therefore, easily identified by even the dimmest or drowsiest pirate watchman. For this reason, the shape of these familiar objects must be concealed by camouflage.

- **Contrast with the Background.** When selecting a position for concealment, a background should be chosen that will virtually absorb the sniper and his equipment. In preparing his position, the sniper must avoid leaving telltale signs of his presence. For example, a parapet of freshly dug earth around a foxhole is as noticeable as a flag waving over it. An area having no vegetation other than a row of evenly spaced bushes leaves little doubt in a pirate observer's mind as to the presence of a defensive position. Another problem when using vegetation for camouflage is that it will eventually wilt and turn brown, thus providing a contrast in background.

b. Stick Camouflage

When available, stick camouflage is effective for covering exposed parts such as the face, neck, and hands. When applying camouflage to the face

Figure 9-9. Leave behind any items that may reflect light.

and neck, two men should team up to ensure a complete and effective job. The color of stick used will depend upon the geographical area in which the individual is operating; e.g., white stick in snow areas; desert sand or sand stick in desert areas; and forest green, olive drab, or black in jungle areas.

c. Field Expedients

The regular issue items of camouflage materials will not always be available to the sailor; therefore, he must be prepared to use what is on hand. Most common of the materials that are available are mud, cloth, and foliage.

    (1) **Mud.** Mud provides excellent camouflage for shiny objects such as belt buckles, but it should not be used on the skin due to its high bacterial content. The same goes for shark chum, discarded coffee grounds, and other refuse to be found in the

vicinity of the pirate crew—though tempting, these should not be used on bare skin.

(2) **Cloth.** Excellent camouflage can be produced by mixing pieces of cloth in a suitable pattern and attaching them to the utilities or cover. The cloth can be obtained from discarded capes, ruffled shirts, greatcoats, breeches, knee-high stockings, packs, ponchos, caps, socks, helmet covers, blankets, or any other material that is readily available.

    (a) **Coloring the Cloth.** Mud, charcoal, burnt cork, charred coffee grounds, prepared pigment, camouflage stick, or dye may be used to vary the color of the pieces of cloth. Use of fuel, oil, grease, and any noxious refuse (e.g., excrement) should be avoided because of their strong odor.

    (b) **Attaching the Cloth.** When attaching prepared garnish to the utilities, the pieces of cloth are stitched loosely overlapping, with an irregular pattern of texture, line, and color. Double-stitching the items together is preferable; however, in a pinch a single tight stitch is acceptable.

(3) **Foliage.** In most cases, natural foliage is preferred to artificial camouflage, but is sometimes difficult to secure to the body and gear. Rubber bands cut from discarded truck, jeep, or bicycle tubes can be used for this purpose. Use common sense in choosing what kind of field expedient camouflage to use. See Figure 9-10.

d. Camouflage in Various Geographical Areas

Effective concealment of the individual depends largely on the choice and proper use of background. Since background varies widely in appearance, each location requires individual treatment to ensure a blending with the background. It must be remembered that an individual may be invisible from the ground but easily seen from the air or, in the case of combating pirate enemies, perched atop a crow's nest or clinging to the rigging.

(1) **Jungle.** In jungle areas, foliage, artificial camouflage, and camouflage stick are applied in a contrasting pattern with the texture relative to the terrain.

Figure 9-10. Foliage makes for excellent camouflage, but only when used appropriately.

(2) **Desert.** The hands and face should be blended into a solid tone using the camouflage stick corresponding to the color of the terrain. A hood is also effective in this terrain. In sand and desert areas, texture camouflage is normally not necessary. This is doubly so because the desert is outside the pirate's ordinary range, and it can be assumed that if he finds himself in this theater of operations, the buccaneer will be in considerable trouble—likely on the run, or hiding out from the anti-pirate assault force.

(3) **Water.** The most common backdrop when combating pirates. When diving in riverine or harbor situations, the individual should use a branch, driftwood, or other floating object (e.g., a tire or refrigerator door) to hide his face behind. See Figure 9-11. His face should also be blackened with camouflage stick. In general, however, the diver's greatest "camouflage" against detection by pirates will be darkness coupled with stealth and effective sniper support.

Figure 9-11. Water camouflage should utilize existing objects to conceal the assault force team member.

e. Preparation of Positions

In preparing his position, an anti-pirate warrior must exercise the same care as in individual camouflage to ensure complete concealment from observation by the swashbuckling enemy. He must not provide the pirate target indicators such as spoiled, wilted, or brown foliage; stripped branches; or bushes in his area. In water situations, he must not draw the pirate's attention to himself by taking cover behind any attention-grabbing object—for example, a floating animal corpse or treasure chest.

(1) **Foxholes.** One of the most effective positions is a well-prepared and carefully camouflaged foxhole. A cover for the hole is desirable to prevent buccaneer detection and to allow safe movement within the foxhole. The cover should be sturdy and carefully prepared to blend perfectly with the surrounding terrain. The foxhole should not be used near an inhabited area since accidental discovery is likely.

(2) **Security and Alternate Positions.** When members of the anti-pirate assault force are preparing positions, one individual must always act as lookout while the others work on the position. An alternate position should then be prepared that, if possible, is accessible from the primary position by a covered route.

f. **Camouflage During Movement**
  (1) **Camouflage Consciousness.** The sailor must be camouflage conscious from the time he departs on a mission until the time he returns. Camouflage consciousness is second only to pirate consciousness on the sailor's priority list. He must constantly observe the terrain and vegetation, changing camouflage as the terrain and vegetation change. He should utilize shadows caused by vegetation, terrain features, and cultural features to remain undetected. He must master the techniques of hiding, blending, and deceiving.
    (a) **Hiding.** In hiding, the individual uses any means available to completely evade detection by the privateer enemy.
    (b) **Blending.** Blending is the art of using camouflage in such a way as to be indistinguishable from the surrounding area.
    (c) **Deceiving.** In deceiving, the pirate is tricked into false conclusions regarding the sailor's location, intentions, or movement. By planting objects such as cans, cartons, or realistic-looking life-size mannequins, the pirate may be decoyed into the open where he can be brought under fire. See Figure 9-12.

  (2) **Footprints.** The sailor must avoid leaving footprints on open ground. While most assault force operations take place in water, where footprints are not a concern, riverine operations and inland incursions typically feature muddy and marshy terrain perfect for retaining footprints. Whenever possible, the sailor must move parallel with such terrain features as rows of vegetation, huts, pirate cove saloons and brothels, and fence lines.

Figure 9-12. The use of mannequins is an ideal way to deceive the pirate enemy.

(3) **Return to Friendly Area.** Probably at no other time during the course of the mission will the sailor have more of a tendency to be careless than when he is returning to a friendly area. Fatigue and undue haste may override caution and planning. The pirate will have more extensive intelligence as the sailor's activities become known. Possessing a greater knowledge of the terrain, the buccaneer may then try to outflank the sailor, beating him back to the land entry point or the boat and lying in wait. Camouflage, concealment, and cautious movement then become of paramount importance. Attention to every detail and careful planning will enable the anti-pirate warrior to return safely to his unit and be available to execute another mission.

Chapter 10

WEAPONS

There are many weapons available to the anti-pirate assault force member as he prepares for his mission against the buccaneers. Some, like the M-16 automatic weapon, are "classics" that the sailor may have encountered elsewhere. Others, like the F-250 flamethrower or the T-1000 pest dispersant gun, are the product of "outside the box" thinking and will require some training prior to use against the corsair foe.

What follows is a brief rundown on each weapon, with an eye toward its particular uses against the swashbuckling enemy.

10.1. M-16E1 (The "Crew Tamer")

This is a semi-automatic/automatic gas-operated shoulder-fired weapon. Its rapid fire capabilities make this weapon ideal for the purpose of neutralizing an entire shipboard of crusty buccaneers—or convincingly presenting the possibility of doing so. The 5.56 ammunition is magazine-fed and the entire weapon is air-cooled. There are three types of magazines, 20- and 30-round with 50-round types available as special orders. Rate of fire is available as special orders. Rate of fire is between 700 and 800 RPM when fired as an automatic. See Figure 10-1.

a. Safety Precautions

There is a mechanical safety on the side of the weapon. When it points toward the barrel, the weapon cannot fire. It has been well established that the pirate enemy, with his throwback firearms, is unfamiliar with the concept of the safety. You may feel free, then, to keep the safety on even while pointing the Crew Tamer at the pirate hoard.

When traveling, carry the weapon unloaded with bolt back and safety on.

Figure 10-1. The "Crew Tamer" automatic weapon.

10.2. 9mm Smith & Wesson ("The Patch Giver")

The 9mm Smith and Wesson is 7½ inches in overall length and has a barrel 4 inches long. Worn in a shoulder holster under the sailor's greatcoat or diving suit, the Patch Giver is an ideal service weapon. It is light, small, and capable of surprising the buccaneer who moves in on an apparently unarmed sailor. It weighs 26½ ounces and the magazine holds 8 rounds (an additional round may be placed in the chamber). The rate of fire is as fast as the trigger can be pulled. The effective range is 50 yards. It has a sliding block–type safety in which a block slides up in front of the firing pin so that even if the weapon is dropped on the hammer it is still safe.

10.3. 50-Caliber Machine Gun ("Buc Amok")

The 50-caliber machine gun utilizes bolt-fed ammunition to function in either an automatic or semi-automatic mode. In automatic mode, it is colloquially known as the "Buc Amok" because of the chaos it instills in any group of pirates on whom it is turned. This is because the gun is primarily used from great distances, beyond the sight range of the swashbuckling foe (often by a sniper stationed on board the base ship, or on a desert island); the appearance of machine gun fire thus causes confusion and terror, leading the targeted pirates to quite literally "run amok." The weapon is recoil operated and air cooled. The sighting devices consist of a leaf-type rear sight and a semi-fixed-blade–type front sight. The 50-caliber machine gun may either be fired from the hip or from a tripod that is provided. Ammunition can be fed either left or right with use of an adapter, female end in first.

a. **Safety Precautions**

The weapon is only safe when unloaded; there are no safety features, so keep your wits about you and be ready to grab dirt should the Buc Amok go off.

10.4. 30-Caliber Machine Gun ("Sea Dog Skinner")

The 30-caliber machine gun utilizes belt-fed ammunition to function in an automatic mode. Ideal for medium-range sniping and arms support, the Skinner creates less havoc than the Buc Amok but can be used with greater accuracy and control. It is recoil operated and air cooled, with adjustable front and rear sights. The 30-caliber machine gun may either be fired from a bipod or tripod. Ammunition can only be fed in one direction.

a. **Safety Precautions**

The only safety for this weapon is when it is not loaded. Keep pregnant women and children away from this thing.

10.5. M-79 Grenade Launcher ("Corsair Cooker")

The M-79 grenade launcher is a single shot percussion-fired weapon utilizing a 40mm round. Its ideal use is in the case of unclearable belowdecks chambers: the Corsair Cooker throws its load down below and any dead-ender pirates who survive the blast will come streaming aboveboard, hands in the air. The launcher has a minimum range of 34 yards, a maximum range of 375 yards, and a casualty range of 10 yards diameter from the point of impact of the fragmentation round. Sighting is by means of a fixed-blade front sight and an adjustable-leaf rear sight. See Figure 10-2. Types of ammo—HE (high explosive), dart round, canister round, illumination round.

a. **Safety Precautions**

Every time the weapon is broke down, the safety is automatically on.

Figure 10-2. The "Corsair Cooker" grenade launcher in action.

10.6. Ithica Shotgun M-37 ("Crow's Nest Crippler")

The Ithica shotgun is the main shotgun in use by the anti-pirate assault force. In general, it is used for everything from guard duty to dove shooting. With regards to the pirate enemy, the Shotgun M-37 is invaluable in detainee capture and movement, as well as in providing covering fire (as suggested by its alliterative moniker).

a. Safety Precautions

When the thumb safety is to the right, weapon is on safe; when to left, the weapon is ready to fire.

10.7. AK-47 Assault Rifle ("Old Faithful" or "Pirate Punisher")

The AK assault rifle is a gas-operated, air-cooled, selective-fire, shoulder-fired weapon. It is no exaggeration to say that the AK-47 is the most crucial weapon in the assault force's arsenal. It remains the weapon of choice for long-distance anti-pirate attacks thanks to its accuracy from great distances and its dependability. The Pirate Punisher is similar to Russian submachine guns but cannot be classified as such since it fires a rifle-type cartridge. The AK is much more accurate over a longer range than any of the normal run of submachine guns. The AK is made in two versions, one using a wooden stock and the other using a folding metal stock; it is also equipped with an 8-inch bayonet.

a. Safety Precautions
The safety is a bolt-locking bar, located on the right side of the bolt.

Note: Anti-pirate assault team members may also consider the weapon used by their brethren in werewolf sniper operations. The W24 Swiper Weapon System is as good an anti-pirate weapon as it is an anti-werewolf weapon. See page 9 of U.S. Army Werewolf Sniper Manual.

10.8. LAAW M-72 ("The Galleon Stallion")
LAAW stands for light assault anti-tank weapon. It was not specifically designed for anti-buccaneer missions, but this muscular weapon has its place among the assault force's arsenal. Two of these weapons, pointed accurately at the side of a pirate ship, can do the work of an entire row of cannons. Moreover, they can do it from some distance away. See Figure 10-3. However, the Galleon Stallion—so named for its ability to send an entire pirate ship toward Davy Jones's locker—is to be used as a weapon of last resort, and/or in the case of kamikaze pirates.

The weapon consists of two tubes, an inner one of high-strength aluminum (mounted at the rear) and an outer one of fiberglass. This outer one contains the rocket warhead, front and rear sight, firing mechanism, and carrying sling. Although the fiberglass tube is extremely tough, this is to protect it from the rough handling in the field rather than from the rocket exhaust. *Note: the weapon cannot be refired.*

The M-18 warhead is employed primarily against armor but, as in anti-pirate missions, may be used against seagoing vessels and entrenched on-shore positions. It can penetrate 11 inches of class "A" armor at 0 degree angle at target, 36 inches of reinforced concrete, or go through one side of a scurvy pirate ship and out the other.

The rocket itself is a high-explosive 66mm fin-stabilized anti-tank M-72 round. Settings are available on the weapon for range in 25-yard increments and lead-time of 15 MPH.

The firing M-412 has a nose cap crimped to the forward end of the warhead. It functions on impact or graze.

a. **Safety Precautions**

Keep foreign matter out of launcher and keep all components corrosion free, especially the flask. Keep the area to the rear and side, 60 meters each way, clear of personnel, vegetation, etc. No one moves while the weapon is being fired. Do not taunt the Galleon Stallion. If readied for firing but not fired, replace rear safety pin or weapon may be accidentally fired. If a malfunction occurs, do not attempt to refire; in fact, you should probably throw it into the ocean at that point, just to have it away from you. Be especially careful of recoil in cold weather.

Figure 10-3. The "Galleon Stallion" in action.

10.9. 45-Caliber Pistol ("Pirate's Poison")

The 45-caliber pistol is the standard handgun used by the anti-pirate assault force, and the military in general. It is highly effective as a shipboard weapon for its substantial firepower and excellent control. It has the added benefit of being visually imposing to pirates. It is a recoil-operated, semi-automatic, magazine-fed, air-cooled hand weapon.

a. **Safety Precautions**

The pistol has three safeties:
  (1) Thumb safety
  (2) Grip safety
  (3) Half-cock safety

Though it may seem redundant, three safeties are necessary, particularly for packing the Pirate's Poison pistol on your person while pursuing pirate prey. Although not a safety, the pistol also is equipped with a disconnector safety feature that disconnects the firing mechanism when the barrel is pushed into the pistol.

10.10. F-250 Flamethrower ("Peg Poacher")

The F-250 flamethrower is the sailor's ace in the hole during the nitty-gritty process of pirate extraction. For use belowdecks when flushing sea rats from their warrens, the Peg Poacher can persuade hardboiled buccaneers to quit the ship before it becomes an inferno. The weapon also comes in handy when attacking pirates from the shore or another ship: Possessing a range of 150 feet, the Peg Poacher can ignite masts, on-deck crates and barrels, or—true to its name—pirates' wooden legs, all without putting the sailor in significant jeopardy. See Figure 10-4.

NOTE: Because of the sea-battered condition of most pirate vessels, the Peg Poacher generally is not effective at igniting the entire ship, as awesome as that would be.

a. **Safety Precautions**

The flamethrower has no proper safety mechanism. It may only be considered safe when the fuel canister is empty; even then, exercise caution, and try not to stand in its way.

10.11. T-1000 Pest Dispersant ("The Sloop Snacker")

The Pest Dispersant is an experimental weapon, not officially sanctioned by the U.S. military and thus not recommended for use. However, due to the frequent (and effective) documented use of the so-called "Sloop

Figure 10-4. The "Peg Poacher" flamethrower lives up to its fearsome name.

Snacker" on anti-pirate operations, as well as the dangers associated with its use, it is to the sailor's advantage to be aware of it. Based off a modified M-79 grenade launcher (or "Corsair Cooker"), the Pest Dispersant is rigged to shoot hollow capsules instead of grenades. Instead of explosives, the hollow capsules are filled with live termites, fleas, baby mosquitoes, and other noxious vermin. This potent mixture drives pirates crazy, as the fleas and mosquitoes feast on their flesh and the termites go after any and all wooden prostheses. See Figure 10-5. The termites often also infiltrate the pirate ship itself, in some cases felling masts and destroying crow's nests, or even eating breaches into the ship's hull.

a. **Safety Precautions**

Keep a healthy distance from the so-called "pest palace" where the vermin are kept and bred in advance of their being weaponized and deployed. Hope your number is not called for "bug farming" duty; i.e., scooping up a capsuleful of pests prior to loading. Keep the ship well stocked with bug spray, and use it to treat the Pest Dispersant's muzzle after it has been fired. See Figure 10-6.

Figure 10-5. The "Sloop Snacker" feasts on another pirate crew.

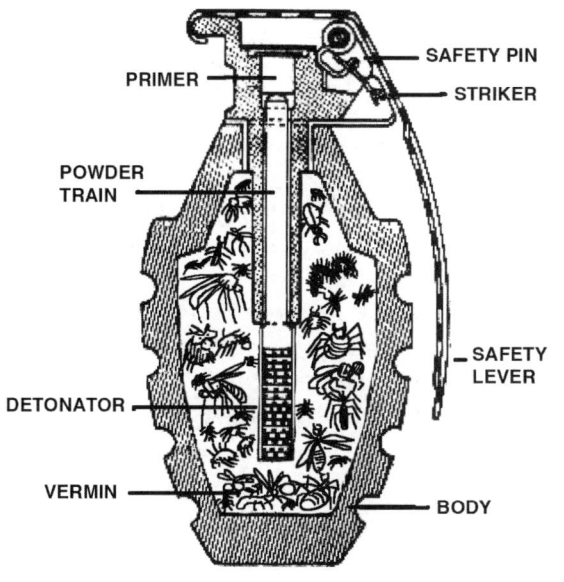

PRIMER

SAFETY PIN

STRIKER

POWDER
TRAIN

Figure 10-6. A cross-
section of the "Sloop
Snacker's" payload.

SAFETY
LEVER

DETONATOR

VERMIN

BODY

10.12. Grenades

When first employed in war, grenades were chiefly weapons for defensive purposes. Today there are grenades for a wide variety of purposes: to produce casualties among pirate personnel; for screening and signaling; for illumination, incendiary action, pirate-ship demolition, and buccaneer-harassing purposes. The hand grenade is a small bomb or missile filled with explosives or chemicals, or it may be an empty container designed for practice in throwing. In exceptional cases, an empty container may be filled with vermin (see T-1000 Pest Dispersant listing, above) and thrown by hand aboard a pirate ship; however, this should be done only with ample precautions, as "blowback"—escaped vermin turning on the sailor—is nasty and almost assured.

a. **Composition**

Although they vary in size, shape, and weight, hand grenades are made up of three main parts:

(1) **Fuse:** This device automatically sets fire to a train of powder that burns at a controlled rate. The burning time is called the delay of the fuse, which prevents the grenade from exploding until several seconds after it is thrown. Some fuses burn into an igniting cap (igniter) which sets off the fillers; these are called igniting fuses. Other fuses burn into a blasting or detonating cap; these are known as detonating fuses. Some detonating fuses are of the silent type. They do not sputter, smoke, or sparkle while the delay fuse is burning. These fuses are identified by a protruding T-lug that holds the safety lever to the top of the fuse body.

(2) **Filler:** The substance with which the grenade is filled may be any explosive such as TNT or any of a number of chemical compounds. In the T-1000, the filler is vermin.

(3) **Body:** This is a container that holds the filler; it is made of metal, glass, paper, or any other suitable material. Grenade bodies have different shapes; for example, the body of a fragmentation grenade is shaped like a lemon, while chemical grenades usually have cylindrical bodies.

b. Operation

When the grenade is to be thrown aboard the pirate ship or in the direction of buccaneer combatants, it is held in such a manner that the fingers of the throwing hand pass around the body of the grenade and the palm is over the safety lever, holding it in place. Before throwing the grenade, the safety pin is removed and the safety lever is held in place by the palm. When the grenade leaves the hand, the safety lever, which is no longer held in place, is thrown clear of the grenade by the action of the striker spring, forcing the striker through its arc. The striker then continues through its arc until it strikes the primer, igniting it. The primer in turn ignites the powder train, which burns for a predetermined time down to the detonator, or igniter, which then explodes or ignites the filler.

c. Grenade Throwing

The grenade should be thrown like a baseball, using the throwing motion that is most natural to the individual. To give the grenade a spinning motion in its flight, it should be allowed to roll off the tips of the fingers and released with a snapping motion of the wrist. As a rule, this method will achieve the most accuracy and distance. The individual should not change his throwing style completely, although minor corrections might be necessary to improve throwing skill.

It is important to remember to follow through when throwing the grenade. This not only improves accuracy and distance, but relieves the strain on the arm. When throwing the grenade from the standing position, an additional step forward should be taken and the thrower should fall to the ground after releasing the grenade.

To prevent injury to the throwing arm, the sailor should not throw from beyond 20 yards from the pirate ship. He also should refrain from throwing the grenade along oblique angles or trying to make "trick shots" (e.g., off the ship's sail, into the pirates' gruel trough), as these hijinks can lead to injuries and arm fatigue. See Figure 10-7. As the anti-pirate assault force member builds experience throwing grenades, trick shots may be attempted.

d. Throwing Positions

In combat, the buccaneer target will probably be in jungles, concealed behind the ship's mast or rigging, or hiding in wooded areas. You may

GOOD THROWING MOTION

BAD THROWING MOTION

Figure 10-7. Good and bad throwing motions for tossing grenades.

have just a fleeting glance of the pirate target. Therefore, the grenade may have to be thrown from any position in which you may find your-self, or one from which it can be placed on the target with a degree of accuracy, depending upon the situation. You must learn to throw the grenade from a standing, kneeling, crouching, or prone position.

Standing. Half face the target with the weight of the body balanced evenly on both feet. With the grenade held in front of you, chest high, remove the safety pin with a twisting-pulling motion. As the grenade leaves the hand, take an additional step forward to follow through. Keep your eyes on the privateer target to observe the strike as you fall to the prone position.

Kneeling. Use the kneeling position when you are protected by a low wall or trench (as in riverine operations). The kneeling position may also be used when taking cover on board a Navy ship and lobbing the grenade onto the deck of the pirate vessel. Don't expect to get as much distance from this position as from the standing position. Half face the target and kneel on the knee nearest the target. Extend and slightly bend your other leg to the rear. Hold the grenade chest high, using the proper grip. Remove the safety pin with a twisting-pulling motion. Throw with a natural motion. If your target is an individual pirate or group of pirates, be aware that you do not have to score a "direct hit." As the saying goes, "almost" only counts in horseshoes and hand grenades. Push off with your rear foot to give added power to your throw. When you release the grenade, fall forward to a prone position, breaking your fall with your hands and arms. Observe the probable strike on the sea dog target and then duck your head.

Crouching. Use the crouch position in built-up areas, woods, or jungles where a certain amount of accuracy is required. This also includes the task of "extracting" pirates from entrenched areas or belowdecks rooms where only a narrow doorway or window is available. For short throws under low-hanging tree limbs or into pillbox enclosures and other openings close to the ground, throw the grenade with an underhand motion. Use the regular grip. Let the grenade roll off the fingertips, as if pitching a softball. Stand and face the buccaneer target and assume a crouching position. Grasp the grenade firmly and hold it chest high. Remove the pin with a twisting-pulling motion. Bring back the arm and throw the grenade with a softball pitching or bowling motion. Fall forward into a prone position. Observe the probable strike of the grenade (if possible—for throwing the grenade into a room, you will likely only see a blast and hear the yowls of the injured swashbuckler) and duck your head.

Prone. This position limits both accuracy and range. Use it when you are pinned down by fire and must keep a low silhouette. Examples include being trapped on a lifeboat or beneath the jungle undergrowth while taking pirate fire. Lie on your back with your body perpendicular to the thrower-target line and your throwing arm away from the target. Hold the grenade chest high as in the standing position. Remove the pin with a twisting-pulling motion. Check your right leg (left leg for left-handed thrower), bracing the foot against the ground. Try to maintain a low silhouette. Bring your throwing arm back straight to the rear, or else cock it over the rear shoulder. At the same time, grasp and hold on to any substantial object within reach of your free hand. This will improve your accuracy and distance. Throw the grenade, pushing with your rear foot. As you release the grenade, roll over on your stomach. Observe the probable strike on the corsair target and then duck your head. See Figure 10-8.

Figure 10-8. Throwing a grenade from the prone position.

e. Types of Grenades

(1) Fragmentation Hand Grenade, M26 ("Old Faithful")
A typical fragmentation hand grenade is the M26. Its strength in anti-pirate missions is its versatility: Effective in jungle and riverine operations, the M26 wreaks havoc when tossed into a ring of pirates dining on gruel and sour mash. This is an improved type of grenade that consists of a thin steel body, approximately the size and shape of a lemon, lined with a wirewound coil, which

replaces the older type (MK 2) cast-iron body. The M26 body is approximately 2¼ inches in diameter at the center and 3 inches long, 3.9 inches long including fuse. This fuse is of the "silent type," which means only that the delay charge burns silently. When the grenade is thrown, the striker under the force of the spring pushes the safety lever free of the fuse and strikes the primer. The primer ignites the delay charge, which, after a 4- to 5-second delay, explodes the detonator and the bursting charge, thereby fragmenting the grenade body. The pedestal base allows the grenade to be stood on end and to be distinguished from the Mark I Illuminating Hand Grenade in the dark. The M26 grenade is painted olive drab, with a yellow band at the neck near the fuse, and yellow markings. See Figure 10-9.

Figure 10-9. The "Old Faithful" hand grenade, "personalized" for the pirate enemy.

(2) Offensive Hand Grenade, Mark 3A2 ("Sea Dog Stinger") This grenade has a body of sheet metal ends and pressed fiber sides. The offensive hand grenade is used for demolitions and is effective against personnel in closed-in places because of its shock effect. While serviceable in jungle and riverine operations, the Mark 3A2 really shines in onboard and belowdecks missions. There, it becomes a highly effective tool in incapacitating and discombobulating the pirate enemy. Its filler consists of 8 ounces of TNT. It uses a detonation type fuse with a delay time of from 3 to 5 seconds. The weight of the grenade complete is 14 ounces. Its color is black with an identifying band in yellow, giving the "Sea Dog's Stinger" its bee-like name.

(3) The Incendiary Hand Grenade, AN-M14 (Thermite) ("The Home Wrecker")

This grenade consists of a body of smooth metal (sheet) with no vents, a filler of thermite, and an igniting-type fuse. When the filler is ignited, it burns with a white-hot flame that develops a temperature of 4,330 degrees F, for 30 to 35 seconds. Due to its intense heat and the fact that Geneva conventions prohibit extreme cruelty toward enemy combatants, the Home Wrecker should not be used as an anti-personnel weapon. The grenade is placed rather than thrown. Since it creates such terrific heat, it is very useful in destroying pirate-abandoned guns and machinery—and, in most cases, inflicting terminal damage to the pirate ship itself. Clamps of steel strapping, which fit around the grenade body, may be used to nail the grenade against an object to be burned. Its color is blue-gray with band and markings in purple. The grenade weighs 32 ounces.

(4) Colored Smoke Grenade, M18 ("Sea Dog Semaphore")

This grenade is used for signaling purposes from ground-to-air and ground-to-ground, and frontline identification. An agreed-upon color will signify that the pirate ship has been taken; a different color signifies that follow-on forces are needed; and a third color indicates that the mission should be aborted immediately. A tapered hole extends through the center of the grenade from the bottom emission hole to the fuse. The starter mixture lines the tapered cavity. The M18 is available in red, hot pink, orange, blue, green, turquoise, teal, yellow, purple, and violet. The body is painted blue-gray with markings and band in yellow. The top of the container is painted the color of the smoke that is produced.

(5) WP Smoke Grenade, M15 (white phosphorus) ("The Patch Provider")

The WP Smoke Grenade, M15, has a drawn-steel cylindrical body similar in size to the burning-type chemical hand grenades. However, the body is made of a heavier sheet metal than the other smoke grenades. The sides and bottoms are pressed out of one piece of sheet steel; no ridge or fold is present where the bottom and sides meet. Its edges are rounded. Its filler is white phosphorus, and has a detonating fuse with delay of 4 to 5 seconds. A detonating type of fuse ruptures the grenade body; this allows the filler to come in contact with the air and scatter over an area of about 15 yards. These conditions make the Patch Provider ideal for use during or just prior to engaging the swashbuckler enemy on the deck of the pirate ship. The white phosphorus filler, upon coming in contact with the air, burns with a dense white smoke that blinds the pirate, giving it the dual purpose of harassing the pirate by screening and of producing casualties. White phosphorus also causes severe burns if it comes in contact with the skin. The body is painted blue-gray, with stenciling and one band of yellow.

(6) HC Smoke Grenade, AN-M8 ("The Corsair Confounder")

This grenade is the burning type. Its main use is as a "smoke bomb," providing a dense, acrid screen and allowing sailors to make a hasty exit from a sticky situation. It comes in especially handy during hostage-extraction and targeted pirate assassination missions, where the objective is not to interact with the buccaneer enemy. Its container is standard except that there are no emission holes in the side, only in the top. Its filler of HC MIXTURE, when ignited by the 1.2- to 2-second igniting fuse will burn from 2 to 2½ minutes, producing a dense veil of opaque smoke. The sheet metal body is painted blue-gray with a band of yellow. The top of the container is painted the color of the smoke that is produced.

(7) Red Smoke Grenade, AN-M3 ("The Bloody Banner")

This grenade is larger than the usual chemical grenades; it measures 3 inches by 5½ inches. It is used for signaling, and its red smoke can be seen for great distances when used against a background of snow. The red smoke grenade is typically used to signify sailor casualties at the hands of pirates. Thus, it is deployed as a call for follow-on forces, including any air support, to "bring the pain," responding with deadly force. Attached to the body of the grenade are three metal flaps that are bent upward to provide additional surface so that it will not sink into the snow, mud, or swampy ground. Its weight is 21 ounces. Other characteristics are the same as the HC grenade.

(8) CN Tear Gas Grenade, M7 ("The Patch Scorcher")

The Patch Scorcher Tear Gas Grenade, M7, is identical to the CN-DM grenade except that it has only a tear gas filler, and its effect is to cause a painful burning sensation in the eyes of the mangy sea dogs. Its principal uses are to flush out pirates hiding belowdecks prior to conducting room clearance, and to pacify unruly corsair detainees (especially prior to relocating prisoners). It is made of smooth sheet metal. The filler is activated with a 1.2- to 2-second igniting fuse and is released by means of holes in the grenade body that are covered with adhesive plaster. The adhesive plaster is burned off as the CN is ignited. This hand grenade is painted blue-gray with a band and markings in red.

(9) CN-DM Irritant Gas Hand Grenade, M6 ("The Puking Pirate")

This grenade is filled with a combination of tear gas and adamsite. This makes the grenade more effective when used for harassing purposes or in controlling buccaneer riots and marauding pirate hordes by causing choking, tears, and nausea. See Figure 10-10. It has a sheet metal body. Its fuse is the igniting type because the grenade contains a burning mixture. In the body are holes or vents covered by adhesive plaster squares that are burned off when the filler is ignited. The body is blue-gray with the markings and band in red.

Figure 10-10. A pirate puking after a run-in with the "Puking Pirate."

10.13. Booby Traps

Booby traps are defensive weapons, used primarily to harass the pirate enemy and delay his movement or attack. They may be used to hold a position while advancing.

a. **Safety**

(1) Be extremely careful when setting a booby trap. Many a booby trap has turned out to be less trap, more booby!

(2) You will have the most use for booby traps during riverine operations and when targeting the pirate enemy in his "safe harbor." These traps should be considered an unconventional weapon or part of "PiPsyOps." If used cleverly, they can "mess with the pirate's mind" by causing him to wonder who is behind these bizarre occurrences.

(3) In arming manufacturers' booby traps, remember that the primary safety device is a positive block between the cocked striker and the cap. Always remove this positive block last. If there is any pressure on the primary pin, its removal will cause detonation.

(4) When rendering a booby trap "safe," insert the primary safety pin first, and then the secondary safety pin. Bend the pins open to prevent them from working back out. Finally, remove the device from the explosive.

(5) On the other hand, when in an area that might have been occupied by the buccaneer enemy, be suspicious of even the most innocent-looking objects. They may be booby-trapped. Also remember that they are usually set in groups of two or more.

(6) Remember that the pirate's technology is extremely outdated. A pirate booby trap will not take the form of a metal-and-fiberglass land mine, but is more likely to be a spike-filled pit covered by a lattice of palms and grass, or a rusty axe attached to a trip wire made of vines.

b. Types of Booby Traps

(1) M1 Pull Booby Trap ("Sky High Sea Dog")

This device is activated by a 3.5-pound pull on the trip wire. The wire is usually stretched across a jungle trail or hut doorway, or attached to an object. Ideal for catching drunken pirates returning to the ship after a night of carousing at cove saloons and brothels. See Figure 10-11.

(2) M1A1 Pressure Booby Trap ("Peg Daddy")

This device is activated by applying 10 pounds pressure on its head. Recommended use is buried on the jungle path and covered with foliage. However, the Peg Daddy is the rare booby trap that may be swiftly embedded on board the pirate ship, placed in a high-traffic area and covered with shipboard refuse. The Peg Daddy will surprise the next privateer who opts to walk through garbage rather than cleaning it up. This booby trap can also often be planted under the loose board of a step, or the like.

(3) M14 Antipersonnel Mine ("Treasure Trap")

This is a simple, safe, and effective device, which can be set around foxholes at night and retrieved in the morning. It can also be used along trails. The genius of the Treasure Trap is that it takes

Figure 10-11. How the "Sky High Sea Dog" booby trap got its name.

advantage of the pirate's natural laziness—specifically, his aversion to digging holes to bury treasure. Seeing the freshly turned soil surrounding the Treasure Trap, the pirate approaches, sensing a relatively easy dig. When stepping on the apparently soft soil, however, he is shocked by a violent explosion underfoot. The trap is activated by a pressure of approximately 20 to 35 pounds. To arm, remove the horseshoe on top, and turn the safe and arm button to "A." To disarm, reverse the procedure. And don't forget to collect the pirate's treasure. He won't be needing it anymore.

(4) The Grenade-in-a-Can Booby Trap ("Hook Harvester")
This is one of the most popular improvised booby traps, and has proven remarkably effective against pirates. It is constructed in the following manner:

    (a) Remove grenade from shipping container.
    (b) Attach container to tree, post, or other object likely to be encountered by buccaneers.
    (c) Attach trip wire to grenade.

(d) Remove safety pin from grenade, and replace grenade in container, leaving the container top off. When the trip wire is pulled, the grenade will be snapped from the container and activated.

The Hook Harvester is effective because of the pirate's innate greediness and curiosity. He will seldom hesitate to stick his hand or face into an unfamiliar shipping container, no doubt expecting to make off with someone else's lucre. No sooner does he do so before the sailor, concealed in the nearby foliage, yanks on the trip wire, giving the swashbuckler a nasty surprise.

(5) **M5 Pressure Release Booby Trap ("Sea Rat Trap")**
This device is found under books, souvenirs, etc., or anything that weighs 3.9 pounds or more. It strongly resembles an immense rat trap. The trap is fired by removing the weight from it. Its one safety pin cannot be removed to arm it, unless sufficient weight is resting upon it. The Sea Rat Trap, like the Peg Daddy, can in certain conditions be snuck on board the pirate ship and successfully hidden, if concealed beneath a parrot cage, a barrel of rum or grog, or the like. See Figure 10-12.

10.14. Pirate Booby Traps
As has been mentioned, the pirate enemy has booby traps of his own. While these are invariably crude, and made of scavenged materials, they are no less deadly. Too often, the scurvy sea dog's intelligence and ingenuity are discounted. The anti-pirate assault force member makes these mistakes at his peril. As the booby trap descriptions make plain, the sailor's greatest asset is his discerning judgment and his self-control. The wily pirate shows his understanding of the Navy enemy in the careful selection of bait designed to appeal to the sailor.

a. **Pitfall ("Sailor Shishkabob")**
A simple but deadly trap, the so-called Sailor Shishkabob is simply a deep pit lined with sharpened bamboo spikes. It is then concealed with a grid of bamboo shoots, palm leaves, and branches. The sailor, attracted

Figure 10-12. The cleverly baited "Sea Rat Trap" claims another victim.

by a piece of "sailor bait" (typically a beer, piece of steak, or pack of cigarettes), traipses onto the flimsy surface and falls through to the gallery of spikes below.

b. Cargo Net ("Navy Net")
Another simple but effective trap, the Navy Net (as the pirates call it) consists of a primitive net made of ropes and vines overlaid by branches and twigs for camouflage. The sailor, again lured by bait of special interest to the Navy man, wanders off the path, and suddenly finds himself hanging upside down inside the net. See Figure 10-13.

c. Dangling Boulder ("Sailor Smoosh")
The simplest of all pirate traps, the Sailor Smoosh is an enormous boulder dangling from a composite of twine, ship's rope, and vines above a crude trip wire. Attached to the trip wire is the sailor bait, which, when moved, allows the boulder to fall, crushing the sailor beneath it.

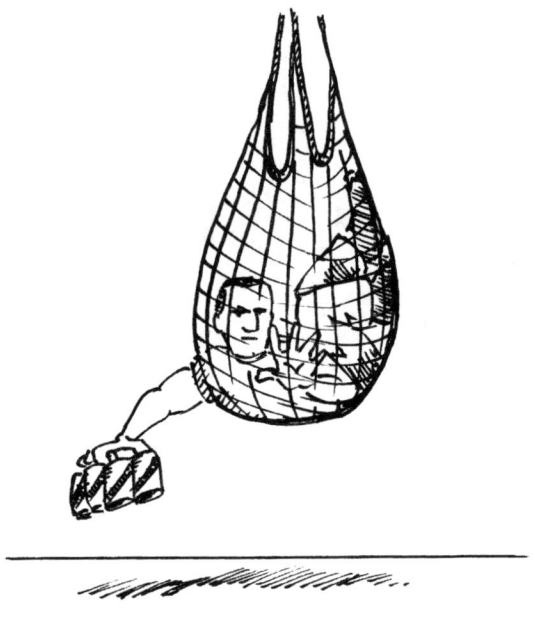

Figure 10-13. The so-called "Navy Net" claims another victim.

Chapter 11

DEMOLITIONS

Demolitions typically play a significant role in anti-pirate assault force operations. While the specific function of explosives may vary—targeting the pirate ship, cutting off avenues of escape from a cove or harbor, or terminating buccaneers—their use is almost always offensive. The information presented here will frequently be used in tandem with the chapter on diving (Chapter 7). The section on unconventional warfare (Chapter 6) may also be consulted, as the typical demolition operation involves "guerrilla," or surprise attack, and techniques from those areas may be readily applied to the deployment of explosives against the swashbuckler.

11.1. Safety Precautions

The sailor's mission in combating pirates is marked by danger at every turn. Too often, the danger begins when handling explosives, well before contact has even been made with the buccaneer foe. Safety in handling explosives can be achieved only through a thorough knowledge of demolition materials and their hazards, the use of good judgment in conducting anti-pirate demolition exercises, and proper application of appropriate safety precautions. This section is by no means a complete list of safety precautions: It lists only those precautions that are most pertinent to anti-pirate demolition operations.

a. General

Do not allow any instructions or any set rules to take the place of caution and thought in conducting anti-pirate demolition missions.

Review applicable safety precautions before each exercise.

Never divide responsibility for preparation, placement, and firing of explosives. One person should be responsible for supervision of the entire project, and should check the area and entire assembly prior to firing. The supervisor should be in close contact with the person or team responsible for pirate reconnaissance, ensuring that the buccaneer's location and capabilities do not change prior to the start of the mission.

Do not use tools for any job other than that for which they were specifically designed.

Smoking will not be permitted at any time in the vicinity of explosives. See Figure 11-1.

Ensure that the demolition area is clear of explosive hazards upon completion of the exercise.

Figure 11-1. Exercise appropriate caution near heavy explosives.

b. **Storage**

Never store blasting caps, primers, detonators, boosters, or pyrotechnics with bulk explosives.

Do not leave exposed explosives unguarded. This is doubly true when the ship is within rowing or swimming distance of the pirate target. Daring counter-raids by audacious swashbucklers are not unheard of.

Do not store or handle explosives in or near an occupied building.

Ensure that explosives are turned over frequently to avoid exudation.

If no permanent magazine is available, ensure that explosives are kept from the direct rays of the sun.

c. Shipping

The BRAVO flag shall be flown in the bow of all boats loaded with or transporting explosives. This rule may briefly be suspended if the Navy ship is traveling within reasonable view of pirates. The commander may wish to keep the force's possession of explosives a surprise. "Reasonable view" should be construed to include potential buccaneer recon missions, or the view of natives who may be assumed to be friendly to the black skull-and-crossbones flag.

All explosives will be securely stowed in wooden boxes on the main deck as far aft in the boat as possible.

All blasting caps and detonators will be stowed securely in a watertight, wood-lined, steel portable magazine as far forward in the boat as possible.

Care will be taken to stow all explosives in such a manner that they cannot move about or be easily confiscated (in the case of pirate incursion).

All explosives shall be protected under a well-secured, fire-retardant tarpaulin. If time and resources permit, the tarpaulin may be made up to look innocuous in order to conceal the presence of explosives, should pirates invade the vessel. Disguise ideas include images of kittens, wizards, or ogres (all of which are known to terrify pirates), or printed words such as "Tax Forms," "Textbooks," and "*Waterworld* DVDs" (all of which are known either to bore or repulse buccaneers). See Figure 11-2.

d. Firing

(1) Non-Electric Firing

- Use electric firing whenever possible. In underwater and close-to-water demolitions,` however, it is imperative that you have the option of using non-electric firing in your anti-pirate assaults.
- Always carry caps in a watertight cap box.

Figure 11-2. Disguise explosives by giving them labels known to repulse pirates.

- Do not blow into or introduce a wire, nail, or similar instrument into a non-electric cap in an attempt to remove foreign matter.
- Avoid kinks in the safety fuse.
- Always cut 6 inches off the end of safety fuse prior to use and ensure a square cut.
- Always time no less than 2 feet of safety fuse prior to use. In general, anti-pirate demolitions should use 1 foot or less, depending on the sailor retreating swiftly. This is so as not to allow the buccaneer a sufficient length of time to detect and potentially dismantle the explosive.
- When operational or training requirements necessitate using lengths of time fuse shorter than 2 feet, do not bend or mash the fuse or allow black powder to spill as this may speed up the burning rate.
- Use dual firing systems whenever possible, and especially if charges are buried or submerged. This requirement may be suspended during certain anti-pirate operations, when a "quick and dirty" or "hit and run" mission is necessitated by environmental or logistical conditions.

- In the event of misfire, observe full waiting time *(full time of fuse plus 30 minutes)*. However, it is advisable that you move on to a "Plan B," because with 30-plus minutes the buccaneer is likely to discover the misfired bomb, thus denying the assault force the valuable element of surprise.

(2) **Electric Firing**
- Never take shunt off leg wires until ready to connect to firing wire. The rule of thumb is that you are not ready to connect to firing wire until you can smell the rank odor of pirates. If you cannot smell the pirate's trademark pungent mix of filth, gunpowder, grog, and salt, you are not sufficiently close to the target.
- Take care not to pull leg wires out of caps.
- The charge placement team or individual shall have in their possession all means of actuating the charge; i.e., hell box.
- Always follow complete check-out procedures for electrical firing.
- Be aware of and take precautions for any electrical sources in the area (static, radio transmitters, thunderstorms, etc.).
- Do not use any means other than a blasting galvanometer containing a silver chloride cell for testing electric circuits.
- In the event of a misfire using plastic explosives, a full 30-minute waiting period shall be observed.

11.2. Demo Kit

Firing wire reel
Nose plugs
Eyeblack or grease (for camouflage)
Cap sealing compound
10-cap "hell box" or blasting machine
Circuit tester (galvanometer)
Friction tape
Condoms
Cap container, (non-electric)
Blasting cap crimper, M2

Firing leads
Metal packing band cutter
Sheath knife
Ruler
MK1 30-cap blasting machine

11.3. Types of Explosives
a. 90/90 Amatol ("Cannon Crusher")
Color: Yellow to dark brown

Composition: A mixture of 80% ammonium nitrate and 20% TNT

Detonation Temperature: 489°F (254°C).

Loading: Cast, extended or pressed depending on the concentration of ammonium nitrate

Melting Point: Does not melt

Sensitivity: Less sensitive than TNT, but is readily detonated by other high explosives

Stability: Very hygroscopic; is usually protected by a sealing pour of TNT

State: Crystalline

Toxicity: TNT is only toxic component

Use: Demolition kit, Bangalore torpedo, M1A1, also used as substitute explosive in 3-inch and 155mm shells. The Cannon Crusher is ideal for destroying pirate weapons caches and especially, as the name implies, cannons. It should be part of the supplies brought on board by the follow-on or second-wave forces, as it is too sensitive to risk bringing into live anti-pirate combat. The Cannon Crusher is then used to disable buccaneer weapons permanently.

b. HBX-1 and HBX-3 ("Ship Shanker")
Color: Slate gray

Composition: HBX-1 HBX-3

Detonating Temperature: 365° to 500°F (185° to 260°C)

Loading: Loaded by casting

Melting Point: 178°F (81°C)

Stability: In storage, good. At temps above 149°F (65°C), desensitizer will exude. Non-hygroscopic and not adversely affected by moisture.

State: Solid mortar-like substance

Toxicity: Produces toxic effects peculiar to its components. TNT is the only significantly toxic component.

Use: Used primarily in underwater ordnance, the Ship Shanker is the diver's first choice when affixing explosives to the underwater hull of a pirate ship. HBX-1 and HBX-3 more than earn their nickname by stabbing enormous holes into the underbellies of pirate vessels. See Figure 11-3.

Figure 11-3. The "Ship Shanker" shanks another ship.

c. **RDX (Cyclonite) ("Wing Man")**

Color: White

Composition: Cyclotrimet-hylenetrinitramine

Detonating Temperature: Approximately 455°F (235°C)

Loading: Always used in U.S. ordnance with a desensitizer; in explosives such as HBX, the RDX is cast with TNT.

Melting Point: 396°F (202°C)

Relative Effect: 1.60

Sensitivity: Sensitivity is appreciably reduced by addition of wax.

Stability: In storage, very good. Non-hygroscopic, and not adversely affected by moisture.

State: Crystalline solid

Toxicity: Not markedly toxic, and generally does not cause dermatitis. If ingested, however, it may affect central nervous system.

Remarks: Most powerful of all military explosives developed by British during World War II. Used primarily as a component of explosive mixtures, the so-called "Wing Man" supports other explosives, rarely acting alone or receiving much notice. Cyclonite is invaluable, however, as a means of supporting other explosives in anti-pirate assault operations.

d. **Dynamite ("Mad Man")**

Color: Straw yellow to yellowish brown

Composition: Trinitrotoluene

Detonating Temperature: 869°F (465°C)

Loading: Usually cast, but may be pressed (tamped)

Sensitivity: One of the most insensitive high explosives, distinctly more sensitive when decomposed by light

Stability: In storage, very good at prescribed temperatures. However, when stored at elevated temperatures, dynamite may exude an oily liquid that is insensitive alone, but when mixed with wood or cotton, forms a low explosive that is easily ignited. While this "homemade" explosive may be used as a pirate trap (e.g., rags smeared in exuded liquid flung into a pirate campfire), it should be taken seriously as a shipboard hazard.

State: A flaked, granular, or crystalline material

Toxicity: Highly poisonous. Is easily absorbed by the skin. Dynamite dust and fumes are toxic when inhaled. Ingestion may also cause poisoning. Causes liver damage and jaundice with fatal results. For these reasons, dynamite has well earned its nickname as an explosive agent, and has also seen reduced usage in anti-pirate combat.

Use: Still, the so-called "Mad Man" of explosives has its uses, not least as an instrument of terror against the buccaneer enemy. See Figure 11-4. The hiss of a burning fuse, followed by the appearance of a long red stick of dynamite tossed over the prow of a vessel on a starry night, has been known to strike fear into the hearts of crusty sea dogs on all seven seas. For that reason, dynamite will likely remain an anti-pirate assault force staple for years to come, "Mad" or not.

Figure 11-4. Good old-fashioned dynamite is an effective tool for striking fear into the swashbuckler's heart.

11.4. Safety Fuse

The fuse is a flexible cord about ¼ inch in diameter. It consists of a black powder core encased in a fiber wrapping that is covered with a waterproofing material (orange-colored wax). The safety fuse is shipped in a paper package containing two 50-foot lengths of coiled fuse. This should be plenty for the anti-pirate assault force. Remember that in almost every instance, a short fuse—coupled with a quick getaway—will be the sailor's preferred choice. Each coil of fuse burns at a fairly uniform rate, which varies between 36 and 47 seconds per foot.

(1) **Use:** The safety fuse provides a burning time delay before ignition of a non-electric blasting cap. It's ideal for anti-pirate operations, whether aboard the pirate ship or in the jungle environs of the pirate cove.

(2) **Safety:** Do not rely upon visual recognition of this fuse, as many foreign time fuses and detonating cords resemble it. Use only a fuse that has been positively identified. Before using, always cut and time at least 2 feet from the roll to be used. No method of lighting fuse should be used that obscures or conceals evidence that the fuse has been lighted. The burning speed of fuse varies due to differences in temperature, altitude, weather storage conditions, character of tamping, and mishandling. In the most typical conditions—i.e., on the high seas in a Caribbean environment—the fuse should burn on the "fast" side of the calculations below. Be aware of this when making your calculations and planning your getaway from the pirate target. See Figure 11-5.

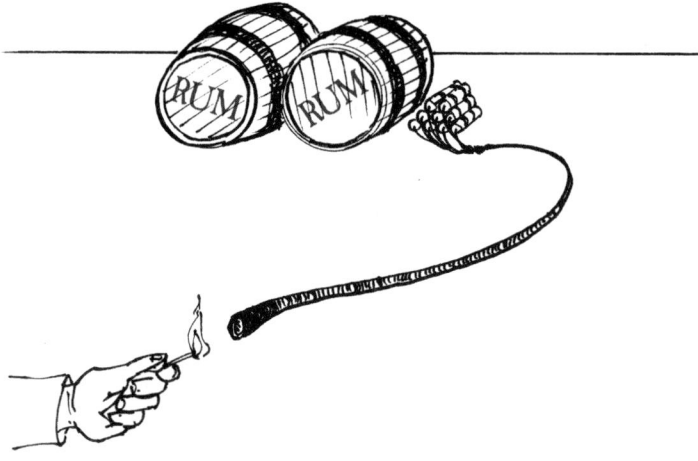

Figure 11-5. The safety fuse in action.

a. **Fuse Length Calculation**
- Well in advance of the anti-pirate mission, burn and time a 6-foot length of fuse.

- Divide that time (in seconds) by 6, to determine the burning rate per foot.
- Divide desired time of fuse (in seconds) by the burning rate (in seconds) to arrive at length of safety fuse in feet and tenths.

NOTE: To convert .1 to inches, multiply 12 by 1.

Example: To obtain a 10-minute (600-second) fuse:
(1) Burn 6 feet. Time consumed (e.g.) 270 seconds.
(2) Divide 270 by 6 to obtain the average burning rate of 45 seconds per foot.
(3) Divide 600 by 45 arriving at a fuse length of 13.3 feet. Convert .3 feet to inches by multiplying by 12. Answer: 13 feet, 3.6 inches.

NOTE: The conditions under which the actual fuse may be burned and those under which the test length are burned may differ. Therefore, do not expect the timing of the fuse to be exact; be sure to allow for some differential. In drafting your getaway from the pirate ship or other swashbuckler target, always err on the side of expecting too little time to escape.

11.5. Blasting Caps

a. Non-Electric Blasting Cap

The non-electric blasting cap is a clear lacquered copper or aluminum tube containing three small explosive charges: ignition charge, priming charge, and base charge. The presence of corrosive salt air and the likelihood of the cap getting wet during anti-buccaneer operations make the non-electric cap the preferred choice. The charges, which are in layers, only partially fill the tube. The remaining portion of the tube is empty, so that the blasting cap can be fitted over and crimped to a time fuse or a coupling base.

Use: Provides the detonating impulse required to explode demolitions. Unlike a lengthy fuse, the non-electric blasting cap is silent and inconspicuous, making the ignition charge the first (and last) sign the scurvy pirate gets that anything is amiss.

b. Electric Blasting Cap

The special electric blasting cap consists of a base charge of PETN (13.5 grains), a priming charge, a bridge wire, and two 12-foot leg wires. The charges and bridge wire are all sealed into the end of a copper or aluminum shell. Although the shell should be watertight, for peace of mind the electric blasting cap should be used in anti-pirate incursions during which there is a reduced risk of the cap getting wet (e.g., inland operations or the rare twenty-years-later-when-pirate-is-in-retirement strike). When current is passed through the leg wires, the bridge wires, strongly heated by the current, ignite the priming charge, which detonates the base charge. Special caps are the only ones that will positively detonate all present military explosives.

c. Delay Blasting Cap

Delay blasting caps are primarily used for extreme stealth missions, when the buccaneer enemy is meant not to know that an assault force member has been there. After planting the delay cap, the assault force member quietly departs, waiting as the oblivious buccaneers go on with their business. In some notable cases, the pirate ship has departed and even lost the pursuing Navy ship, only to be surprised some time later by the sudden destructive blast of the concealed explosive. See Figure 11-6.

Figure 11-6. An extreme example of the delay blasting cap in action.

Special delay blasting caps are the same as special electric caps except that a delay is obtained by embedding the bridge wire in a burning charge instead of an explosive charge, or by inserting a short piece of time fuse between the bridge wire and priming charge. Special delay caps are issued in ten different delay periods.

11.6. Explosives Packages

a. Bangalore Torpedo ("Pirate Pathblazer")

Consists of ten Bangalore torpedoes packed in a wooden box. Each torpedo is a 5-foot olive drab steel tube. The Pirate Pathblazer is useful for combat in the jungle areas surrounding a docked pirate ship, when a safe path must be cleared quickly. See Figure 11-7. The Bangalore contains about 9 pounds of 80/20 amatol. Each end of the tube is filled with a booster charge of crystalline TNT. Both ends have a threaded activator well to provide means of priming with a blasting cap and priming adaptor or standard demolition firing device. Torpedoes can be linked together to provide for a charge of any length desired.

Use: To clear a path through minefields, barbed wire, or other lightweight obstacles. May also be used underwater to clear sandbars, shipwrecks creating obstacles, or dead coral. Though unorthodox, the

Figure 11-7. The Bangalore torpedo quickly blazes a path through the hostile jungle.

Bangalore can also be linked together across a river entrance and used as an impromptu mine.

b. Ammonium Nitrate ("Cove Clearer")

This combination is primarily for post-assault cleanup, including destroying pirate galleons, demolishing buccaneer-friendly saloons and brothels, and clearing jungle land suspected to be mined. The kit consists of 40 pounds ammonium nitrate charge in a sealed metal can. Contains a booster of TNT to ensure detonation. A lowering ring is provided on one end for attaching a line when lowering the charge in a hole.

A cap well (unthreaded) and a detonating cord tunnel are attached to the side of the container to accommodate either an electric or a non-electric cap.

Use: Post-assault demolition. Used principally for earth moving, not suitable as a cutting charge.

Safety: Do not puncture the container, as ammonium nitrate readily absorbs moisture.

c. 2.5-Pound Block ("Stern Slicer")

A 2.5-pound block of composition C-4 packed into a rectangular plastic container, which is sealed at each end by a plastic plate. Each end has a threaded blind hole to receive a blasting cap with a priming adaptor.

Use: As a general demolition charge, including underwater demolitions. The Stern Slicer is famously effective as a cutting or breaching charge. When affixed to the stern of a pirate ship, the resulting explosion destroys the poop deck and produces a slow, cinematic sinking of the pirate ship, with the bowsprit gradually rising until it points directly upward. See Figure 11-8.

Safety: Do not detonate in closed spaces. C-4 produces poisonous gases when it explodes.

d. Flexible Linear Demolition Charge ("The Fullback")

The MK 8 MOD 2 flexible linear-type demolition charge consists of a 25-foot length of 2-inch diameter rubber hose, with a main charge of 50 pounds of 70/30 Composition A-3 and aluminum powder. The charge contains an MK 8 MOD 0 booster in the female end, and a MK 12 Mod 0 booster in the male end. Each booster contains 76 to 79 grams of granulated TNT. The MK 8 MOD 0 booster contains an activator well.

Figure 11-8. An enemy vessel after the "Stern Slicer" has gotten done with it.

Use: Clearing channels through sandbars and coral reefs. Can also be lashed to or wrapped around irregularly shaped obstacles. The use of the Fullback is also irregular. It is reserved for instances when either the primary Navy ship or one or more larger subsidiary vessels must enter the pirate cove or pass close to an island ringed by coral, or with an unusual amount of debris (e.g., shipwrecked vessels) resting on the sea floor. Like its football counterpart, the Fullback clears the way, allowing these ships safe passage.

e. **One Pound Block ("The Ventilator" or "Feng Shui")**
The 1-pound TNT block consists of two ½-pound blocks enclosed in an olive drab, water-resistant, fiberboard container, which has metal end closures. One end is provided with a threaded activator well. The fiberboard container can be cut to provide two ½-pound uncovered blocks, each with an activator well.

Use: Used either as a main charge for small demolition operations, or as a booster charge for a major demolition operation. May be used underwater. The Ventilator earned its name by being supplemented with additional pounds of TNT, C-4, and any other explosives near to hand. Affixed underwater on one side of the ship, the Ventilator creates an opening from port to starboard (or vice versa). The drastic "redecoration" of the pirates' sleeping quarters gives this destructive compound its alternative nickname, "Feng Shui."

Safety: When using, take adequate cover, as metal ends fly when fired.

f. MK 135 Demolition Charge ("Joe the Plumber")

The MK 135 consists of a haversack packed with ten individual MK 20 MOD 0 demolition charges. The MK 20 is composed of a 2-pound block of Composition C-3, contained in a canvas bag. The booster and explosive lead are made of 11 feet of reinforced primacord. Five feet of detonating cord act as a booster, and the remaining 6 feet extend from the block to form an explosive lead.

Use: General demolition operations, including underwater operations. An unassuming explosive, Joe the Plumber is remarkably versatile, pairing with a number of flashier explosives to bring down galleons and wreak havoc in the pirate community. When affixed to the underside of the pirate ship, Joe the Plumber earns its nickname by doing serious work on the sloop's plumbing. See Figure 11-9.

Figure 11-9. The strategic use of explosives sends pirates flying.

11.7. Charge Estimation and Placement

Depending upon what type of explosive you are going to use, and upon the specific nature of the anti-pirate mission, there are either one or two steps involved in determining exactly how much explosive you will need for a particular job:

(1) Apply the appropriate formula to determine the necessary amount of TNT.
(2) If using an explosive other than TNT, apply the appropriate relative effectiveness factor to your answer to determine the amount of your particular explosive necessary to meet the anti-pirate objective.

The next few paragraphs present the most commonly used formulas, and the final paragraph in this section shows how to use relative effectiveness.

a. **Cutting Masts and Rigging**
Use the following formula to cut the masts, fo'csles, and rigging aboard the pirate ship:
P=3/8 A, where
P=pounds of TNT necessary, and
A=the cross-sectional area to be cut (in square inches)

b. **Cutting Stern and Bow**
The thinner wood used in the rest of the pirate ship can be cut either with an untamped, external charge, or a tamped, internal charge. While the former can be placed much more easily and rapidly than the latter, an internal charge will produce the same results, with much less explosive. The untamped, external charge formula is as follows:

P=D240, where
P=pounds of TNT required, and
D=diameter of the wood in inches

NOTE: For wood having diameters larger than 25 inches, increase P by ¼. When diameter exceeds 36 inches:
P=D2250, where
P=pounds of TNT or plastic required, and
D=diameter, or least cross-sectional dimension at the point where the explosive was placed (in inches)

c. Felling Trees to Create an Obstacle

During riverine operations, you may gain a strategic advantage by "boxing in" the pirate, preemptively sealing off his avenues of exit before launching your attack. An ideal way of achieving this is by felling dense jungle trees and other foliage to prohibit river passage, or to seal off footpaths. See Figure 11-10. The following formula applies when using an untamped, external charge to fell a tree but leave it attached to its stump:

P=D250, where

P=pounds of TNT required, and

D=diameter of the tree in inches

NOTE: For trees having diameters greater than 24 inches, increase P by ¼.

Figure 11-10. Felled trees can be used to box in the pirate enemy.

d. Breaching Walls
In the case of targeting known pirate "safe houses," buccaneer-friendly saloons, brothels, and the like, use the following formula to breach walls of concrete, masonry, rock, or similar material:

P=B3KC, where
P=pounds of TNT required
B=breaching radius, in feet
K=material factor
C=tamping factor

NOTES: For breaching walls 1 foot in thickness and over, increase the total calculation by 50 percent. For charges under 150 pounds, add 10 percent.

11.8. Coral Blasting
Coral blasting, while less glamorous than demolitions of pirate ships, is a crucial part of the success of the mission. Coral presents a major obstacle to the movement of Navy vessels into and out of pirate coves, and thus gives the wily sea bandits a distinct "home field" advantage. With the combination of reconnaissance and preparatory coral blasting, the assault force can "level the field."

a. Selecting Type of Explosive
Explosives with low detonation velocities, such as ammonium nitrate, are the best explosives to use against coral when powder points are not used. TNT, Tetrytol, and plastic explosive, however, have all been used with success. Powder points ordinarily are loaded with plastic explosive, Nitramon, or blasting gelatin.

b. Placing Charge on Coral Heads
In order to keep packs of demolition charges in position about either type of coral head, they should be saddled together by their haversack straps. Packs should be secured so that the detonating cord will be moved against the coral by wave action as little as possible. The sharp edges in coral growths can cut detonating cord as would a knife.

If the detonating cord leads are not long enough to be tied together, additional detonating cord should be placed in one of the packs before it is placed in the water. A float should be connected to the detonating cord lead of this pack so that the pack can be identified.

It must be stressed that coral-blasting missions should be conducted under the guise of official cove business, or under cover of darkness. The pirate's suspicion will be roused by the explosive detonation of coral walls encircling his cove, regardless of the preventive measures taken. If there is a "cover story," however, and enough time is allowed prior to the anti-pirate mission, the blasting of the coral may be smoothed over and even forgotten by the corsair enemy. Cover stories should be kept consistent, repeated to locals and inquisitive swashbucklers, and always be straightforward. Annual coral maintenance and trimming, the discovery of a tropical coral disease, or complaints about the overgrowth and excessive sharpness of coral all are suitable examples of cover stories.

c. Powder Points

Coral may be blasted with explosive charges dropped into powder points. They are used in place of drilled boreholes for coral, because coral particles clog a drill. Powder-point blasting requires less explosive per cubic foot of coral than any other type of blasting. Except during assault operations, it is usually the most practical type of coral channel blasting.

d. Bangalore Torpedoes

Bangalore torpedoes may be used, either singly or in bundles, to blast channels in coral. Because Bangalore torpedoes may be needed at a later point during the anti-pirate mission, however, they should not be the explosive of first resort for blasting coral. Bundles of torpedoes can be prepared in advance and either carried by hand or floated into position. A bundle of as many as nine lines of torpedoes can be carried by a column of men with ease if each man has only a 3- or 4-foot length to support.

When a bundle is floated, it is lashed to light wood spreaders and enough buoyancy for a nine-line bundle. When a bundle is in position over the coral, it is cut loose from the float.

CAUTION: *Do not place explosives in crevices that may be present. In most cases, explosives placed in a crevice toss large coral boulders into the bottom of* *the channel. This completely defeats the purpose of clearing the coral, as these boulders have been known to scrape and even breach the hulls of passing Navy ships en route to the pirate cove.*

e. Determining Amount of Explosive

Underwater mushroom-top coral heads require about 5 pounds of TNT, or 4 pounds of either Tetrytol or C-3, per cubic foot of coral. Underwater solid coral heads require more explosive than this.

When demolishing above-water coral, however, pause to ask yourself: Will a pirate notice the disappearance of this coral wall? If so, is there an alternate route, requiring only the demolition of underwater coral, that I can blast? To the fullest extent possible, pains must be taken not to alter the buccaneer's physical water environment.

11.9. Cold Weather Demolition

Cold-weather encounters with pirates are exceedingly rare—but they are not unheard of. Largely the province of desperate swashbucklers on the run from formidable foes, the cold-weather assault mission adds a new set of wrinkles for the anti-pirate assault force team. Among these are the peculiar qualities of certain explosives in cold weather. See Figure 11-11.

Figure 11-11. Though very rare, encounters with buccaneers in arctic terrain are not unheard of.

a. **Effects of Cold Weather on Explosives and Explosive Materials**
Since extremely low temperatures cause changes in various articles, it is important to foresee these changes and handle them properly.

(1) **Explosives:**
  - **C-3:** Becomes jumpy and difficult to mold at 30°F. Loses much of its plasticity after 48 hours at 15°F.
  - **C-4 and TNT:** Perform normally at low temperatures.
  - **Primacord:** Becomes brittle below 0°F.

(2) **Explosive Materials:**
  - **Electric Firing Cable:** Rubber insulation becomes brittle, more easily cut, and more difficult to splice, at low temperatures.
  - **Friction Tape:** Loses its adhesive quality below 35°F. Back up tape with marlin or copper wire.
  - **Fuse Lighter:** The pin breaks and jams at low temperatures.
  - **Galvanometer:** Silver chloride cell may be rendered useless by extreme cold. Keep next to body.
  - **Hell Box:** May be rendered useless by extreme cold. Keep next to body.
  - **Non-Electric Caps:** Often misfire below 15°F.
  - **Safety Fuse:** Is rendered brittle by cold, and is easily broken. Measure fuse while it is warm, and keep it as warm as possible. Use electric firing whenever possible.

b. **Effects of Explosives on Ice**
Although data on ice demolition is conflicting, the following information can be used for general guidelines when beginning an ice demolition task.

Surface blasting is relatively ineffective.

All ice blasting is incredibly noisy. Be ready to toss the idea of sneaking up on the buccaneer enemy out the window, if you engage in ice blasting.

Under-ice blasting is eight times more effective than surface blasting, and it produces much less flying ice. To place packs under the ice, bore a hole in the ice, or work in from the edge of a floe. Place inflated flotation bladders in the packs to keep them against the underside of the ice. If anti-pirate divers are equipped to perform sub-ice dives, they may also perform the explosive placement. (This is useful in the case of a pirate ship stuck in ice, when a diver might use the ice as cover, swimming beneath it to plant an explosive beneath the pirate ship.) However, as is widely known, diving beneath solid ice is an incredibly risky proposition.

With that said, strategic ice blasting can have the tactical effect of painting the pirate into a corner. Getaways previously available now become impassable. Ice floes and free-floating mini-glaciers seal off the pirate ship's planned exit path. The better-stocked, more warmly clothed Navy force waits for the freezing, hungry, increasingly desperate pirate enemy to make a move.

11.10. Advanced Demolitions

As you should be well aware by now, the name of the game when combating pirates is creativity and adaptability. The explosives and demolitions packages listed above should cover most situations, but not all. In the case of wily and intransigent buccaneers, certain advanced techniques must be deployed.

Charges constructed employing advanced techniques generally produce more positive results, while using less explosives than required by conventional or standard formulas. The disadvantages of advanced techniques charges are that they usually require more time to construct, and once constructed they are usually more fragile than conventional charges. This can be a detriment when hiding the explosives; the pirate enemy, upon finding the charge, will have an easy time dismantling the weapon. Following are rules of thumb for various charges and the swashbuckler targets they are designed to destroy.

a. Saddle Charge ("Maroon 5")

This charge can be used to level the masts of pirate ships, effectively "becalming" the vessel and trapping all corsair inhabitants on board. In the case of Saddle charge deployment while the pirate ship is docked in a cove, the weapon will generally have the effect of dispersing all buccaneers throughout the jungle village and environs. The pirates lose all sense of cohesion as a fighting unit, as they are effectively marooned (thus giving the explosive its colorful name). See Figure 11-12. The Maroon 5 has a blasting capability up to 80 inches in diameter. Dimensions are as follows: The short base of the charge is equal to one-half the circumference of the target. Thickness of the charge is ⅓ block of C3 or C4 for targets up to 6 inches in diameter. Use ½ block thickness for targets from 6 to 8 inches in diameter. Prime the charge from the apex of the triangle; the target is cut at a point directly under the short base by cross-fracture. Neither the Saddle nor Diamond (see below) will produce reliable results against non-solid targets, such as gun barrels. These charges benefit from prepackaging or wrapping, providing that no more than one thickness of the wrapping material is between the charge and the target to be cut. Heavy wrapping paper or aluminum foil are excellent, and parachute cloth may be used if nothing else is available.

Figure 11-12. The "Maroon 5" destroys the pirate vessel's ability to move, marooning all on board.

b. Diamond Charge ("The Sea Dog Sequesterer")

Especially useful for riverine operations, the diamond charge effectively destroys the dock and riverbank where the pirate vessel is moored. When deployed strategically, the Sea Dog Sequesterer can be used to prevent the majority of the pirate crew—who may have wandered into the village in search of food, drink, and companionship—from returning to the ship to help defend it. The Diamond charge's dimensions are as follows: The long axle of the Diamond charge should just touch on the far side. The short axle is equal to one-half the circumference. Thickness of the charge, is ⅓ block C3 or C4. To prime the charge both points of the short axle must be primed for simultaneous detonation. This can be accomplished electrically or by use of equal lengths of detonating cord, with a cap crimped on the end that is inserted into the charge. As detonation is initiated in each point of the Diamond and moves toward the center, the detonating waves meet at the exact center of the charge. The Diamond charge is more time-consuming to construct, and requires both more care and more materials to prime. Transferring the charge dimensions to a template of cardboard (or even cloth) permits relatively easy charge construction. (Working directly on the target is extremely difficult and, with pirates in the vicinity, extremely risky.) The completed wrapped charge is then transferred to the target and taped or tied in place, ensuring that maximum close contact is achieved. The template technique should be used for both the Saddle and Diamond charges.

c. Ear-Muff Charge ("The Brothel Buster")
The uses of the Ear-Muff charge fall under "PiPsyOps," as this explosives package is often deployed to make the pirate's cove life a little less comfortable. As the name suggests, the Brothel Buster is used to destroy concrete buildings: not only brothels but, potentially, saloons, opium dens, and other establishments that give solace to the weary pirate. The Brothel Buster may be used in conjunction with a covewide sweep for pirates, a targeted swashbuckler assassination, or again, simply as a means of harassing the buccaneer enemy. Little is more irritating—or, indeed, embarrassing—than for a pirate to be exposed in a private moment by the explosion of an exterior wall. See Figure 11-13.

Within its limitations (which are quite restrictive), the Ear-Muff charge offers dramatic savings in explosives for destroying reinforced concrete targets. The rule of thumb for construction is as follows: For each foot of target thickness (up to a maximum of 4 feet), use 1 pound of C4; for fractions of a foot, go to the next higher pound. Divide the total amount of C4 exactly in half, placing one half of the charge on each side of the target, diametrically opposite each other. (This brings up one limitation: the requirement to have two sides of the target accessible.) Prime the two charges to detonate exactly simultaneously, and the target will be destroyed as the shock waves meet in the center of the target and, if effective, cause it to virtually explode from within. This charge is effective and reliable only against targets that are approximately square, and not much more than 4 feet square.

Figure 11-13. The "Brothel Buster" works its magic.

11.11. Improvised Demolitions

Preparation is paramount in combating the pirate enemy. However, the anti-pirate assault force ought always to be prepared for contingencies. In the realm of explosives, that entails knowing how to improvise effective demolitions tools.

NOTE: *This is not MacGyver; these improvisations are not magically cobbled together from everyday ingredients, but require some explosive materials to be on board. However, these solutions are ideal for situations when there is "a little of this, a little of that" in the way of explosive materials on board.*

a. **Improvised Time Fuse**
Boil equal parts of potassium chlorate and sugar in water. Dip cotton

string in the solution and let dry. Burning rate is approximately 60 seconds per inch.

b. Improvised Blasting Cap
Seal off one end of copper tubing or pipe. Pour in tetryl (finely ground). Fix carbon or lead from a pencil between two wires and insert into tubing. Seal off other end and detonate electrically.

c. Improvised Black Powder
Mix 3 parts charcoal powder, 10 parts sulphur, and 25 parts perchlorate (potassium nitrate). Wet and let stand. When almost dry, granulate by forcing through a piece of fly screen. Spread thinly and allow to dry. Black powder, when seen in real life, is remarkably similar to its portrayal in *Looney Tunes* cartoons. The powder is ideal for "dividing and conquering" pirates during a shipboard battle, creating a line of fire that separates a buccaneer from his fellows. See Figure 11-14.

Figure 11-14. Improvised black powder turns the deck of a pirate ship into a minefield.

d. Improvised High Explosive

Mix 3 parts potassium chlorate and 1 part granulated sugar. Confine in any container, and prime with time fuse.

e. Improvised Thermite

Combine 1 part aluminum powder, 3 parts potassium chlorate, and 1 part sugar; or combine 1 part ferric oxide and 1 part aluminum powder.

f. Improvised Cratering Charge

Materials: 25 pounds ammonium nitrate fertilizer in pellet form, 1 quart any type motor oil.

Procedure: Pour pellets in hole and add motor oil. Prime with a 1-pound block TNT. The improvised cratering charge is an ideal improvised explosive for sinking pirate vessels.

g. Improvised Shaped Charges

Material: Plastic explosive and any cylindrical container.

Procedure: Pack plastic explosive into container so that the cone is approximately as deep as half its diameter, and the standoff is approximately half its diameter.

h. C-4 and Vaseline

Combined in the proper mixture, it can be made to stick to almost anything. This is an ideal improvised solution when attempting to attack the integrity of the pirate ship's hull.

Part Two

DEFENSIVE STRATEGIES

It is for good reason that the word *Combat* appears in the title of this manual: The emphasis of this book, and the foremost thought in the sailor's mind, should be on actively fighting pirates.

But attention must be paid to defending against murderous corsairs. It is at your peril that you underestimate the buccaneer foe; they have not survived for centuries on the high seas by being pansies who faint at the sight of blood.

Some aspects of defense, such as hand-to-hand combat and the detection of pirate mines and booby traps, have been covered. This section pertains to defense defined broadly. This includes warning against crucial, often deadly errors made by anti-pirate personnel, and illustrating the appropriate emergency measures to be taken in these and other situations.

As ever, though, the best defense against scabrous pirates is a good offense: An emphasis on defense should never be taken for an encouragement to sit back and be passive. The endless struggle against the swashbuckler will be won not by caution and restraint but by daring, aggression, and a singular lack of mercy toward the seafaring criminal class.

Chapter 12

CONTINGENCY PLANNING

12.1. Effect of Environment and Organization

Your response to emergencies and unforeseen situations during the anti-pirate campaign will vary greatly depending on the theater of operations. As a rule of thumb, however, you may think of the riverine theater as having all the potential problems of open-water campaigns—drowning and hypothermia, shipboard accidents and fires, ship-to-ship attack by buccaneers—plus a number of river-specific pitfalls. Thus, this section will discuss all likely emergencies, with the understanding that all may apply to riverine operations, but only some to open-water campaigns.

Environmental conditions in riverine operations and the unique composition of the mobile riverine force require certain modifications to normal contingency procedures.

The following paragraphs concern aspects of emergencies, disaster control, and Search and Rescue as they apply to riverine operations.

12.2. Emergencies

a. **Man Overboard**

All craft will be prepared for man overboard. Frequent drills to aid rapid identification of a man overboard are indicated. Rapid small craft is mandatory in riverine currents in order to be effective.

At least one man should be designated as "cover man." At the signal for a man overboard, the cover man goes to a designated position, ideal for providing covering fire, and readies himself to respond to any pirate volleys with return fire. In this way, the cover man provides the recovery team a necessary security buffer as they rescue the man overboard. See Figure 12-1.

Figure 12-1. A "cover man" should always be utilized when rescuing a man overboard.

b. **Fire**

Depending on the severity of the fire, it may or may not be necessary to debark troops. If it is necessary, rehearsed emergency debarking procedures will be followed and designated craft will assist with debarkation and fire fighting. The possible necessity for grounding the craft that is on fire should be considered.

Again, one or more "cover men" should be standing at the ready to provide protective return fire against pirate attacks. In the case of the craft needing to be grounded, or personnel debarked, in an area heavily populated by swashbucklers, more cover men will be needed. As soon as possible upon debarking, a security perimeter should be erected, sealing off the group's temporary base of operations from assault by privateers.

c. **Breakdown**

All riverine craft and ships should be prepared to tow other craft and ships in the event of a breakdown.

In the event of a breakdown, which would require slowing the entire formation, a decision will be made whether to declare the disabled ship a straggler or slow the formation. The detachment of escorts for stragglers may be necessary. It is imperative that one or the other course be chosen. No ship should be permitted to fall far behind the others, as this would immediately present an opportunity for assault by pirates.

Preselected temporary anchorages may be used in the event that a slowed speed of advance detains the whole formation and prevents it from reaching its destination on schedule.

d. Emergency Sortie

An emergency sortie is an emergency relocation of the afloat base of operations forced by pirate action or inclement weather conditions. Planned withdrawal of shore perimeter defense troops and equipment and disposal of inoperable craft are executed, and withdrawal fires and emergency destruction plans are executed if the sortie is forced by action on the part of the buccaneers.

If a riverine assault operation is in progress, subsequent rendezvous will be conducted in accordance with instructions given in the operation order.

12.3. Disaster Control and Emergency Assistance

Disaster control and emergency assistance procedures are executed in accordance with current directives and standard operating procedure (SOP).

The assault force commander is responsible for:

- Conducting disaster control measures and operations in areas where the force is located.
- Rendering assistance in local emergencies to other U.S. agencies and activities.
- Rendering assistance to the friendly local government and population in emergencies.
- As a "last priority," rendering assistance to pirates and buccaneer-friendly local "stooge" governments, should they be the victims of natural disasters or other non-combat emergencies.

The assault force commander will be prepared to provide disaster control forces to the extent possible, on the basis of noninterference with essential operations.

a. **Coordinating Instructions**

The assault force commander will:

(1) Support other commanders as requested by providing forces and material assistance consistent with the requirements of his mission.

(2) Exercise economy of forces consistent with the mission assigned.

(3) Support disaster recovery operations of other U.S. and friendly government agencies, consistent with the requirements of own missions.

(4) Support disaster recovery operations of the buccaneer enemy and pirate-friendly "stooge" governments, pursuant to the drafting and notarization of a ceasefire or non-aggression agreement.

Component commanders will:

- Coordinate plans, training, and operations for evacuation and disaster recovery with foreign military and civil defense authorities as directed by higher authority.
- Provide for own disaster control operations, as appropriate.

b. **Communications**

Established communications will be used as required. Maximum coordination will be effected as necessary with all U.S. military and other communication agencies.

Commercial communications facilities may be used to augment government facilities as required and available.

NOTE: One luxury afforded the anti-pirate assault force, when it comes to communications, is the primitive nature of the pirate's technologies. The crew of an anti-pirate mission need never fear that the buccaneer enemy has tapped into the line or picked up the radio signal.

12.4. Search and Rescue

Search and Rescue (SAR) is the use of aircraft, surface craft, submarines, and other special equipment employed in search and/or rescue of personnel. SAR may be deployed following clashes with the pirate enemy. The SAR team may also be used to find and rescue personnel, equipment, or craft lost during the normal course of duty. See Figure 12-2.

Figure 12-2. Be prepared to conduct "Search and Rescue" missions in the wake of clashes with pirates.

a. Execution

SAR operations should be conducted in accordance with NWP 37, the National Search and Rescue Manual, and as set forth in this section.

b. Responsibility

The assault force commander assumes specific responsibility for direction of SAR operations. In addition, the parent command of ships and/ or small craft and aircraft in distress retains the responsibility for the safety of its own personnel.

This does not alter the responsibility of any commander to engage in rescue operations on his own initiative, as the circumstances may require and operations permit. Independent action must be immediately reported to the assault force commander and coordinated with the appropriate SAR regional commander or his designated representative.

Security for the SAR team likewise experiences an "overlap": The SAR team should have its eyes and ears open at all times, and assign at least one man to return fire in the case of piratical aggression. However, the assault force commander should, given adequate personnel, assign one or more craft to "shadow" the SAR mission, defending against rearguard attacks by crafty corsairs.

Chapter 13

DEFENSIVE COMMAND AND CONTROL

13.1. General Considerations

During execution of riverine operations, many related actions will be experienced by the anti-pirate assault force. Much of this field manual contains doctrine specifically directed toward riverine assault operations, waterway interdiction and surveillance and security operations, special operations, and logistics. This chapter contains information directed toward those actions and considerations that affect the entire mobile riverine force.

13.2. Movement of the Anti-Pirate Assault Force

Two types of movement made by the anti-pirate assault force are relocation of the force to a new base of operations and the movement of all or part of the assigned forces in a riverine operation. Any movement of the assault force or its subordinate elements must be controlled and coordinated. Standard tactical control measures, such as checkpoints, phase lines, boundaries, and objectives, may be used. Assault force commanders must ensure that the location and purpose of control measures are understood by all elements of the task force.

Security of the forces during movement is a primary consideration during planning. Threats include water mines, water obstacles, ambush, harassing fire, cannon fire, and direct and indirect fire. Armed helicopters may escort all water movements to provide reconnaissance, fire support, and communications relay. Close air support should be available when required (the jungle canopy is so dense as to prohibit aircraft from coming in close to the river). Whenever possible, waterborne movements should be preceded by reconnaissance and security operations conducted by all available means. Troops should be thoroughly briefed on security plans, with emphasis on typical pirate guerrilla tactics, counter-ambush strategies, and maximum use of security measures. All personnel should be apprised of the pirates' legal status within the given cove or island nation, and of the corresponding rules of engagement, prior to battle. As a humorous pirate-fighters' saying has it, "What the swashbuckler's cutlass can't do [i.e., defeat the sailor], the red tape of the bureaucrats can."

Plans are made for counter-ambush reaction during the water movement so that all assault force personnel are prepared for immediate, coordinated action. Plans should include:

- Designation of counter-ambush maneuver elements
- Command and control measures
- Fire support
- "Pirate rousters"; i.e., security personnel "beating the bushes" surrounding the riverbank, flushing out any buccaneers lying in wait (See Figure 13-1)
- Security
- Identification and recognition of committed elements
- Recovery and reorganization of the committed force.

Provisions must be included for security of watercraft when the major assault force elements have been committed to counter-ambush missions. Actions may range from complete commitment of the waterborne anti-pirate force to evasive action and continuing movement. Responsibility for immediate action rests with the commander designated by the assault force commander.

During water movement, assault craft should be organized to provide an advance guard including mine countermeasures craft, flank and rear guards, a group of two to three "cover men," and a main body. This facilitates control and provides tactical integrity of the assault force. The objective of the organization for movement is to provide uninterrupted movement and security for the entire anti-pirate force.

13.3. Riverine Afloat Base Movement

The riverine afloat base of operations normally will be relocated as necessary in support of riverine operations. Emergency relocations may be

Figure 13-1. Pirate "rousters" should be used to ensure no pirates manage to hide close to the assault force base.

made at the discretion of the anti-pirate assault force commander, keeping all concerned informed.

As with all other maneuvers, support coverage is paramount when moving the afloat base. "Cover men" should be enlisted, as should "pirate rousters"—sailors to "beat the bushes," flushing out any buccaneers who may think to hide in hopes of launching a sneak attack. (This is of particular concern when conducting helicopter landings.) Even in defense, being aggressive and taking the initiative will help ensure that no swashbuckler takes your skull as a trophy (literally or figuratively).

The limited hydrographic data available on most rivers and tributaries, as well as rapidly shifting depth, sand bars, and mud banks, make river navigation difficult. Strong currents are not unusual. Navigational aids may be few and inaccurately charted; ships should ensure that navigation charts are corrected to include the latest available data. Commanding officers must exercise caution in navigation when underway. Navigation teams should be well trained and highly proficient in piloting.

During all movements, each ship of the riverine assault force will be escorted by designated river assault craft. See Figure 13-2. Rivers will be swept along the movement route where threat of mining is believed to exist. Assault force units may be pre-positioned in high threat areas along the route of advance. Air and artillery support should be available. Ships of the force will take hostile targets ashore under fire only as permitted by the rules of engagement. Caution must be exercised at all times to ensure that any firing conducted against the pirate enemy does not endanger other friendly craft or troops ashore.

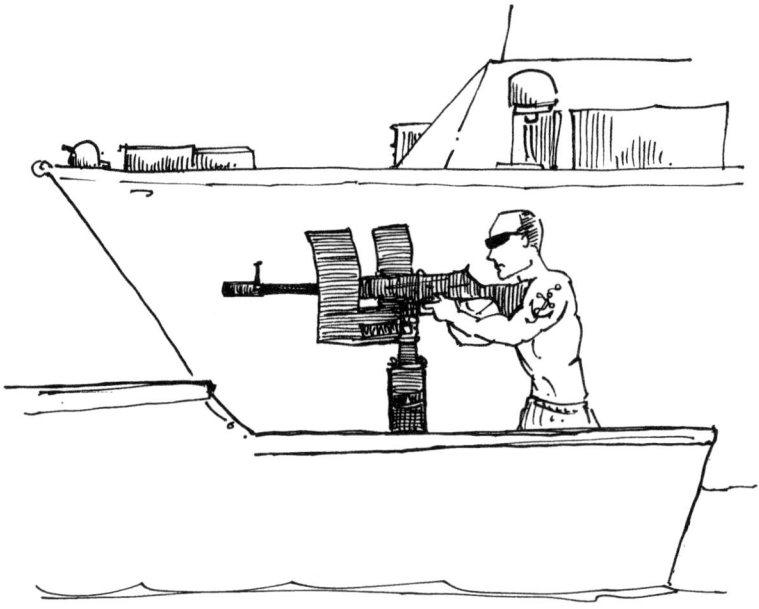

Figure 13-2. Movement of the floating base should be accompanied by an armed escort.

Riverine assault craft will be stationed in accordance with the movement order for each change in location of the riverine base. Escort craft may be used for:

- Predeployment along the route in locations of greatest threat
- Forward, rear, and flank escort
- Establishment of base defense patrols and clearance of new anchorage areas
- Minesweeping in areas of suspected mining threats.

River assault squadron units that are not engaged in escort of ships during movement of the riverine base will be directed to proceed ahead or astern of the formation to the new base site. These ships should consider anti-pirate reconnaissance part of their mission, and report back any and all relevant information to vessels traveling behind them.

13.4. Measures to Prevent Mutual Interference

Measures to prevent mutual interference among anti-pirate personnel should be promulgated by the assault force commander. Mutual interference between friendly units, including aircraft, must be prevented by close coordination between units conducting riverine assault operations and waterway interdiction and surveillance and security operations. Information exchanged between the operations control centers should include:

- Proposed transits of friendly units through areas assigned to other friendly units, and frequent (at least hourly) position reports of units making the transit.
- All known locations and weapons capabilities of pirate enemies.
- Proposed operation plans in areas where overlaps occur.
- Other information that will assist friendly units in identifying each other. This coordination may require the establishment of havens and transit lanes.

Commanders of forces in adjacent areas, those operating within a tactical area of responsibility (TAOR), or those operating in conjunction with the assault force should be provided copies of all operation orders. If this is precluded by security requirements, provisions for continuing liaison with these commanders should be made.

Commanders should ensure that all pre-operations briefings include:

- All available information about friendly units that may be encountered
- All available information on the location, capabilities, and habits of the local pirate enemy
- Applicable intelligence reports
- Challenge and reply codes
- Light array sequencing

- Established havens and transit lanes
- Chain of operational command
- A review of rules of engagement
- All known environmental information (tides, currents, moon, terrain, and so forth)
- Replenishment information
- Rally points
- Communications instructions
- Supporting arms coordination
- Combat service support arrangements.

This information should be updated as additional data become available.

Particular caution must be taken near operation area boundaries. All available means should be used to determine the hostile character of any contact before commencing destructive fire. See Figure 13-3. This is a particularly sensitive matter in coves and other inland areas where pirates may technically be considered "privateers" and enjoy some

Figure 13-3. Exercise restraint in dealing with locals who may use the same waterways as the anti-pirate assault force.

governmental protections as such. Odious as it may sometimes be, strict compliance with local rules of engagement is mandatory.

Ambushes established by friendly forces must be coordinated with appropriate operations centers.

Small craft operating within the riverine base of operations during the hours of darkness may be easily mistaken for indigenous watercraft. This is especially true of small motorized craft. Since indigenous watercraft normally are prohibited by curfew from using most rivers at night, any unidentified craft in the vicinity of the riverine base is highly suspect. To prevent firing on friendly craft, regulations should be established within the riverine base from sunset to sunrise concerning movement of all craft. The following considerations apply:

- No craft should be underway except those authorized by the operations center, and all craft authorized to be underway will normally be accompanied by at least one other craft.
- Craft authorized to be underway should be familiar with, and prepared to respond immediately to, the recognition and identification code when challenged.
- The operations center should advise patrol units concerned of all authorized craft movements within the riverine base area.

Chapter 14

MEDICAL EVACUATIONS (MEDEVACS)

Medical evacuation and casualty care are responsibilities shared by all anti-pirate assault force personnel. All personnel assigned to the unit must be aware of casualty facilities and medical evacuation procedures (MEDEVAC). A well-developed MEDEVAC plan will not only save lives but will also ensure the unit is ready for present and future anti-pirate operations. The loss of personnel because of a poor MEDEVAC plan is inexcusable and can result in a disastrous lack of firepower when it is most needed. This chapter covers in depth the setting up of a landing zone, the landing zone brief, the medical evacuation request, and the medical evacuation procedures.

14.1. Landing Zone/Site/Points

A helicopter landing zone (LZ) is a specified ground for landing helicopters to embark or disembark troops or cargo. A landing zone is designated by a code name. It may include one or more landing sites. See Figure 14-1.

14.2. Preparation of the Landing Zone

When planning the preparation of an LZ, you should take several factors into consideration. First, you should know what type of helicopters will be using the landing zone. The Combat Operation Center (COC) can provide this type of information. Second, you must consider the assault force's position in relation to the enemy pirate force. Security troops must establish a 360-degree perimeter around the landing zone to defend the LZ from attack by buccaneers. Do not discount the use of pirate cannon fire as an anti-aircraft weapon. A third factor is the time it will take to prepare the landing zone. And a fourth factor considered is the equipment needed to prepare the LZ.

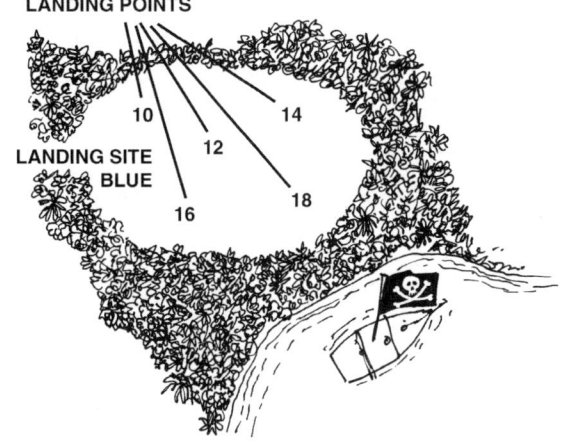

Figure 14-1.
Helicopter landing zone for MEDEVAC emergencies.

a. Approaches and Exits

The ground approaches to the LZ and exits from the LZ must be free of major obstacles that might obstruct landing or takeoffs, such as tall jungle trees, village huts or cow pastures, or pirate-loyal establishments. Approaches and exits should also be clear of obstructions that are 10 meters or higher, extending at least 50 meters in the direction of approach and exit paths. The rule of thumb for determining the distance required between the landing point and a high obstruction is a 10:1 ratio. This means that the distance a landing point is located from a tree is ten times the height of the tree. See Figure 14-2.

Example: A helicopter landing or taking off near a 30-foot tree needs at least 300 feet of horizontal clearance.

b. Ground Obstacles

Obstacles on the ground, such as stumps or rocks, should not exceed 1 foot in height on level ground and should be less on sloping ground.

c. Gradient (Slopes)

Ground slope has a considerable effect on selecting a landing site or landing point within the LZ. A helicopter cannot land safely in locations where the ground slopes more than 14 degrees. When pilots land on a slope, they prefer to land uphill because of the tail down attitude of the helicopter.

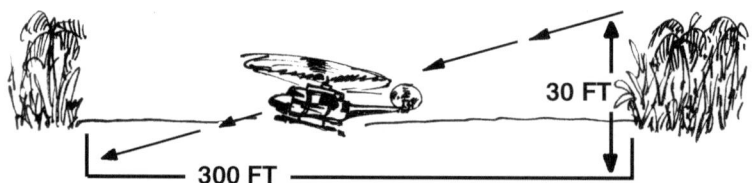

Figure 14-2. Horizontal clearance needed to land a MEDEVAC chopper.

d. Surface Conditions

Mud, excessive dust, and loose debris are considered undesirable surface conditions for helicopters. Mud causes a helicopter to become bogged down. Excessive dust reduces visibility and compromises the location of the site. Loose debris is dangerous because it is sucked up into the rotor blades or turbine intakes, causing serious damage. Shallow water, less than 18 inches deep and with a firm bottom, can be used as a landing site. In most anti-pirate operations, landing in shallow water may be your best bet.

e. Winds

When the wind at ground level exceeds 10 knots, the helicopter must land into the wind.

14.3. Marking the Landing Zone

Once you have established the LZ, you need to direct the helicopter to the location of the LZ. The proper marking of the LZ will aid the pilot in locating it. Recommendations for marking an LZ and for guiding a helicopter to an LZ are as follows:

a. **Daylight landing:** The landing zone is equipped with a means of showing wind direction and velocity. This is usually accomplished by the use of smoke or by verbal radio message. Expedient methods for determining wind direction and velocity are as follows:

   (1) **Grass drop method.** Extend your arm straight out and drop the grass from your hand. Point the extended arm at the

dropped grass on the ground. The angle between the arm and the body divided by four is the wind velocity in knots.

(2) **Angle of smoke method.** Observe the angle at which smoke blows. The wind speed is as follows:
- If smoke goes straight up, no wind.
- If smoke blows at a 30-degree angle, wind is 3 to 5 knots.
- If smoke blows at a 60-degree angle, wind is 5 to 7 knots.
- If smoke blows along the ground, wind exceeds 8 knots.

Use smoke and landing zone panels to mark a landing zone by day. Both should be the same color as the designation of the landing zone. This will aid the pilot in locating the landing zone. Mark obstacles that cannot be removed within the landing zone with single red panels staked to prevent uprooting by rotor wash.

SECURITY CAUTION: If smoke is used to mark the landing zone, use only as needed and do not tell the pilot the color of smoke; ask the pilot to acknowledge the color after the smoke grenade is set off.

b. **Night landing:** The organization and use of an LZ at night or during periods of low visibility is more complex compared to daytime operations. Use special lighting equipment or field expedients as required.

(1) You must indicate outlines of landing zones by low-intensity markers.
(2) You must show obstacles near the landing zone with low-intensity markers or voice radio instructions.
(3) It may also be advisable to set up a second, wider security perimeter encircling the landing zone in order to prevent pirates from seeing the lights and attempting to attack.

Another method of guiding the aircraft to the zone is vector instructions. This is simply relaying instructions to the pilot by radio. For example, the radio operator spots the helicopter. Using a compass, the radio operator shoots an azimuth of 135 degrees from the LZ to the helicopter and quickly computes a back azimuth of 315 degrees. The radio operator then transmits the following message:

"HOME WISH, THIS IS HOOK HANDLER . . . VECTOR THREE ONE FIVE TO LANDING ZONE HAWK . . . OVER."

The pilot then acknowledges the message and takes up the correct heading of 315 degrees. The term *vector* is always used in a situation like this to prevent misunderstanding. As the helicopter approaches, minor corrections will probably be necessary. These are given as corrections to the original heading by the following:

"HOME WISH, THIS IS HOOK HANDLER . . . COME RIGHT FIVE DEGREES OF PRESENT COURSE . . . OVER."

When the tactical situation does not allow the use of a compass, you can vector the helicopter to an LZ by using the clock system:

"HOME WISH, THIS IS HOOK HANDLER . . . MY POSITION IS AT YOUR NINE O'CLOCK . . . OVER."

The aircraft would then execute a 90-degree turn to the left.

14.4. Landing Signalman Enlisted (LSE) Signals

Once the pilot has located the LZ, you can now help the pilot land the helicopter. These signals are visual arm-and-hand signals used by personnel to "talk" to the pilot of the landing helicopter. The confidence of the pilot in the LSE's signals depends on the precise manner in which the LSE gives the signal. Movements must be sharp and precise. For this reason, it is imperative that the signal man not be troubled by pirate interlopers—a sudden "What was that?" jerk of the head, or an errant movement of one arm to ward off a cutlass blow, could be fatally misleading to the helicopter pilot. LSE signals are executed exactly as prescribed. See Figure 14-3. The LSE must always remain alert for signals from the pilot. During night operations, LSEs must use illuminated wands. During a landing approach, the LSE's functions are as follows:

Inform the pilot of the approaching helicopter that you are the LSE. You do this by means of the Prepare for Direction signal.

Indicate the landing point to the pilot by positioning yourself 25 meters in front of and 10 meters to the right of the landing point as the pilot looks at it. If fears of attack by swashbucklers prevent you from stationing yourself this far from the landing zone, get as close as you can. You may have to stand on the landing zone itself, simply preparing to move quickly once the helicopter locks in on the landing site.

Aid the pilot in landing safely. The pilot is responsible for the approach and landing of the helicopter. However, the pilot relies heavily on the LSE to provide warning of conditions of which he or she is not aware of and to direct the helicopter to a safe landing point.

The only signal that the LSE must give to the pilot on the deck is the Wave-Off signal. The Wave-Off signal is given when it is not safe for the helicopter to land.

Indicate to the pilot when it is safe to take off.

PREPARE
FOR
DIRECTION

HOVER

LAND

STOP - PIRATE ENEMY
SIGHTED: CAUTION

ACTIVE ENGAGEMENT
WITH PIRATE ENEMY -
REMAIN IN HOLDING PATTERN

Figure 14-3. Hand signals for guiding a helicopter in the landing zone.

Chapter 15

SURVIVAL AT SEA

During the anti-pirate operation, you will face a variety of potential emergencies whenever you cross expanses of water: ships, watercraft, and amphibious assault vehicles (AAVs) can sink; aircraft can crash into the sea; or you can accidentally fall into the water. This is to say nothing of the instability of fighting aboard the buccaneers' ship, potentially while it catches fire and/or parts of it explode. However, there are some basic precautionary measures you can take to maintain your safety and reduce your chances of becoming a water casualty. Determine the following information as soon as you board any type of vessel. Knowing this information may save your life or the life of your fellow shipmates.

- *How many life preservers and lifeboats/rafts are on board?*
- *Where are the life preservers and lifeboats/rafts located?*
- *Are the life preservers and lifeboats/rafts trustworthy? (Especially relevant when boarding a pirate vessel, as their maintenance and safety habits are substandard.)*
- *What type of unit survival equipment is on board?*
- *How much food, water, and medicine do the survival kits contain?*
- *When was the last time the contents were inspected for proper quantities and shelf-life expiration?*
- *Is there sufficient survival equipment available for the number of personnel?*
- *What are the egress procedures for the ship, boat, watercraft, AAV, or aircraft?*

15.1. Abandoning Ship

When you embark on a Navy ship, you will receive abandoning ship instructions from Navy personnel. If given the order to abandon ship, report to your designated assembly area and put on a life preserver. *Do not* inflate the life preserver until you are clear of the ship. Torn life preservers will not inflate and inflated life preservers can block you, and those behind you, from exiting the ship. A flotation device that has been inflated may also burst if you jump from a significant height.

Do not remove your clothing, boots, or shoes before abandoning ship. Your trousers and blouse may be the only flotation devices available if your life preserver is faulty or becomes damaged, and your clothes can provide some insulation from cold water. However, remove your soft cover and place it in a cargo pocket for later use. The soft cover is both lightweight and good protection against sunburn caused by the sun's rays reflecting off the water.

If possible, one or more men should remain on board as long as possible, serving as "cover men." Again, the intention is to provide return fire on buccaneers who may be in position to take potshots at the men abandoning ship. After all other personnel have abandoned ship, the cover men have exhausted their ammunition, or the condition of the ship no longer permits them to stay aboard, the cover men should then proceed rapidly to abandon ship themselves. In some cases, it may be logistically more advantageous for the cover men to hold off the murderous corsairs long enough for a patrol ship or helicopter to arrive on the scene. This backup force should be able to provide covering fire at a minimum, and in many cases will provide the cover men with a quick getaway.

a. Jettisoning Equipment

Equipment should be kept properly packed and waterproofed in case you have to abandon ship. If entering the water from a height greater than 30 feet, wearing your equipment (e.g., pack, helmet, gas mask) could cause injury. Upon impact with the water, the helmet will "cup" air inside of it. The chin strap may also create a "hanging effect" as you submerge from the force of the fall. This effect could break your jaw. Therefore, you should remove your helmet and gas mask before abandoning ship.

If you are unable to maintain buoyancy due to the amount of equipment secured to your pack and body, then jettisoning some of your equipment may become necessary. Equipment that you should always retain includes canteens of fresh water, first-aid kit, soft cover, and survival kit. The survival kit should include first-aid items, water purification tablets or drops, fire starting equipment, signaling items (e.g., flashlight, strobe light, chemlights), food procurement items, and shelter items. Other items in a survival kit include sunburn lotion and lip balm, knife, goggles/sunglasses, plastic bag, matches and lighter, and a mirror. While the presence of the pirate enemy may tempt you to keep your service pistol with you, its usefulness cannot justify the added weight—the more so because it's about to get wet and may be unusable thereafter. See Marine Corps Reference Publication (MCRP) 3-02F, *Survival*, for a detailed list of survival items and applications.

All measures should be taken to keep materials and equipment safe and watertight prior to jettisoning them. This way, they can be recovered later by the Search and Rescue (SAR) team. However, if there exists a strong likelihood that pirates may recover and use the equipment before the SAR team can regain it, the equipment should be dumped and considered lost.

b. Abandoning Ship Technique

When abandoning ship, safety considerations must be observed. See Figure 15-1. Use the following technique when abandoning ship without your combat gear:

(1) Place your hands on their opposite shoulders, forming a criss-cross pattern.

(2) Step to the edge of the ship's deck and check the water below for pirates or pirate vessels, sharks, debris, or other survivors. If the water is clear, look straight ahead and prepare to jump. If the water is not clear, move to another location.

NOTE: Do not hold your nose as you abandon ship. If you do hold your nose, the force of impact into the water could jar your arm and hand and cause you to break your nose.

(3) Step off the side of the ship with a smooth, 30-inch stride. *Do not dive off the ship. Do not look down at the water. Look straight ahead.* Looking down at the water can render you unconscious or cause injuries upon impact.

(4) Bring your trailing leg forward during the fall. Cross your trailing leg behind your leading leg.

(5) Keep your head parallel to the water's surface until hitting the water.

Figure 15-1. The proper way to abandon ship.

You should remain in the "abandon ship position" until your descent into the water has almost stopped. However, the weight imbalances in your body may cause you to be in a J shape under the water.

Once your downward motion has ceased, your feet may be parallel with the ocean bottom or you may be nearly inverted with your feet over your head. To counteract potential disorientation, you should pause briefly and allow the natural buoyancy of your torso to bring your body to a nearly upright position.

Floating debris can cause hazards. Therefore, you should swim upward, extending one arm (hand shaped into a fist) upward to feel for obstructions. If you encounter debris, try to push it away or surface in a different location. See Figure 15-2.

Swim away from the ship. *Do not look back at the ship.* Looking back could slow your movement away from the area. Be sensible and aware of the presence of pirates and pirate vessels, but do not expend undue energy casting your gaze about, searching for buccaneers. Focus on swimming forward. Remember, your objective is to leave the area as quickly as possible because:

- Equipment and debris may be falling from or spilling out of the ship.

- Swashbucklers know that the highest-percentage area for picking off swimming assault force members is in the perimeter closely ringing the sinking ship.
- Sharks and other predatory sea creatures are also drawn to the tumult of the sinking ship. (This goes double if there happens to be blood in the water.)
- Additional casualties can occur if individuals abandoning the ship fall on top of swimmers already in the water.
- Swimmers close to the sinking ship may get pulled underneath the water by the suctioning effect of the ship as it goes under.

Figure 15-2. When surfacing, avoid debris from the ship.

c. Modified Abandoning Ship Technique

When abandoning ship while wearing full combat gear (weapon, helmet, and a properly waterproofed pack), safety considerations must be observed. The modified abandoning ship technique is used while wearing full combat gear and exiting from a height less than 30 feet.

Warning

When exiting from a height greater than 30 feet, remove your helmet and pack. Fasten the helmet to the pack or place it inside the pack before jettisoning. If jettisoning gear from the ship or aircraft, check the water below for survivors before throwing the gear forward of the intended jump area. Once in the water, retrieve your gear and swim out of the area.

- Place your weapon over one shoulder, muzzle down, with the weapon parallel to your side.
- Place your arm and hand along the weapon and hold it to your side.
- Take your free hand and place it on top of your helmet to prevent neck/spinal injury from the force of the water pulling upward on the helmet as your body enters the water.

NOTE: *An alternate method is to place your weapon over one shoulder, muzzle down, with the weapon parallel to your side. Reach across your body and grasp the sling of your weapon and hold it to your body. Take your free hand and place it on top of your helmet.*

(1) Step to the edge of the platform and check the water below for debris and survivors. If the water is clear, look straight ahead and prepare to jump. If the water is not clear, move to another location.

(2) Step off the side of the platform with a smooth, 30-inch stride. *Do not dive off the ship. Do not look down at the water. Look straight ahead.* Looking down at the water can render you unconscious or cause injury upon impact.

(3) Bring your trailing leg forward during the fall. Cross your trailing leg behind your leading leg.

(4) Keep your head parallel to the water's surface until hitting the water.

You should remain in the modified abandoning ship position until your descent into the water has almost stopped. The buoyancy of a properly waterproofed pack will immediately pull you to the surface. Once you break the water's surface, unsling your weapon and loop the sling over your head. Be certain to look around you for pirates or pirate vessels (such as a lifeboat). If either is present, you should first attempt to duck down, remaining out of sight of the buccaneers. If spotted, you will want to brandish your weapon while floating on your back. Regardless of whether or not your weapon has been ruined by water, having a service pistol or rifle pointed at him is enough to give even the most brazen swashbuckler pause. It might just buy you a little extra time.

NOTE: *You may also remove your pack (unsnap the quick-release strap on one side of the pack and pass the strap to your other hand in order to maintain contact with the pack, which is functioning as your flotation device). Remain horizontal in the water with your pack under your chest. Perform a breaststroke kick.*

d. **Surface Burning Oil Swim**
After you have abandoned ship, rise to the surface using the techniques shown earlier. However, you must remember that fuel from sinking ships or from the stolen supplies in the hold of the pirate ship will float on the surface of the water. Therefore, you must move clear of the floating fuel by swimming away from the ship as rapidly as possible. Either swim upwind (into the wind) of the ship or swim against the current. Either method allows you to move away from the fuel, and the wind/current will push the fuel past you. To properly execute a surface burning oil swim:
- Extend your arms overhead as far as possible.
- Wave your arms back and form vigorously to splash a hole while moving upward.
- Splash as long as possible to push burning fuel away from the surfacing area.
- Use your arms and hands to sweep away fuel and debris. See Figure 15-3.

- Kick your legs in a constant breaststroke kick.
- Extend your arms (palms outward) forward on the surface, arms shoulder-width apart.
- Stop your hands in front of your face and rotate them so that your palms face forward (roughly halfway out of the water).
- Sweep your arms forward to a full extension at shoulder width. This splashes debris, oil, or burning liquids aside. To reduce the chance of fatigue, use two short splashes to the front to extend the path.
- Repeat the preceding step as necessary while swimming clear of the area.

Some of this advice may seem inadvisable in the event that pirates are in the vicinity, as it will serve to draw their attention to you. However, the risk of being broiled in a conflagration of burning fuel outweighs the risk of pirate attack. Remember that there are procedures for everything—including being taken captive by pirates. Do not "put the cart before the horse" by worrying about fighting pirates while you are meanwhile being burned alive. See Figure 15-4.

Figure 15-3. Surfacing in burning oil.

Figure 15-4. Swimming in burning wreckage. Despite the presence of pirates, the sailor's first objective is to avoid being burned.

15.2. Surviving with a Pack

If packed properly, your pack will float, and it is your key piece of equipment for staying afloat and overcoming water obstacles. See Figure 15-5. If the pack's contents are properly waterproofed, it can support you (with a combat load) in the water. Buoyed up by a waterproofed pack, you eventually emerge from the water with all your equipment (e.g., boots, helmet, flak jacket, weapon, survival items).

Your pack floats based on a scientific principle known as Archimedes' principle. This principle states that an object submerged in a liquid is buoyed up by a force equal to the weight of the liquid displaced (pushed aside) by the object. If the weight of the displaced liquid is greater than the weight of the object, the object floats. If the weight of the displaced liquid is less than the weight of the object, the object sinks. For example, a machine gun sinks in the water, but it still weighs less in the water than it does on land. Even though a machine gun sinks, it is still buoyed up by a force equal to the weight of the water it displaces. For this reason, you should not try to hold yourself or your equipment any higher out of the water than they would naturally float; doing so wastes both energy and body heat.

Figure 15-5. The sailor's pack can be invaluable as a flotation device.

15.3. Staying Afloat with a Life Preserver

The best form of flotation is to find any kind of floating object that will keep you and your equipment out of the water or minimize your exposure to the water. One exception to this, of course, is when there is a significant buccaneer presence in the water. In that instance, you may wish to use driftwood or other floating detritus both as a flotation aid and as a blind behind which to duck, concealing yourself as long as possible.

Life preservers are the best flotation method, as they allow you to wear your clothes for heat retention and sunburn prevention. Sailors use two basic classes of life preservers: inherently buoyant life preservers and inflatable life preservers.

a. Inherently Buoyant Life Preservers

Inherently buoyant life preservers are either vest-type (worn like a jacket) or yoke-type (worn around the neck). The preserver's outer envelope is either a cotton or water resistant material that encloses a removable fibrous glass or plastic foam filling.

For the anti-pirate assault force, the most common type of inherently buoyant life preserver is the vest-type with collar, known as the kapock preserver. Typically the vest-type life preserver will be a visible orange color, allowing the floating sailor to be spotted by his comrades. However, this has its disadvantages as well, as the bright color of the life preserver may serve to attract the attention of pirate scavengers. Caution should be exercised when wearing the kapock life preserver.

The kapock consists of collar straps, upper front chest straps, leg straps, and waist drawstrings that secure the preserver to you. The leg straps, which are fitted on both sides of the life preserver, ensure that the preserver remains around your chest while you are in the water. A chest strap is attached to the life preserver to facilitate lifting you out of the water. The strap can also be attached to other survivors or to lifeboats to reduce the fatigue that results from holding onto a floating/secured object by hand.

b. Inflatable Life Preservers
The anti-pirate assault force also has inflatable life preservers on board. The inflatable life preserver is known as the life preserver personal (LPP). The LPP is capable of both oral inflation and CO_2 cartridge inflation. See Figure 15-6. The LPP consists of buoyancy chambers, CO_2 inflator, and an oral inflation tube.

The buoyancy chamber is deck gray in color and is made from a neoprene-coated nylon fabric. This presents problems that are the mirror image of those encountered with the kapock life preserver. While pirates cannot easily spot the floating sailor, neither can rescue personnel. Alternative means of drawing rescuers' attention, such as flares or gunshots (if neither has been lost or ruined by water), loud whistling or bird calls, or frantic arm signaling, should be used instead.

CAUTION: *Do not inflate the life preserver until you are clear of the aircraft, ship, or vehicle. Torn life preservers will not inflate and inflated life preservers can block you, and those behind you, from exiting the aircraft, ship, or vehicle.*

15.4. Staying Afloat without a Life Preserver
In the event of catastrophic circumstances—e.g., pirates have won the day, including sinking the main Navy ship—rescue personnel may not immediately find you. You may be in open water without any floating objects or a life preserver to help you survive. If so, uniform blouses and trousers can be made into expedient flotation devices.

a. Floating with an Inflated Blouse
It is possible to float by using a bubble of air trapped in the shoulders of your blouse. The look is laughably outdated—it resembles 1980s

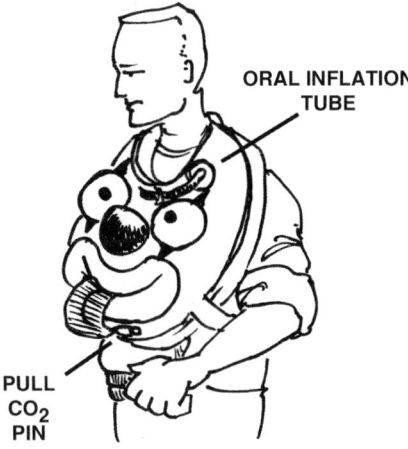

ORAL INFLATION
TUBE

Figure 15-6. The proper way to
inflate a life preserver.

PULL
CO$_2$
PIN

women's fashions, with their large shoulder pads—but it just may help you survive. The air rises to the back and shoulders of the blouse and supports you at the water's surface. An inflated blouse can also be a temporary flotation device used by weaker swimmers while trying to remove their trousers. To create a bubble of trapped air in a blouse:

- Turn the collar inside the blouse to help create a seal.
- Unbutton top button and pull collar around mouth and nose.
- Take a deep breath and bend forward slightly at the waist. Exhale one-half to three-quarters of a breath into the blouse.
- Grasp and twist the color with one hand to create a seal; this prevents air from escaping out from the collar.
- Use your free hand and feet to stroke and kick to the surface.
- Gather and hold the blouse tightly at the collar and stomach level to prevent the blouse from losing air if it floats up too high.
- Splash water on the blouse periodically to prevent the material from drying; dry material allows air to escape.
- Repeat inflation as required.

b. Floating with Inflated Trousers

In warm water, where 98 percent of all anti-pirate operations will take place, trousers can be used as a primary expedient flotation device, as their removal will not put you at risk of hypothermia. However, in cold water, submerging your head to remove and inflate your trousers results in heat and energy losses that negate the benefit of using the trousers as a flotation device.

Once your trousers are inflated, you float motionlessly as if wearing a life preserver. If needed, assume the "heat escape lessening posture" (known as the HELP position) to slow heat loss. As trousers dry, air leaks out of the legs. To slow this process, occasionally splash water on the fabric. Reinflate trousers as needed.

(1) Sling Method

The sling method works if you are a strong swimmer or naturally very buoyant. Take the following steps to inflate trousers using the sling method (see Figure 15-7):

- Take a deep breath, bend over, and remove your boots. *NOTE: Retain your boots. Tie the bootlaces together and suspend the boots from your blouse or hang them around your neck so that they rest on your chest.*
- Remove your trousers. Button or zip the trouser's fly closed. This allows you to control airflow.
- Tie the bottoms of the trouser legs in a square knot.
- Ensure that the front (fly) of the trousers faces you.
- Hold the trousers above the water's surface and behind your head. Grasp both sides of the waistband and open with both hands.

Figure 15-7. In extreme situations, the sailor can remove and inflate his own pants to stay afloat.

- Kick strongly to stay on top of the water while slinging the trousers overhead in order to trap air into them.
- Once the waistband is submerged in the water, air is trapped in the legs.
- Hold and seal the waistband underwater.
- Slip the inflated legs over your head. Hold the waistband in toward your chest, the fly facing your body. To prevent air from escaping from the trousers, seal the waistband by either folding it or twisting it.
- Lie back and relax, resting the back of your neck against the knot.
- Splash water on the trousers periodically to prevent the material from drying. Dry material allows air to escape.

Chapter 16

ESCAPE FROM CAPTIVITY

While it is far from inevitable that you will be captured by pirates, the possibility does exist. The buccaneer enemy is called "the cockroach of the sea" for good reason: He knows how to survive. Whatever his handicaps, the swashbuckler is a tough and intelligent enemy, and in the unending battle between corsair and society, the corsair has had his triumphs.

Fortunately for the captured sailor, a part of the buccaneer's intelligence is his recognition that a U.S. Navy prisoner constitutes a bargaining chip. Therefore, instances of summary execution by pirates are rare. Treatment is barbaric, however. Between malnutrition and unsanitary conditions (pirates openly scoff at the notion of "invisible monsters," i.e., germs), the captured sailor's odds of surviving decline day by day.

Thus, the sailor's best bet is to construct a plan of escape as soon as he is captured, and to effect that plan as soon as circumstances reasonably permit.

The materials given here pertain mainly to escapes made from the pirates' cove. Unfortunately, escaping from a pirate ship is easy but inadvisable—except in certain situations, the buccaneers' sloop will not be within sight of land. Even the strongest swimmers are advised to bide their time until the ship is docked.

16.1. Escape and Evasion in Jungle

When evading or escaping, and before making contact with an escape net or other assistance, the evader must fend for himself.

The more that can be learned and applied of the general principles of survival, the greater will be the chance of reaching safety. This section deals with proper escape and evasion (E&E) conducted in the jungle.

The first rule of E&E is: Upon escape, get away from your buccaneer captors as soon as possible. Sometimes this may require several miles; at other times, just a few yards.

Plan your escape; do not run blindly. Use your head; there is no substitute for common sense. Use the hours of captivity to sit down, think out your problem, and recall what you learned in training. Do the pirates periodically leave the ship or docking area? Where do they go? Do they seem to follow a trail? Do they interact with natives, for commerce or other purposes? What is the nature of the pirate-native relationship? You must ask yourself these and other questions, probing the situation for weaknesses and openings that you can turn to your advantage.

If you have a map, study it closely. Roads and trails can be used as guides, but never travel on them. Stay alert. Natives remain on trails by preference. A few feet from the trail you are quite safe. Conceal yourself upon the approach of any other person until he passes or until you determine if he is friendly. See Figure 16-1.

The easiest traveling is often on the crests of ridges. Remember, however, that crests are more exposed than hillsides, and because of ease of travel, they are apt to be traveled more frequently than other areas. Crests and ridges may make good lookout posts from which to determine whether any buccaneers are following you. Do not overuse this tactic, however.

Figure 16-1. To avoid recapture, stay off paths as much as possible and use camouflage.

Rivers or streams can make good roads, but remember that the majority of native villages and encampments are on water. Rafts attract attention. Floating on or close to a log or drifting bush may be the simplest way to travel. Keep to the middle of the stream. If using a native boat, sink it during periods when not in use.

When close to known pirate locations, limit movement right after sunset or just before sunrise. At these times there is sufficient light to avoid pirate installations, minefields, sentries, etc., but sufficient darkness to prevent recognition by the buccaneer enemy. Do not discount the danger of pirate-friendly (or pirate-fearful) natives. Arrange your clothing, weapons, etc., to present a profile as similar as possible to the natives of the area. See Figure 16-2.

DO   DON'T

Figure 16-2. Arrange your attire to present a profile as similar as possible to area natives.

Be quiet. Noise carries far and natives are alert to any strange noise. Bury your refuse. Any sign of your presence may lead to your capture.

Do not sleep near your fire or your water supply. Get far enough away to be concealed.

If lost in grass that is so tall you cannot see over it, follow this procedure, as a last resort. Cut down enough grass to give you some freedom of movement and, using your machete or any other tool, dig a hole to crawl into, then set fire to the grass. Take every precaution not to get burned by fire or asphyxiated by smoke.

The jungle provides hiding places. You may have to use them. Bamboo thickets are excellent. Because of the nature of bamboo, you cannot be approached without being alerted by the noise of dry bamboo.

When approaching a native camp, use extra caution, for the camp is probably being watched.

At all times when hiding or remaining in one location for a period of time, be sure to plan more than one exit in the event of discovery by buccaneers.

It is difficult for a person unfamiliar with the jungle to live in it without native assistance. Conceal your weapons outside a strange village before entering. Get to a known friendly village as soon as possible.

If it is a pirate-friendly village, your weapons will be taken from you.

Your goals in surviving and moving through the jungle are straightforward: 1) Remain alive; 2) Put distance between yourself and the pirate enemy. Buccaneers' courage and abilities are known to "dry up" on land, and there exists a vague "tipping point" when going farther inland is not worth their trouble; 3) Make it back to your comrades.

a. **Miscellaneous**

Take time, after the initial adrenaline-fueled stages of your escape, to stop and repair your clothes. It helps to prevent insect bites and further tearing of clothes.

Examine your surroundings carefully. Many of your needs are there. Thorns broken from trees can be used for needles. Strips of vines can be made into thread. If you need rope, vines will also do. Your food and shelter—in fact your life—may depend on your ability to make use of things that are all around you.

Be careful. Do not use trees and vines to pull yourself up hills, as thorns, ants, scorpions, etc., may be encountered and can cause sores that may become infected. Use a walking stick to push aside vines and bushes.

Poisonous reptiles and large mammals of the jungle will cause few problems. Given a chance, they will avoid you.

Many jungle diseases are insect-borne. Use insect repellent freely, if available. If not, be vigilant against insects, and sleep under netting—makeshift, if need be—or otherwise concealed from insect attacks.

b. When Requesting Native Assistance

- Show yourself and let the natives approach you.
- Deal with recognized headman.
- Do not approach groups.
- Do not display weapons.
- Do not risk being discovered by children.
- Treat natives well. There is much you can learn from them.
- Determine whether the natives are sympathetic to the pirates, or live in fear of them. Do this before offering any opinion of your own.
- Respect local customs and manners.
- Learn all you can about woodcraft.
- Take their advice on local hazards.
- *Never* approach a woman. See Figure 16-3.

Figure 16-3. While on the run, avoid women and children.

16.2. The Survival Kit

Whenever possible, carry a survival kit with you when traveling. It is more likely, of course, that after escaping from the buccaneers' captivity you will have nothing. In that case, consider this a "shopping list" of items you should gather and keep with you as you make your way through the jungle:

- A knife
- Flint
- 10 feet wire (copper or steel)
- Fishhooks
- A small mirror

You can, if you wish, carry more articles. However, with the list given here you can accomplish a great deal, if you use your head.

Advice to Those Considering Piracy

Occasionally, news stories appear of anti-pirate assault force members taken captive, experiencing "Stockholm Syndrome" and joining up with a band of crusty pirates. Unfortunately, the wayward sailors who make these decisions are often painted by the media as romantics, yearning for the freedom of the open seas. The freewheeling, anarchic life of the swashbuckler is placed in stark contrast to the rigidly hierarchical shipboard routines of the anti-pirate assault force member. Often a photograph will be printed of the AWOL sailor in his uniform, his composed expression meant to suggest a great depth of emotion suppressed behind that even stare.

While the swashbuckler, like all worthy enemies, deserves your respect, his way of life does not stand up to scrutiny as an object of envy or desire.

All anti-pirate assault force members, at one time or another, daydream about life on the other side. The freedom from society's rules and customs; the gleeful profanity, violence, and drunkenness; the straight-forward power dynamics on board the Jolly Roger—all hold immense allure to the assault force member.

Yet tempting as it may be, while chained to a wall belowdecks, to contemplate "switching sides," you must consider your family and friends, your fellow sailors, and your country itself. (This is to say nothing of the U.S. military, which will immediately court-martial you and try you for treason should you be recaptured as a swashbuckler.) Consider a bar of soap and a hot shower. Consider a T-bone steak served on a plate too hot to touch. See Figure 16-4. Consider the luxury of having all your limbs and eyes, and shaving with a hot towel and plenty of foamy shaving cream. Consider clean and friendly women (or men) and the floral scent of her hair as she brushes past you to get to the bar. Consider maintaining your teeth, regular check-ups from a licensed physician, and the pleasures of avoiding scurvy, malaria, and insect-borne tropical maladies. Consider the moral rightness of a job well done and a paycheck honestly obtained.

Weigh these considerations against the purported "freedom" and "ease" of life under the black skull-and-crossbones flag. Think hard on the matter, as you pick larvae out of your day's serving of gruel. Think carefully, sailor—and then fight your way back.

Figure 16-4. When piracy tempts you, remember the comforts of home.

APPENDIX A

Nautical Abbreviations

Naval watercraft operators must be able to read and understand their charts rapidly and accurately. How much information they get from a chart will depend on how well they read it and interpret the various symbols and abbreviations. Even though there is limited space, much information must be shown on a chart for the safe navigation of vessels. For this reason, symbols and abbreviations are used. The abbreviations in this chart are approved for use on nautical charts and are used on charts published by the U.S. military.

Acronym/Term Definition

1LT	First Lieutenant (Deck Department Head)	DC	Delivery Cutter
		EOW	Engineering Officer of the Watch
ABS	American Bureau of Shipping	FOWK	Fuel, Oil and Water King
AEL	Allowance Equipage List	GAR	Green, Amber, Red (Risk Assessment Tool)
AFAS	Astern Fueling At Sea	IAW	In Accordance With
ANSI	American National Standards Institute	LT	Line Tender
		MDE	Main Diesel Engine
APAF	Anti-Pirate Assault Force	MIL Spec	Military Specification
BSAR	Buccaneer Ship At Rest	MOB	Man Overboard
		MPPS	Musket-Packing Pirate Ship
CEPS	Cutlass-Equipped Pirate Ship	NVR	Naval Vessel Rules
CF	Cannon Fire	NWP	Naval Warfare Publication
CO	Commanding Officer	OIC	Officer in Charge
CW	Corsair Weaponry	OOD	Officer of the Deck
DBN	Double-Braided Nylon	OPAREA	Operational Area
		OPTEMPO	Operational Tempo

ORM	Operational Risk Management	SRAC	Sea Rover Auxiliary Craft (e.g., lifeboat)
PBPS	Pistol-Brandishing Pirate Ship	STBD	Starboard
PFD	Personal Flotation Device	TCT	Team Coordination Training
PLOA	Pirate-Lousy Oceanic Area	TLI	Tank Level Indicator
POIC	Petty Officer in Charge	TP	Technical Publications
PPE	Personal Protective Equipment	USNS	United States Naval Ship
PPO	Pirate Psycho-logical Operations ("PiPsyOps")	UW	Unconventional Warfare
PQS	Personal Qualifica-tion Standard	WLB	Coast Guard Buoy Tender (225')
PV	Pirate Vessel	WLL	Working Load Limit
RAPO	Riverine Anti-Pirate Operations	WO	Winch Operator
RC	Receiving Cutter	WPB	Coast Guard Patrol Boat (110' or 87' cutter)
SAA	Swashbuckler Ambush Attempt	WPC	Coast Guard Patrol Craft (179' cutter)
SAL	Swashbuckler Ambush Likely	WQSB	Watch, Quarter and Station Bill
SDC	Sea Dog Cove		
SO	Safety Observer		
SPE	Severity, Probabil-ity, Exposure (Risk Assessment Tool)		

APPENDIX B

Seabag Checklist (Minimum Outfit)

The minimum outfit of articles of uniform and accessories prescribed for enlisted men, other than chief petty officers of the Regular Navy, is as follows:

Item	*Quantity*
❑ **Belts:**	
❑ Black	1
❑ White	1
❑ **Caps:**	
❑ Blue, working	1
❑ Blue, service	1
❑ Watch	1
❑ **Clothes stops**:	3 pkg.
❑ **Drawers:**	6 pr.
❑ **Gloves, black:**	1 pr.
❑ **Hat, white:**	4
❑ **Insignia (as required):**	
❑ Jacket, blue, working	1
❑ **Jumpers:**	
❑ Blue, dress	1
❑ Blue, undress	2
❑ White, undress	4
❑ **Neckerchief:**	1
❑ **Peacoat:**	1
❑ **Raincoat, blue:**	1
❑ **Seabag:**	1
❑ **Shirt, blue chambray:**	3
❑ **Shoes:**	
❑ Black, dress	2 pr.
❑ Black, service	1 pr.
❑ Gymnasium	1 pr.
❑ **Socks, black:**	8 pr.
❑ **Sweater, blue:**	1

- ❑ **Towel, bath:**
  - ❑ Large   2
  - ❑ Small   2
- ❑ **Trousers:**
  - ❑ Blue   3 pr.
  - ❑ Dungaree   3 pr.
  - ❑ White   4 pr.
- ❑ **Trunks, swim:**   1 pr.
- ❑ **Undershirt:**   6

The following articles of the uniform are optional:

Ascot, any color
Belt, khaki
Captain's hat, for satirical skits
Eye patch, also for satirical skits
Gloves: blue, working
Helmets, tropical: khaki, white
Lanyard, white
Overshoes
Scarf, blue
Shirt, white tropical
Shirt, blue-and-white striped
Shirt, printed with anchor motif
Shoes, white canvas
Shorts, tropical: khaki, white
Turtleneck, black or charcoal

APPENDIX C

Loadout Lists
The following lists indicate supplies that each individual assault force member should have packed and ready to go prior to deployment.

Standard Individual Operational Loadout
The following Warbag equipment shall be in the possession of every anti-pirate assault force member. It shall be "ready to go" at all times:

1. Pencil flare kit   1 ea.
2. MK-13 flare   1 ea.
3. Strobe light w/IR. cover   1 ea.
4. Battery strobe light, extra   1 ea.
5. Chemlight white, high intensity   3 ea.
6. Signal mirror   1 ea.
7. UDT life preserver   1 ea.
8. Flight suit   1 ea.
9. Bulletproof vest w/plates   1 ea.
10. Gunshot kit, waterproofed   1 ea.
11. IV kit, waterproofed   1 ea.
12. Canteen, 1 qt   1 ea.
13. Diy harness, climbing   1 ea.
14. Handcuffs   1 ea.
15. Tieties, large   12 ea.
16. Gas mask   1 ea.
17. Knife   1 ea.
18. Bungie cord   1 ea.
19. Flight glove, pair   1 ea.
20. Fastrope leather glove, pair   1 ea.
21. Flashcrash pouch   1 ea.
22. Holster quickdraw   1 ea.
23. M-16 ammo pouch for CS grenade   1 ea.
24. CQB assault vest handcuff pouch   1 ea.
25. Magazine sig P-226   3 ea.
26. Web belt   1 ea.
27. Redlens flashlight   1 ea.

28. Plastic ziplock bag, large	4ea.
29. O.D. triangular bandage	3ea.
30. Magic marker	1ea.
31. Flashcrashes	4ea.
32. Gunshot kit pouch	1ea.
33. IV kit pouch	1ea.
34. NOMEX flameproof hood	1ea.
35. Canteen pouch	1ea.
36. MP-5N flashlight	1ea.
37. Protective eye wear	1ea.

Ammunition/Explosive Loadout	**45-day Deployment**
1. 9mm ball	20,000
2. F-250 flamethrower	1ea.
3. 5.56mm ball	500
4. 22-cal. long rifle match	300
5. T-1000 pest dispersant gun	1ea.
6. Fragmentation hand grenade, M26	100
7. Offensive hand grenade, Mark 3A2	100
8. Flare hand, red starcluster	10
9. Flare hand, white para	10
10. Flare hand, green starcluster	10
11. The incendiary hand grenade, AN-M14	25
12. Smoke hand, red	5
13. Smoke hand, yellow	5
14. Smoke hand, green	5
15. Grenade hand, riot control cs	16
16. Grenade hand, stun	138
17. Grenade hand, concussion	32
18. Colored smoke grenade M18	15
19. WP smoke grenade, M15	10
20. Electric caps	10
21. Non-electric caps	20
22. HC smoke grenade, AN-M8	1
23. Time fuse can	1
24. M60 fuse igniters	30
25. Red smoke grenade, AN-M3	30
26. CN tear gas grenade, M7	10

27. CN-DM irritant gas hand grenade, M6	15
28. M1 pull booby trap	2
`29. M1A1 pressure booby trap	2
30. M5 pressure release booby trap	2
31. M14 antipersonnel mine	2
32. Grenade-in-a-can booby trap	2
33. 90/90 amatol	100 lbs.
34. HBX-1 and HBX-3	150 lbs.
35. RDX (cyclonite)	75 lbs.
36. TNT	50 lbs.
37. Ammonium nitrate	60 lbs.
38. Bangalore torpedoes	10
39. C-4	45 lbs.
40. MK 8 MOD 2 flexible linear- type demolition charge	5
41. MK 135 demolition charge	5
42. Saddle charge	5
43. Diamond charge	5
44. Ear-Muff charge	5
45. Grenadier's vest	1ea.
46. NVG goggle	1ea.
47. 40mm CS riot control	2ea.
48. Vaseline	25 64-oz. jars

Medical Departmental Loadout

Issued to each member of platoon

1. Morphine serets	16ea.
2. Trauma bag, medical	1ea.
3. IVs, extra	5ea.
4. Gunshot kits, extra	10ea.
5. Plastic ziplock bags, large box	1ea.
6. Gas mask	16ea.
7. Combination locks	2ea.
8. Updated shot recorded	16ea.

NOTES ON DEFENSIVE STRATEGIES

_____
_____
_____
_____
_____
_____
_____
_____
_____
_____
_____
_____
_____
_____
_____
_____
_____
_____
_____
_____

NOTES ON DEFENSIVE STRATEGIES

NOTES ON OFFENSIVE STRATEGIES

ALSO AVAILABLE FROM LYONS PRESS

The official U.S. Army field manual—with more than 100 illustrations, all the combat skills it takes to survive and win the battle against the Undead

The United States Army is prepared for every kind of combat. This is the soldier's zombie combat field manual. It explains how to perform the combat skills needed to survive on the battlefield against the hordes of the Undead. All soldiers, across all branches, must learn these basic skills in preparation for battle against reanimated corpses.

In the confusion and fear of zombie combat, if you uphold your Warrior Ethos and follow the training provided in this book, you can help win in war against the Undead and return home with honor. The book covers a breadth of topics, including:

+ **Individual Readiness**
+ **Zombie Combat Care and Preventive Medicine**
+ **Environmental Conditions**
+ **Cover, Concealment, and Camouflage**
+ **Fighting Positions**
+ **Movement**
+ **Urban Area Procedures**
+ **"Every Soldier Is a Sensor"**
+ **Zombie Combat Marksmanship**
+ **Communications**
+ **Survival, Evasion, Resistance, and Escape**

U.S. Army Zombie Combat Skills
Department of the Army
US $14.95 / CAN $18.95
ISBN 978-1-59921-909-7

LYONS PRESS
Guilford, Connecticut
An imprint of Globe Pequot Press